PRAISE FOR

"*Mending Education* is the third book in a trilogy geared towards education and the systems engulfing the processes of education. The book is important for educators but also people from multiple disciplines, e.g., business, leadership, health care. Every profession thrives on the messages found within *Mending Education* through its stories of hope, creativity, resiliency, and vision. Educators were role models through the pandemic, showing creativity and positive examples of not just surviving but thriving in hard times. The authors have beautifully highlighted the tangible stories that give hope for education even though the profession is filled with crisis from within and outside. Likewise, the book provides a blueprint that other professions can use to scaffold their own vision, creativity, hope, and resiliency."

—**Barbara H. Long,** dean, The Rev. Wilfred E. and Dr. Joyce A. Nolen
School of Business and Professional Studies, Bridgewater College

"In their new book, *Mending Education*, Karen Gross and Ed Wang provide us with a readable yet authoritative review of the challenges and opportunities our education system faces in the aftermath of the pandemic and in the context of multiple ongoing stressors. While never dodging the severity of the issues, they offer a treatment plan built on lessons from the experience of social and emotional learning and from what we have gleaned from resilience studies as applied to the scholastic setting for students and teachers alike. This is a timely and necessary book."

—**Gregory Fricchione,** MD, director, Benson-Henry Institute
for Mind-Body Medicine, Massachusetts General Hospital,
and professor of psychiatry, Harvard Medical School

"*Mending Education* is a book for our times—it recognizes the watershed moment created by the COVID-19 pandemic and examines how to embrace it moving forward. Old paradigms simply no longer fit the current landscape educators are facing. This book addresses the 'now what' for educators by offering hope, clarity, and innovative strategies."

—**Douglas Behan,** director of continuing education and associate
professor of professional practice, School of Social Work,
Rutgers, The State University of New Jersey

"*Mending Education* is a must-read for veteran educators, preservice educators, and teacher educators. Drs. Gross and Wang center the voices of educators and affirm the multiple ways educators benefited their students and families during the pandemic. By doing so, educators who lived that experience find their creativity with online learning, their novelty for engaging students, and their focus on connecting with students and families not only highlighted but recognized as a path forward."

—**Elizabeth McAdams Ducy,** associate professor, education specialist,
and ECSE-AA adviser, Department of Educational Leadership
and Special Education, Sonoma State University

"We have all bemoaned the COVID pandemic and its lasting negative effects, but Karen Gross and Edward Wang turn that pessimism on its head. This book defines the positive outcomes from the pandemic for education writ large and provides ways to create stickiness for lasting change. The coauthors' extensive experience in education is augmented by the priceless data gathered through their research survey of teachers and educators. Along with their upbeat voices, their own delightful and smart original artworks are used to engage the reader and illustrate their points throughout, making this a must-have for educators everywhere."
—**Chris Messina-Boyer**, educational crisis manager/crisis communications consultant, 20Buttonwood PR Solutions LLC

Mending Education

Mending Education

Finding Hope, Creativity, and Mental Wellness in Times of Trauma

Karen Gross and Edward K. S. Wang

TEACHERS COLLEGE PRESS

TEACHERS COLLEGE | COLUMBIA UNIVERSITY

NEW YORK AND LONDON

Published by Teachers College Press,® 1234 Amsterdam Avenue, New York, NY 10027

Front cover: plant forms from Cannavale / Noun Project, late 19th-century Japanese textile from Wikimedia Commons, paper texture by Efe Madrid / Freepik

Library of Congress Cataloging-in-Publication Data

Names: Gross, Karen, 1952– author. | Wang, Edward K. S., author.
Title: Mending education : finding hope, creativity, and mental wellness in times of trauma / Karen Gross and Edward K. S. Wang.
Description: New York : Teachers College Press, [2024] | This book is the third in a trilogy whose previous volumes are: Breakaway learners and Trauma doesn't stop at the school door. | Includes bibliographical references and index. | Summary: "The authors focus on how sudden and forced changes to teaching and learning created "Pandemic Positives" which can be captured and brought to scale across pre-K-adult settings"— Provided by publisher.
Identifiers: LCCN 2024013601 (print) | LCCN 2024013602 (ebook) | ISBN 9780807786000 (paper ; acid-free paper) | ISBN 9780807786017 (hardcover; acid-free paper) | ISBN 9780807782545 (ebook)
Subjects: LCSH: Educational change—United States. | COVID-19 Pandemic, 2020- — Social aspects. | Creative teaching—United States. | Students—Mental health— United States. | Teachers—Mental health—United States. | Well-being.
Classification: LCC LB2822.82 .G757 2024 (print) | LCC LB2822.82 (ebook) | DDC 370.973—dc23/eng/20240531
LC record available at https://lccn.loc.gov/2024013601
LC ebook record available at https://lccn.loc.gov/2024013602

ISBN 978-0-8077-8600-0 (paper)
ISBN 978-0-8077-8601-7 (hardcover)
ISBN 978-0-8077-8254-5 (ebook)

Printed on acid-free paper
Manufactured in the United States of America

To all the students of today and tomorrow who can benefit from the pandemic positives

Contents

Acknowledgments

Books do not write themselves—that's for sure. We want to thank the many educational and other nonprofit institutions and the educators, students, and community members who have informed our work on this book. It is their voices that we have heard and hopefully understood, and this book would not exist without these institutions and individuals.

In particular, we thank our Virtual Teachers' Lounge (VTL) cofounders, Pat Neal and Sakina McGruder, for their insights and wisdom, which continue to illuminate our work, and we feel deeply privileged to continue our work with them. They conducted workshops with us, and insights from these and from their participants have frequently found their way into this book. We also thank Elizabeth Tarner and Carol Linscott for enabling the smooth functioning of VTL and the workshops, which they moderated with grace, and for repeatedly reaching out to many educators to share about these opportunities. We could not have managed without them.

Conducting a survey was a challenge on many levels but it was critical to supporting our observations and ensuring that we recognized and understood the role of educators. Thanks to Emily Feltham for her work in formatting and disseminating the survey and compiling the results. We are grateful to Hong Wang Fung from Hong Kong Metropolitan University for his quality and timely analysis of the survey data and for enabling us to share the survey results.

Thank you to the reviewers of the manuscript for their thoughts and comments. They have enriched the book.

For both coauthors, individuals in their personal and work lives enriched their understanding of education and the difficulty of and concentration needed in writing a book. There are too many to name and we do not want to leave any out—we are deeply appreciative of them all. That said, certain individuals must be named.

Karen Gross extends special thanks to Lisa Carnavale and Audrey and Karen Donovan for allowing quiet time in which to write. Her Cape Ann neighbors were always there to help, offering delicious meals. Bill Reeve regularly shared ideas and articles and was open to almost daily discussions as the book progressed. Nancy Scattergood Donavan brought forth insights in weekly phone calls and provided much-needed perspective. The coauthor's favorite mathematician, Joseph A. Sgro, not only listened to and engaged in conversations daily about almost every aspect of the book (including the selections of art and the survey challenges), but also gave unwavering support and gracious and always wise insights and perspectives.

Finally, thank you to GK, who believed there needed to be a trilogy; no book by this coauthor will ever be written without him.

For his part, Ed Wang extends special thanks to Ed Malone, Sandra McCroom, and Pam Ogletree of Children's Services of Roxbury; without their continued support of his work, he would never have learned so much about the plight of children and their families who experience trauma and toxic stress. He thanks the families and staff with whom he consulted for their patience and for sharing their experiences. The natural inquisitiveness of his granddaughters, Brook and Breeze, inspired his dedicated attention to brain science and child development. The expertise of his wife, Kathleen McLean, in healing the mental sufferings of others is appreciated. He is grateful for the sacrifices his parents made to come up with a one-way ticket and a semester's tuition to enable his sojourn to the United States 50 years ago. His brother, who died by suicide while in college, established his passion for advocacy to improve students' mental health and he dedicates this book to him.

Finally, the coauthors thank each other. This remarkably successful collaboration has led to a friendship that will endure and has resulted in a book that truly speaks to and for us and our life's work.

Note to Readers

Endnotes, providing support, studies, and additional material, appear at the end of paragraphs (rather than the end of sentences), for ease of reading. This placement means that an endnote may refer to various content in the preceding paragraph and thus may address different topics.

We opted for robust endnotes so readers can find support should they need it for convincing leadership of their institutions. It is our belief that some educators spend time searching for support for new initiatives. With this book and these endnotes, the searching and support will be vastly easier and more accessible.

A Related Sources list is available through the QR code found at the end of the book.

The figures in the published book are in black and white. In the online version the illustrations are in color, which may enhance one's understanding of the artwork itself.

The voices of educators who responded to our survey appear in italics throughout the book. While these are not the only voices we reference, the survey voices speak volumes. Their words are available for verification and viewing (while preserving privacy) on request from the coauthors.

Our survey of teachers, which generates the charts and responses found throughout the book, is accessible through the QR code at the end of the book.

Prologue

Molting Matters

Long, long ago, there was a lobster that went to a doctor because its shell was regularly molting. The doctor observed that the lobster was experiencing stress and prescribed various drugs to alleviate all its anxiety. The doctor said that this would enable the lobster's shell to harden and stay the same over time. The lobster was relieved, and at first it seemed as though its shell issues were fully resolved; its shell did not molt. (We are using "it" and "its" for ease in referring to a lobster but we know lobsters have multiple possible genders!) But over time, the lobster sensed that its shell was getting tighter and much heavier. The shell felt confining and the lobster was struggling, even to breathe. The lobster felt miserable. So it went to another doctor to complain about its shell, including about the prior doctor's unfulfilled claim that the lobster's shell would remain unchanged. The new doctor examined the lobster and observed that the shell was actually the same size it had always been, although perhaps a tad thicker with age. Then the new doctor paused and said, "What has changed is you; you have grown and developed and adapted without even being aware of it. The point of the molting shell is that it allows for growth, even if that is inconvenient and at times uncomfortable." Now it was the lobster's turn to pause and it then asked the new doctor: "So if I allow for the possibility of change, I can shed the old shell and develop new shells that are better suited to me?" The new doctor smiled and answered first by restoring the lobster's capacity to molt repeatedly and then by noting calmly that change is hard and makes one vulnerable, but adversity and growth often go together. And the lobster returned to the sea and for all the years since, this lobster and all its compatriots over generations and generations have been growing and molting, just as the new doctor said they would.

Even in a nation as divided as ours, few would disagree with this statement: Our educational system writ large is failing far too many students. This has been true for at least the past decade, despite improvements at the margins. And our educators, whether working in or outside classrooms or in leadership positions, are struggling mightily.

Add to this the negative impacts of the COVID-19 pandemic and its continuing effects on our already struggling educational landscape. The well-publicized failures range from students' missing developmental milestones; to lower test scores; to a growing equity divide based on race, class, and ethnicity; to record numbers of students dropping out or not reenrolling; to educators retiring early or simply quitting. And that's just the start.[1]

1

We know from research studies that students and educators have been struggling with declining mental wellness, which was exacerbated by the pandemic. We have witnessed student dysregulation and dissociation inside and outside school buildings. Students have overdosed in high school bathrooms, requiring Narcan to be revived. Students have been injured or killed, including in school and university shootings. Millions of students have experienced the anxiety of school lockdowns, which sometimes result from fake threats of violence, known as "swatting."[2]

One repeated scenario stands out for us as an exemplar of the negatives in our educational system. In some schools, as the pandemic continued, teachers were supplied with red pieces of paper. When their struggles rose to such a high level in their classrooms that they could no longer function, these teachers took out the red paper; walked out of the classroom; handed the paper to a teacher in the next classroom, to the principal, or to someone in the office; and exited the building, staying out for the rest of the day. That left the other teachers with the task of taking over the abandoned classroom, filled with students. And each time we, the coauthors, heard this story, we kept asking ourselves: Who took care of the teacher with the red paper who left the building, and who helped such teachers if and when they returned? Who helped the teachers who never left? We remain haunted by the need for those red pieces of paper. Something is very wrong if we need emergency exit plans for educators. And something is very wrong if we don't have approaches for teachers to find their equilibrium when they return. The tenuous state in which we found ourselves in the midst of the pandemic is reflected visually in Figure P.1.

We are aware of how difficult it is for people and institutions to change, even in the presence of failure. We also are cognizant of how hard it is to alter social and cultural norms in schools and communities. Personal and institutional change make us anxious and uncertain, a state compounded by the instability and fear stoked by the pandemic. Those old worn-out slippers feel mighty comfortable when we think about tossing them aside.[3]

It's like the lobster that didn't want its shell to molt. Even when people see a need for change, thinking about and acting on change are light years apart. Further, when the benefits of change are not felt immediately, we are less inclined to take action or maintain it over extended periods of time. Humans generally have a preference for short-term thinking.

Despite the many known negatives in education, the lobster parable offers several critical lessons. First, even when it is essential, change is hard, though we know it fosters growth and improvement. Second, growth and the resulting change are often accompanied by adversity. And this is where the parable teaches us the most.[4]

A crisis (or, as in the parable, adversity) supplies a unique opportunity for growth and making changes. To be sure, not all crises lead to change. But the pandemic offers us a once-in-a-generation chance to make lasting change, in part because the pandemic was widespread and presented the risk of illness or death for millions, touching all ages, races, ethnicities, religions, and political affiliations.[5]

In the field of education, the necessity for change and the speed with which that change was required by the pandemic's effects forced educators to alter what they did in unanticipated, sometimes dramatic, positive ways. The pandemic created

Figure P.1. Karen Gross, *Hanging by a Thread*, 2021

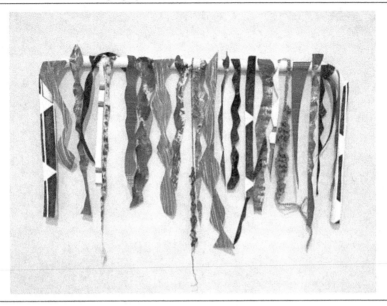

more than a single game-changing moment. If we can get the positive changes to stick, the pandemic will indeed be a game changer that will improve education systemically into the future.[6]

This gets us to the point of this book, with the lobster parable being a constant reminder. We are in a unique moment in time; we can call it *molting season*. A far-reaching crisis has profoundly impacted our educational system. We can use this crisis to bring about that which would not otherwise be likely: systemic, positive, replicable, and scalable improvements in education. Instead of focusing on the negatives the pandemic caused in education, we choose to see an opportunity to "molt" education's existing shell, knowing full well that in some institutions before the pandemic, just as with the lobster, change was starting. Molting for lobsters and education is not instantaneous.

Yes, although our conclusion is counterintuitive for many, we assert that a negative can create remarkable positives. We can help not only the current generation of students but also students of future generations, just as the lobster did for other lobsters. Join us as we share how to enable this educational molting to happen. The pandemic has presented all of us with a window of opportunity in which change can happen, and for us, this is a moment that cannot be lost; in a sense, the pandemic has inspired a clarion call for action in myriad fields, including education, our focus in this book. And we ask our readers, if molting is not possible now in education in light of the pandemic and its aftermath, when will education's shell change?

Part I

THE ORIGINS OF THE EDUCATIONAL PANDEMIC POSITIVES

CHAPTER 1

The Perspective of Positives

THE LENSES WE WEAR

This book addresses what transpired in our educational system from early childhood through adulthood during and after the pandemic through lenses markedly different from those currently employed by most commentators. This book is *not* seeking to tackle and remediate the negatives the pandemic wrought in education over so many months; attempting that is often an effort to restore, whether by design or instinct, the status quo ante.

This book is the third in a trilogy whose previous volumes are *Breakaway Learners: Strategies for Post-Secondary Success with At-Risk Students* and *Trauma Doesn't Stop at the School Door: Strategies and Solutions for Educators, PreK–College*. Reading the earlier volumes is by no means necessary, as this book can and does stand on its own. On occasion, however, the current book draws on the earlier two, and its approach is similar in four important respects: It is based on in-the-trenches experiences, it is a recognition of missed opportunities, it is replete with concrete steps that will move the proverbial needle if we are willing and daring enough to change, and it is grounded in trauma theory and emphasizes the importance of mental wellness.[1]

In the present book, we seek to uncover what many have not recognized or identified and, further, is too often unaddressed in existing studies: positives the pandemic brought to education and an explanation of their impact on practice and how those positives need to be gathered together, replicated, and scaled with stickiness (by which we mean long-lasting changes) to improve our educational system. For us, the majority of the positives we have identified have not yet become formidable game changers in education, although they could become just that if and when they gathered the needed stickiness. In short, we want to demonstrate how the positives from the pandemic can work to *mend* education, a theme in Part III. We have seen these positives ourselves and recognized them in the voices and experiences of educators that have been shared with us. Figure 1.1 expresses the benefits of working toward mending our world in the midst of a crisis through the use of shards, which we discuss in detail in Chapter 12.

We acknowledge that the positives we identify and advocate implementing are not viewed as positives by all. And there is no set number of these positives, although we have identified several dozen of them. Our view of education's ultimate

Figure 1.1. Karen Gross, *Mending Is a Challenge*, 2021

goals—student academic success and quality social and emotional balance—undergirds why we see the many changes we identify as positive.

For those who see educational success differently or place different value on social and emotional learning or the role of education in righting social wrongs, our positives can be perceived as negatives. True enough, but resolving national political and philosophical belief systems in a divided nation is neither our role nor the function of this book. Instead, we overtly support and advocate for education as a pathway to opportunity and wellness, from childhood into adulthood.

To date, the positives we have identified (and there are others: A Brookings report identified 3,000 positives—that's not a typo—globally) have not been studied or written about in detail. These positive changes are slipping away through attrition or are being discarded now that the pandemic crisis has ostensibly passed. It is as if these positives served their intended, limited purpose, tolerated during the pandemic but with no current utility or worth. We label these positives and how they operate in practice as the *pandemic positives*, recognizing that positives from the pandemic exist far beyond the field of education. We believe that this is the first time this particular phraseology has appeared as a defined term in the literature in any consistent and developed manner.[2]

OUR STORIES

The uniqueness of our approach toward positives is furthered by our perspectives. Our racial, ethnic, and socioeconomic backgrounds; our origins; and our formative years of education in two different nations and the differing worldviews of these locales influence the vantage point from which we see the pandemic, among many issues. Our individual and deeply personal experiences of trauma and toxic stress in our early years also inform our perspectives. Both of us are keenly aware that it is possible for students to hide the abuse and mental illness they witness or experience in their own homes; we did this in our own early years.[3]

For one author, the experience of living in the United States as a first-generation immigrant from Hong Kong offers a diversity perspective. His experience of returning to Hong Kong after the height of the pandemic adds further nuance. When he was a student in Hong Kong in primary 1 (equivalent to 1st grade in the United States) 62 years ago, there was a strong educational emphasis on math, Chinese and English language, and penmanship. After primary 6, in form 1 (7th grade), the annual core curriculum added science subjects through to graduation. Students who excelled in science had better opportunities for higher education and career choices. Interestingly, many of the author's classmates who did very well in science entered careers that were not associated with the subject. When the author visited an educational agency in Hong Kong during the pandemic, its director asked how social and emotional learning could be incorporated into its STEAM (science, technology, engineering, arts, and mathematics) program. The author was surprised that a recognition of whole-child development in education was catching on in a system so focused on STEM (science, technology, engineering, and mathematics) for many years.

For the other author, her background of living in a home where she spoke a language in addition to English with her Swiss stepfather (and not her biological mother, who spoke nary a word in a foreign language) presents an opportunity for cross-cultural awareness and knowledge of familial boundaries, as well as the experience of difference vis-à-vis her family members and friends. And there were plentiful summers in Europe for more language practice and cultural awareness; these trips were designed for learning, rather than as vacations, though the latter was how they were perceived by many.[4]

To this are added the differences in the authors' professional disciplines, expertise, and separate but related careers. These all come together in this book to provide strikingly similar perspectives on education, especially when it comes to the essential development of the whole-brain child (sometimes referred to here as the *whole child*), as well as on the import of social and emotional learning, the effect of trauma and toxic stress on content learning, and the capacity for ongoing personal and life goal success. Learning and mental health are deeply intertwined.[5]

Importantly, we share a sense of public stewardship for eliminating racial and ethnic disparities and inequities in education and for prioritizing mental health care. We have been involved in introducing and then implementing difficult changes in public policy at the state, national, and global levels. We get the import of stickiness of change from our years of work challenges. Moving the needle of change is tough going.

To add to all these factors, our in-the-trenches life experiences contribute to our capacity to understand the educational world we are seeking to improve. This isn't theoretical discourse: For us, this book is more than an academic or intellectual exercise. The impact of our personal narratives and the changes the pandemic wrought in us individually and in our work are incorporated into this book. In a very real way, our own stories are part of the storytelling that undergirds the book—the story of how crises can enable change that has stickiness.

In a policy article for the Harvard Kennedy School of Government, "A Journey of Public Stewardship on Asian American and Pacific Islander Mental Health: Massachusetts's Approach to Addressing Disparities," one of the authors revealed that his brother, after suffering from depression in silence, had died by suicide in college 50 years earlier. His brother did not seek help until the burden of his mental illness became so severe that others took notice. His academic adviser persuaded him to seek treatment in the hospital, where his acute symptoms were resolved but the deeper issues were not addressed. He quickly signed himself out of inpatient care. He was too ashamed because of the shadow of stigma to follow through with his care. His invisible wound of mental illness and the shadow of stigma continued to the end. The loss of his brother resulted in the author's advocacy for improving students' mental wellness.[6]

Fast-forward 50 years, when the Centers for Disease Control and Prevention's Youth Risk Behavior Surveillance System sampled high school students from 2011 to 2021 and found that the percentage of students across every racial and ethnic group who felt persistently sad or hopeless had risen over those 10 years. The percentage of female students who seriously considered suicide, made a plan, and then attempted suicide also increased during this period.[7]

Poor mental health and attempted suicide among students continue to rise. Students' mental problems are not new for educators. The good news is there is more openness to talking about mental illness than there was 50 years ago. Educators must address the mental wellness of students the moment these students enter the school doors. The time is now. We can and must do more to promote mental wellness in schools.

Add to this that one of the central reasons for our conducting a survey, the results of which are referenced throughout the book, is our belief in the importance of listening to and learning from the voices of educators who were working in the trenches before the pandemic and continued to do so during the crisis and in its waning years. The Virtual Teachers' Lounge (VTL), an online forum, also brings the perspectives of educators working with students, parents, and leaders. Personal experiences and stories enrich our understanding and provide scaffolding for the many concrete suggestions we offer and for their implementation.[8]

CONTEXT AND CHANGE

We have been struck, in the context of the pandemic's effect on business, economics, health care, and particularly education, by the new acronym VUCA. We live in a VUCA world, one filled with *v*olatility, *u*ncertainty, *c*omplexity, and *a*mbiguity. Each of us, authors and readers alike, could use other words for the acronym's letters to reflect how individuals feel and experience the current world, such as *vulnerable*, *unequal*, *confused*, and *anxious*. It is in this VUCA context, a world filled with permacrises, that we seek to assess, understand, and improve education.[9]

The shared feelings of anxiety because of the unknown, not being in control because of uncertainty, and a sense of disconnect because of social distancing and masks made us engage differently. These are all hallmarks of trauma. The work shown in Figure 1.2 represents the world before and after trauma.

It is for all these reasons, among others, that we deployed both our left and right brains to write this book, recognizing the complexity accompanying brain functioning. In our quest to emphasize the critical development of the whole-brain child, we have paid attention to students' and teachers' emotions and creativity, features generally located in the brain's right hemisphere, and the reasoning, logic, and science of the left hemisphere. We compiled evidence-based practices and present them throughout our chapters to support the positive strategies used during, and even before, the pandemic. We also looked at the root causes of educational inequality and included practice-based evidence focused on its elimination or, at least, its amelioration.[10]

We found countless examples of individual, family, and community acts of resilience (defined as emerging from forward-looking capacities premised in large part on hope and a positive mindset and not returning to the status quo ante) and lasticity (elasticity, plasticity, pivoting right, reciprocity, and belief in self) during

Figure 1.2. Karen Gross, *Becoming Disordered*, 2022

the pandemic. We balanced our negative and positive emotions during a time of fear and uncertainty, loss and grief, work and financial struggles, social distancing and civil unrest. All this happened while our government was managing an unprecedented public health crisis, last experienced with the 1918 Spanish flu. We will share, in the context of education and of whole-child development, how the pandemic activated our capacity to not merely cope but experience improvements. The key is to be open to seeing these improvements.[11]

We worry that these opportunities will be lost in the push to find normalcy—which doesn't exist, at least in its prior form. We are losing the perspective of the pandemic, discussed in Part III. This book is an effort to highlight and share the positive benefits so they are leveraged and used when we mend education. The book is an invitation to reflect on, recognize, and implement what the pandemic has taught us through its impact, including most specifically trauma and mental wellness—which we can do if we become willing learners with the capacity to continue to see and then incorporate change in the educational landscape.[12]

PRE-LAUNCH VISTA

As we launch, consider this sentence: *The pandemic brought positive changes to our educational system.* Many would simply discard this assertion (and this book, which addresses positive change) as patently untrue. Some would find the sentence uncomfortable, even if it contained kernels of truth. Still others would question, as noted earlier, whether what we call *positives* are truly that. Some educators might disagree with this whole notion of positives, given what they are presently experiencing in their classrooms. Others would ask, How could the pandemic, so filled with collective stress and wide-ranging individual trauma, bring about improvements in education? For some, discovering educational positives arising from the pandemic is as problematic as identifying personal positives growing out of traumatic experiences, a related phenomenon.

As explored in Chapter 2, the positive changes in education are grounded in two distinct though related notions: hope and creativity. If educators had hope, they were able to achieve remarkable creativity. And even if they lacked hope or were unaware of what was driving their change-making capacity, their actions and strategies altered their educational offerings in positive ways.

Before we move forward, we want you to consider an educator's words from the survey we carried out, words that exemplify the possibility of positives in the midst of a crisis:

> The [p]andemic changed how I see myself as an educator because I became more aware of the full spectrum of needs students have. I am now more conscious of student needs not only academically and how they individually learn but also emotionally and how that effects [sic] their ability to learn in a classroom, interact with peers, and grow as an individual.

CHAPTER 2

Hope and Creativity

THE UNSPOKEN GREATS

We had two underlying questions in creating this book: What enabled some educators to develop pandemic positives? and What facilitated their creation? We are fully aware that not all educators developed these positives. If we want to enable the replication, scalability, and stickiness of the pandemic positives, we need to know how these many positives came into being and how and why they worked. With this understanding, we can better understand Part II of this book, where the pandemic positives are detailed, and Part III, which addresses how to make the positive changes enduring.

As alluded to in Chapter 1, we want to focus on two terms that have not received concentrated attention in the discussions of education during the pandemic: *hope* and *creativity*. We approached this book based on our own hope and creativity as well. Add to this our awareness that it was not an easy task to synthesize these two terms.[1]

Defining the two terms and then applying them to the educational setting is our path toward explaining the origins of the pandemic positives. And as we have been doing in our teaching in this pandemic era and as a response to trauma's impact on our memory and concentration, we start with our conclusions. That way, if readers get lost or tune out, they can see where we end up.

Hope and creativity are, in some sense, the greatest of the pandemic positives we uncovered, although they have gone unheralded and unlabeled. Hope and creativity are precursors of the development of concrete pandemic positives that have arisen in educational institutions and been manifested (whether consciously or not) among some leaders and educators.

The survey referred to earlier was a broad one, conducted online. Its purpose was to gather educators' views across the K–12 landscape during the pandemic. The survey's demographics and approach are described in Chapter 3, and we use the results throughout the book. Several of our findings show how respondents expressed the inclusion of both hope and creativity during the pandemic and their ongoing presence.

Hope and creativity can be developed and nurtured in individuals and organizations through culture and leadership; they can be quashed the same way. Surely we want to find ways to enable the former outcome and curb the latter; if we accomplish this, there will be fertile soil for future positives during inevitable coming crises, large and small. We most assuredly do not believe the pandemic positives are or should be perceived as unicorns.

SOME CAUTIONS

Before turning to the definitions of each term, we have several cautionary messages to share.

First, there are no universally accepted definitions of the terms. We culled definitions from literature, research, and data largely outside the education field and applied the definitions to education. While plentiful research exists on hope and creativity elsewhere, in education—especially when related to the pandemic crisis—it is less robust.

The pandemic tested our sense of hope. How do we, and educators in particular, foster hope in the context of omnipresent adversity? We saw hope demonstrated by teachers' optimism, motivation, can-do attitude, and goal-directed actions, even in the most challenging of situations. After all, they came up with the pandemic positives detailed in Part II.

Second, although there is no consensus on this, a critical interrelationship exists between the two terms. Consider these questions as the starting point for seeing this interconnection: Is hope a precursor of or prerequisite for creativity? Alternatively, is creativity a precursor of or prerequisite for hope? Can we have hope without creativity and creativity without hope? Do these two concepts overlap in important and perhaps unrecognized ways? These are questions we probe throughout this book, questions with which we hope readers will wrestle too.

Third, we are not addressing hope in the context of its religious implications. Education is predominantly nondenominational and while hope and faith are connected in religious contexts, that interrelationship is beyond the scope of this book.

Fourth, with respect to creativity, we are not limiting ourselves to the arts but are looking more broadly at creative approaches across various disciplines.

Fifth, those who have hope and creativity may not be aware that these processes are at work within themselves. The outcomes derived from hope and creativity are what we have seen as and after they occurred. Our application of these terms is our after-the-fact nomenclature, employed to provide explanations for actions we witnessed or experienced.[2]

WHAT IS HOPE?

Most definitions of *hope* signal the concept that hope is about a person's belief in the future. This framing is supported by a coauthor's work with adolescents. Asking them about their feelings of hope, connectedness, and trust, he posed the questions "Do you feel hopeful that what upsets you will get better?" "How many people do you trust to stand by you when things are tough?" and "Do you look to others for help and comfort?" The majority of children responded to all three questions positively, paving the way for their hope in the future.

The coauthor also uses hope as one of the fundamental principles in his curriculum Trauma-Informed Care: Hope, Strengths, Resilience, Growth, and Healing. This knowledge- and skill-based training curriculum is for providers, educators included, who work with children. It integrates the science of toxic stress and trauma, science-based practice, and culture-based evidence from diverse racial and ethnic communities. An example of collaboration and its applicability across sociocultural and historical contexts is his work with Dr. Carlos Velazquez-Garcia, executive director of the Psychotraumatology Institute of Puerto Rico and an expert in treating trauma; this work was successful because sociocultural and historical contexts were not forgotten.

Besides individual hope, there is institutional hope, manifested primarily through leaders and governing boards. Hope, whether individual or institutional, is grounded in the aspiration that, even in a crisis, there is the possibility of change and positive improvement. And without hope, it is hard for either individuals or organizations to be motivated to make change or exhibit creativity. One is forced to ask in such situations, Why should we care and why does it matter?

The American Psychological Association defines *hope* as "the expectation that one will have positive experiences or that a potentially threatening or negative situation will not materialize or will ultimately result in a favorable state of affairs." As Drew Boyd, a renowned researcher and psychologist of hope, has stated, "A rainbow is a prism that sends shards of multicolored light in various directions. It lifts our spirits and makes us think of what is possible. Hope is the same—a personal rainbow of the mind." Visually embodying this sentiment, the work in Figure 2.1,

Figure 2.1. Karen Gross, *Refractions and Reflections*, 2021

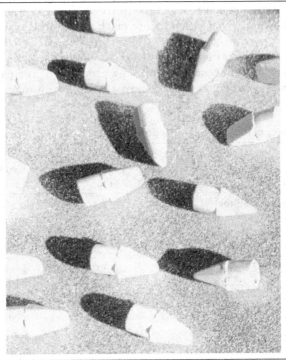

from a series shown to students using ordinary objects (here, pencil erasers), shows light, shadow, and reflection.[3]

Citing a recent study conducted by a number of scholars, Boyd observed that hopeful employees exhibited greater creativity (a term that was subjective in the study and one we will define and address shortly). And citing Darren Webb, he noted that there are different forms of hope, including estimative hope (obtainable and goal oriented) and resolute hope (seen in creating one's own sense of the possible despite the odds and high hurdles). The deeper point from this and similar studies is that hope can and should be nurtured, given its wide-ranging benefits, as it is not a static condition; hope's presence is also contextual.[4]

It is noteworthy that there are substantiated psychological and physiological benefits of hope. If we have hope, we can diminish anxiety and depression and other negative feelings; further, hope can reduce perceptions of physical pain. It can boost both respiration and circulation and reduce blood pressure. It can increase our sense of predictability, a factor of real value in times of crisis when control is reduced or seems to be lost. The survey respondents recognized the value of hope, as evidenced in Table 2.1.[5]

As we reflect on hope and its meaning, we are drawn to Jane Goodall and Douglas Abrams's aptly titled *The Book of Hope: A Survival Guide for Trying Times*. Four factors behind the book's appeal tie in with how it offers a useful architecture for us in thinking about hope in the educational arena.

First, the book was released during the pandemic; as such, it is reflective of and responsive to the difficult times in which we are living now, including but not limited to the pandemic. That's useful, since much of the literature on hope predates the pandemic.

Second, the book takes the form of a dialogue: Goodall answers thoughtful questions and responds to comments from Abrams. Questioning is a pandemic positive and a key tool for education, as we note in Part II. We use the dialogue of educators

Table 2.1. Frequency of Responses on "Hope"

Statement	Strongly disagree (%)	Disagree (%)	Agree (%)	Strongly agree (%)	Agree or strongly agree (%)
Maintaining hope during the pandemic was a key motivator to enabling educators to continue effective work with students.	0.6	7.5	53.5	38.4	91.82
I believe my ongoing belief in hope is essential to my effective work as an educator.	2.5	5.0	49.1	43.4	92.45
I have the resources to deliver such an approach.	1.3	10.1	58.5	30.2	88.68

in the form of their voices throughout this book. And our epilogue is a tribute to this dialogic approach as we answer and respond informally to each other's questions about our book and its wider appeal outside the realm of education.[6]

Third, Goodall sees hope in stories related to experiences she had, witnessed, or heard about. Although she recognizes the literature, studies, and data on hope (cited at the end of her book), she reveals hope's existence and operation through describing how people, nature, and animals behave and through noting her interaction with them. She grounds her work in her in-the-trenches experiences, something that we do in this book as well with respect to the pandemic positives.

Fourth, we share Goodall's belief in the importance of hope. As she advises her readers: "Hope is contagious. Your actions will inspire others. It is my sincere desire that this book will help you find solace in a time of anguish, direction in a time of uncertainty, courage in a time of fear." We agree with these sentiments; they undergird our work on mending education.[7]

Goodall sees hope as "what enables us to keep going in the face of adversity. It is what we desire to happen, but we must be prepared to work hard to make it so." That is, while we can have hope without action (say, being imprisoned with no option for release, an example she offers), most hope requires action and agency. Hope, she asserts, is not an emotion; she sees it as a survival trait. She observes it in youth and their capacity to act in coming decades.

Her ideas suggest to us, as it does to Abrams, that we can develop hope even if we did not have it earlier or had lost it. Hope is not mere wishful thinking. Nor is it the same as optimism. As Goodall explains, "Hope . . . is a stubborn determination to do all you can to *make* it work" (emphasis in the original). It is not a denial of all the hurdles one faces—it is what brings light to the darkness, a concept reminiscent of Drew Boyd's hope as a rainbow, mentioned earlier.[8]

Goodall notes that hope rests on social support; it is hard to go it alone in times of crisis. We need one another. And while she believes in spirituality, she sees no need to foist her views on others. She carries with her tangible symbols of hope and shares them with others so they can see the power the future holds. One of the coauthors of the present book does the same. She always has with her a ceramic stone etched with the word *hope*. She also gives replicas to many of her students and workshop participants. Goodall ends her book with a poignant plea to readers: "Please rise to the challenge, inspire and help those around you, play your part. Find your reasons for hope and let them guide you onward."

Holding that broad definition and underlying explanations in mind, we have ways of reflecting on hope in education, which fit well with Goodall's approach. We have communication; we have the capacity to rebound and adapt; we have the voices of youth; and throughout the pandemic, we saw educators exhibiting how education could thrive despite rapid change and the many obstacles involved in educating students. And our examples are filled with humor, whether found in dancing, singing, or doodling.

With that frame, we can now turn to a definition of *creativity*, something that is even more nuanced and subject to many more misunderstandings than hope.

WHAT IS CREATIVITY?

Let's begin with what creativity isn't. It is like the age-old story of how to carve an elephant out of stone: One gets a huge rock and chisels away at everything that isn't an elephant—what's left is an elephant made of rock. While a negative definition may seem odd and perhaps not fulfilling, it does allow us to wrestle with what makes creativity what it is. As with carving the elephant, we take away—remove—what isn't creativity, just as we took away that which wasn't the elephant. And more broadly, we are carving the future of education by removing what didn't work before the pandemic and allowing the pandemic positives to shine.

To begin, creativity is not just about the arts. There can be creativity in business, medicine, philosophy, mathematics, technology, and education. Creativity is not a gift possessed by some and not by others, and it can manifest in individuals at any age and stage of development. It is not necessarily grand in scale, and it is not a one-time occurrence.

So what is creativity and how can we find it and sustain it?

Creativity is a process, not an ability; that's why it's inaccurate to assert that some have it and others do not. We just may not see it or it may be nascent. Next, creativity is more than a way of thinking; it is about problem solving and not only thinking outside the box but also discarding the box itself—there can be creative action. Further, creativity is not limited to new or original ideas; it can transform what others have done or connect things from the past in new ways.

Moreover, creativity is about more than the development of an idea, object, or method. It is about the deployment of such elements into a form that enables their utilization. Yes, creativity can occur in the privacy of one's mind, but for it to achieve its full power, its products need to be seen, recognized, or used. Thus, creativity is more than a state of mind or a thought; it is what the mind produces that can be used.

Creativity clearly is not limited to those who have lived a long life: Children are creative from an early age and, indeed, we may stifle their creativity as they age, including through overly doctrinaire educational practices. While viewing creativity as a force has appeal, it is not always generated by a major epiphany.

Creativity comes in different sizes and shapes. Some seek to define creativity according to the size of what is created. It does not need to be large in scale, as alluded to earlier. Small-scale—"little-c"—creativity, notes Dean Keith Simonton, is about "everyday problem solving and the ability to adapt to change." "Big-C" creativity is what leads to Nobel prizes. In defining creativity, some suggest it must create value, others that it must be spontaneous, and others that it must be new.[9]

In sum, different types of creativity exist and they appear in different contexts. Here, we are looking at creativity that arises in a crisis, when what worked before the crisis no longer does and a solution is required for progress to be made. Literature on the increase in creativity in the presence of drastic negative changes has been growing. Examples of creativity during negative circumstances are when individuals battling injury or illness generate creativity and when artists create their best work in times of struggle. Of course, not all creativity comes from crisis and desperation; it can originate in joy and beauty—and hope.

Marie Forgeard asserts that creativity is activated when circumstances force us to lose the illusion of control and consider a world of new possibilities. "Adverse events," she writes, "can be so powerful that they force us to think about questions we would never have thought of otherwise." Richard Tedeschi and Lawrence Calhoun suggest that our creativity in a crisis is akin to what occurs in an earthquake. Everything as we knew it disappears and we are forced to create new paradigms for survival.[10]

This is what occurred during the pandemic, including in education: Adversity led to creativity. The pandemic and all that it caused fit within the construct of reflecting on creativity in the midst of crisis. In understanding how creativity arises in a crisis, we are better able to comprehend how the pandemic positives came about. Note too that our survey respondents recognized the presence of creativity during a crisis—the pandemic—as reflected in Table 2.2.

Creativity can arise in a crisis in several ways, one growing from the necessity that we develop strategies for dealing with the crisis. Creativity acts as a salve: It is what we do to withstand or address the horrors of what has occurred. Conversely, terrible happenings cause internal changes that can open doors to creativity of which we were not previously aware. In short, crises can be both responsive to and generative of creativity. Further, there is no universality, in that creativity emerges for some people and not for others. It is not a matter of intelligence or emotional wellness. Its presence is unpredictable, and it does not follow the patterns of creativity seen outside a crisis period that involve preparation, planning, and processing. The mixed-media work in Figure 2.2 reflects the boldness and positivity of creative moments in time, even during the pandemic.

This has led us to devise a definition, not of creativity in general but of creativity in a time of crisis—such as the pandemic. And the name we give to our definition is *crisis creativity*. Our definition is as follows: Crisis creativity occurs in a time of profound uncertainty, urgency, and anxiety. It enables individuals and organizations to respond to such circumstances by developing new, combinational,

Table 2.2. Frequency of Responses on "the Power of Creativity"

Statement	Strongly disagree (%)	Disagree (%)	Agree (%)	Strongly agree (%)	Agree or strongly agree (%)
Instruction during the pandemic increased opportunities for students to develop and nurture their creativity.	5.7	20.8	45.3	28.3	73.58
I will continue to include creativity as an integral part of my work as an educator.	0	3.1	59.7	37.1	96.86
I have the resources to deliver such an approach.	2.5	11.9	62.3	23.3	85.53

Figure 2.2. Karen Gross, *Creativity Unbounded*, 2022

or transformational ideas, products, and solutions that foster positive forward movement, large or small.

This new term and its definition were a product of our creativity as we worked in crisis venues during the pandemic together and separately. It is exemplified by the artwork in this book, most of which was created during the pandemic. With this newly created definition, we can look at the interrelationship of crisis creativity and hope, edging us toward a discussion of how these two key factors enabled educators to produce the pandemic positives.[11]

THE INTERCONNECTEDNESS OF HOPE AND CRISIS CREATIVITY

In an educational setting, hope can be found in several locations. It can be in individual educators. It can be in schools or school systems, through the messaging and behavior of leaders. And it can be in larger communities touched by education. In the absence of hope, it is difficult, if not impossible, for educators to generate creative solutions, because they are fighting against the tide—resistance from within the educators themselves, the institution, and society.

Assuming, however, that hope exists in one of these three locations, educators can exercise crisis creativity. If educators believe they can act without being disciplined or criticized, they can develop solutions to aid their students' progress, and when they see success in their students, it inspires continued crisis creativity. This can occur among educators who previously were highly successful with students and also among those who had adhered to the approaches of their training, their school system, and predominant societal norms.

This we know: Those who have hope are more likely to be creative, and those who are creative are more likely to be hopeful. This in part hinges on the concepts of agency (granted by leadership) and autonomy (capacity to act without permission from leadership). If we feel unempowered or completely without support, it is hard to be creative. If we worry about our creativity being viewed as harmful, not productive, or outside the rules of work or society, it is harder to demonstrate creativity. By contrast, if we are supported, encouraged, and enabled to solve problems and then come up with solutions and use them, we are more likely to create them.

In other words, creativity flourishes, even in crises, given fertile soil in which ideas, products, and solutions can grow, and we can feed the soil to promote the presence of creativity. And what flourishes in the soil of a crisis differs across people, places, and organizations: There is no one pathway toward or one single product rendered by creativity. In the context of a crisis, a strong link exists between hope and creativity, and a synergistic overlap creates the opportunity for pandemic positives to grow.

The art educator Kate Mochon captures the essence of crisis creativity in the context of her students: "Each of [the students] is also struggling with isolation, feeling unmotivated, and not knowing how to connect. I have been heartened by the creative projects they embarked upon on their own. . . . I remind my students that creativity can happen anywhere, and that the important part is the *process*, not the *product*. They are actively building skills that keep them resilient now, and for the future" (emphasis in the original).[12]

CHAPTER 3

The Root System

NAMING

The architecture of the remainder of this book begins by identifying and explaining the operation of the positives that occurred in educational institutions across the country, many if not all generated by hope and creativity, as described in Chapter 2. We call this a naming task, the naming of what we have termed *pandemic positives*. Naming is more than labeling: It is showing how the positives functioned in educational settings, making their importance real for readers.

It is not as if during the pandemic educators were naming what they were doing as they were doing it. We are identifying the changes the pandemic engendered after the fact, after they were tried by educators. That is why we look at where the pandemic positives originated rather than beginning with their points of impact.

Naming and the recognition of its significance are not a new task for us. We wrote *The Feeling Alphabet Activity Set* during the pandemic, heightened racial tensions, and uncertainty. We recognized that if individuals at all ages and stages could identify—name—*what* they were feeling, that very act of identification would help them and those around them move forward. Feelings—negative or positive—matter. Naming our feelings is the first step in processing them and transforming them into positive thoughts and behaviors. The same is true with pandemic positives. If we name them, we are on the path to making them a part of education.[1]

We identified pandemic positives from numerous sources, the most important of which is the lived experiences of educators working in the trenches during the pandemic. We categorize and describe these concrete pandemic positives according to the space in which they originally occurred and in the approximate time setting: (a) at-home learning, when schools were shuttered; (b) online learning via Zoom or other platforms; and (c) in-person learning with masks and social distancing and some online integration. The word *originally* matters. What we saw in the three settings can be replicated in and adapted to other situations. And we know too that there were differing timetables for each setting among institutions and some settings were passed over altogether. The detailed description of timelines appears when we examine the pandemic positives in detail in Part II.

WHY THE PANDEMIC POSITIVES WORKED

Any detailed description of the pandemic positives requires an understanding of why they worked, weaving together threads to explain why these positives were effective when implemented. Five "root systems," linking theory to practice, explain why the pandemic positives improved education when they were put into practice:

1. The theoretical understanding of trauma (including its definition in education) and studies revealing its impacts and effective proven strategies for its amelioration
2. The theoretical understanding of mental wellness (including its definition in education) and studies revealing its import for learning and social and emotional learning and effective proven strategies for its maintenance
3. The extant literature describing, studying, and reporting on the experiences of K–12 students and educators during the pandemic, with a focus on that which has demonstrated the presence of pandemic positives with effectiveness
4. Stories of the lived experiences of educators in the trenches, including the experiences of the authors and the educators with whom they worked in an online forum called the Virtual Teachers' Lounge
5. The results of the previously noted survey that was provided to active educators on their observations and experiences during the pandemic, including but not limited to their perspectives on the positives the authors identified and the capacity for these positives to be replicated and scaled

TRAUMA THEORY

The Substance Abuse and Mental Health Services Administration defines *trauma* as follows: "Trauma results from an event, series of events, or set of circumstances that is experienced by an individual as physically or emotionally harmful or threatening and that has lasting adverse effects on the individual's functioning and physical, social, emotional, or spiritual well-being." We are hardwired to resist threat and danger. Our responses can be adaptive or maladaptive.[2]

The International Society for Traumatic Stress Studies differentiates between the collective stressful experience and the individual traumatic experience during the pandemic. We saw and worked with individuals who had preexisting conditions that affected their well-being, among them adverse childhood experiences; mental, emotional, behavioral, and learning challenges; poor health; and dysfunctional families. These preexisting conditions made some individuals more vulnerable during the pandemic.[3]

For our purposes here and in the context of education in particular, we define *trauma* as the occurrence of an event or events causing individuals to experience sufficient psychological distress such that they are unable to perform successfully in their day-to-day lives within the educational system.[4]

There are several key additive factors when reflecting on trauma beyond its definition. First, trauma affects both the brain and the body, and trauma can cause changes in both, as is powerfully expressed by Bessel van der Kolk in *The Body Keeps the Score: Brain, Mind, and Body in the Healing of Trauma*. Trauma truncates neural connections, although thankfully, with the right approaches, pathways can be rebuilt because of our brain's remarkable plasticity. Hold the thought about connections, as this element will keep reappearing in Parts II and III.[5]

Second, trauma symptomology is produced and can be acute and deferred, although its manifestations are often dismissed by the individual experiencing them and those who are bearing witness. We often mistake trauma symptomology for a host of other explanations, including but not limited to learning differences, mood or thought disorders, physical illness, and individual overreaction. *Hysteria* is an old-fashioned word to describe, and deprecate, trauma symptoms experienced by women. Being able to name trauma is a critical first step in its amelioration. And when we witness traumatized individuals, we would be wise to recognize that behavior is commonly the language of trauma, giving us a clue about what someone is experiencing. For the person bearing witness, that can have an effect too, resulting in secondary trauma, or what Nancy Sherman calls "moral injury."[6]

Acute symptomology typically is revealed through the senses in one or more of the traditional three *f*'s: *f*ight, *f*light, or *f*reeze. But this paradigm of reactions, produced by the autonomic nervous system, is not the entire picture. Two other *f*'s, *f*awn and *f*aint, are also involved. *Fawning* is the overattachment of the traumatized individual to another person or place; the individual who fawns frequently wants to please and to keep doing more of whatever activity is needed to produce positive responses. Call it obsessive obsequiousness. Sadly, in education fawning is often mischaracterized as a positive response because compliance is seen as a plus in an otherwise volatile classroom setting. *Fainting* is literal: A person affected by trauma momentarily loses consciousness.[7]

In Judith Herman's work on trauma, her central concepts of hyperarousal, constriction, and intrusion explain the neurobiology of trauma. Her triphasic model of treatment focuses on the trauma survivor's behaviors, including dysregulation, low frustration tolerance, quickness to anger, avoidance of emotion, withdrawal from others, reliving events with emotional intensity stimulated by "triggers," and in more extreme reactions, different levels of severity of dissociation.[8]

We used Herman's three concepts—hyperarousal, constriction, and intrusion—to characterize the milder dysregulation, overregulation, and dissociation of students. The population she was concerned with was diagnosed with posttraumatic stress disorder (PTSD), a diagnosis we do not ascribe to most students.

But we note the prevalence of adverse childhood experiences (ACEs); the data on ACEs reveal that approximately 64% of adults reported at least one ACE incident. ACEs are part of the invisible backpack students carry. The work shown in Figure 3.1 essentializes the intertwined burdens we all carry, burdens often invisible to others and even to ourselves.[9]

Educators and parents are seeing an abundance of both dysregulation (a loss of control that can lead to shouting, throwing, stomping, and hitting) and voluntary

Figure 3.1. Karen Gross, *Burdened With Complexity*, 2022

dissociation (daydreaming, the separation of a person from the group, and at its worst, separation from the person's internal feelings through looking at a screen too much or staring distractedly out a window or at the floor or ceiling). As observed earlier, we tend to ignore overregulation, which is similar to fawning, because individuals with this symptomology are compliant—in fact, they are overcompliant. They do as they are told. A traumatized person can demonstrate one or all of these behaviors over the course of a day, a week, or a month.[10]

Third, trauma never disappears, though it can be ameliorated by trauma-responsive practices. And earlier trauma can be "retriggered" by subsequent trauma, setting off what we call a "tuning fork orchestra." So even if we try to pretend trauma did not occur or try to ignore it, we will not succeed in stamping it out. It will reappear, often suddenly, leaving us bewildered, saddened, and symptomatic.[11]

Fourth, the many trauma-amelioration strategies detailed in books, reports, and articles can be loosely encapsulated by these seven *d*'s: *d*elight, *d*ance, *d*istract, *d*azzle, *d*emonstrate, *d*ignify, and *d*onate. Type out the *d* words and put them on the wall or write them on a whiteboard. Commit to executing them when you see them detailed in Part II. The *d*'s are in principles, values, and approaches found in trauma-responsive schools.[12]

Collectively, these *d*'s are intended to allow the brain to move away from the trauma and for others to recognize an individual's struggle by believing in them and their future. Using the senses helps. Creativity helps. Encouragement helps. Maintaining trust and stability help. Consistency and the absence of abrupt change help. Pleasant distractions help. Play helps immensely and not just for elementary school students. Giving to others (as in *donate*) helps. This last reality strikes some as odd, wondering how helping others helps us. It does so because of our mirror neurons, our empathy engines, which get activated when we give to others and which enable us to feel better because we enabled others to feel better. Writing, music, and movement help. Fostering connections with others, both peers and those younger and older, helps.[13]

MENTAL WELLNESS THEORY

The World Health Organization (WHO) defines *mental wellness* as "a state of well-being in which the individual realizes his or her own abilities, can cope with the normal stresses of life, can work productively and fruitfully, and is able to make a contribution to his or her community."[14]

Despite the appeal of WHO's definition, we are looking more specifically at what constitutes mental wellness in the context of education. So we need a narrower definition, one that focuses on a school climate that supports the mental health of students, all others in the education sphere, and those who engage with students outside school. A strong relationship exists between the quality (or lack thereof) of a positive school climate and students' and teachers' well-being.[15]

To that end, we have identified eight categories to describe what is needed to create and sustain mental wellness for students; the amalgam of these categories provides our guideposts for bettering the lives of students. These categories are adaptations of long-established psychological domains applied generally for achieving psychological well-being. The categories are what are needed to enable and support the mental wellness of students in the context of education. And as we assess the pandemic positives and their stickiness, we can look at them through this mental wellness lens.[16]

The categories are as follows:

1. Emotional: balancing positive and negative emotionality and forming satisfying relationships in and outside schools
2. Social: developing a sense of connectedness and belonging inside and outside the support system, preventing social media exploitation
3. Intellectual: expanding knowledge and skills, recognizing and developing creative abilities
4. Learning: enriching one's learning and feelings of achievement and satisfaction, using healthy apps and ChatGPT in a discriminating way
5. Environment: providing a safe, secure, stable, supportive, and stimulating school climate for learning
6. Physical: promoting exercise, sleep, nutritious eating, a healthy lifestyle, and overall physical wellness
7. Spiritual: developing and forming a sense of purpose, belonging, and meaning in learning and developing identity
8. Financial: supporting basic needs to live, learn, and play, including internet and hardware accessibility

Erik Erikson's Stages of Psychosocial Development theory undergirds these eight mental wellness categories in education. According to Erikson, the essential challenges for children's developmental growth between the ages of infancy and 3 are "trust vs. mistrust" and "autonomy vs. doubt"; for ages 3 to 6, they are "initiative vs. guilt"; for 6 to 12, the challenges are "industry vs. inferiority"; and for teenagers, "identity vs. role confusion." Stages of psychosocial development adjust and grow with age and the quality of the protective environment of children. Early childhood to middle school and through to high school are critical periods for applying Erikson's stages theory. Teachers who use the theory must focus on these developmental challenges to ensure that the eight categories of students' mental wellness listed above are met.[17]

In our work, we witnessed students miss or poorly establish Erikson's developmental milestones, the impacts of which are challenging for learning and the psychosocial development of a whole child. But here's the kicker: Mental wellness is disturbed by trauma and toxic stress, both of which affect how we think, feel, act, and relate to others. And that is what the pandemic did: It disrupted the stages of development as well as the eight mental wellness categories; this hampered the ability of schools to nurture these stages/categories in all students. In contrast, what the pandemic positives did was to enable educators to pay attention to the developmental stages and the eight categories with respect to their students. Educators often accomplished this without intentionality.[18]

SOCIAL AND EMOTIONAL LEARNING

Social and emotional learning (SEL) is a well-known approach for developing mental wellness within and beyond the educational arena. SEL develops self- and social awareness, relationship skills, and responsible decision-making; for an example, look at the work of the Collaboration for Academic, Social, and Emotional Learning (CASEL), an organization dedicated to the implementation of SEL curriculum. SEL is a systematic schoolwide approach to teaching and learning throughout the school day and can be extended to out-of-school time and used in partnership with families and communities.[19]

Importantly, SEL does not focus simply on depositing skills onto students (to borrow Paulo Freire's observation about education); instead, it promotes a school culture that fosters mental wellness and creates opportunities for educators to engage in efforts to lift, rather than blame, students. It helps students directly, and also indirectly, through improving educators' engagement with students. SEL is not like grit or traditional resiliency, which prompts students to pull themselves up by their bootstraps. Rather, it is a broader approach, situating students where they are and boosting their capacity to grow and flourish, a critical distinction developed in both *Breakaway Learners* and *Trauma Doesn't Stop at the School Door*.[20]

SEL competencies in educational settings help students identify and regulate emotions, develop and maintain positive self-identity and peer and teacher relationships, solve problems, and improve their mental wellness and general well-being. Developing students' competencies reduces disruptive behavior and emotional distress and promotes engagement and learning. In sum, SEL creates a school climate that enhances the whole child's cognitive and emotional development and academic success. Social and emotional competencies have been standardized and used in more than half the states in the country. Research demonstrates the impact of SEL on various child outcomes, among them well-being and behavioral and academic measures. High-quality SEL programming positively impacts teachers and other school staff and improves school culture and climate.

Teachers have to be trained and coached in SEL as one of their professional development goals. To ensure progress, schools have to monitor that there is continued quality improvement in SEL programming. Our survey respondents supported the need for this type of professional development, as shown in Table C, available through the QR code at the end of the book.

We appreciate that SEL will not solve all that ails education; that said and as noted above, in the context of trauma and toxic stress, SEL's benefits are empirically verified and are worthy of implementation. The respondents to the survey recognized the import and impact of SEL implementation, as indicated in Table 3.1.[21]

We recognize that there is a reluctance to implementing SEL from some parents, educators, and leadership in parts of the United States. But many teachers embedded SEL practices in their daily instruction, both online and in classrooms, during the pandemic with success. Our survey highlights for us the educators' commitment to continuing their SEL practices, employing them to teach and model decision-making, conflict resolution, taking responsibility for one's behavior, naming and taming negative feelings, redirecting negative thoughts and behavior, and using mindfulness strategies.[22]

One of the authors has developed two knowledge- and skill-based training curricula: Trauma-Informed Care: Hope, Strengths, Resilience, Growth, and Healing,

Table 3.1. Frequency of Responses on "Sustaining Change in Social and Emotional Learning"

Statement	Strongly disagree (%)	Disagree (%)	Agree (%)	Strongly agree (%)	Agree or strongly agree (%)
I made changes during the pandemic that improved the social and emotional development and learning of my students.	1.9	6.9	63.5	27.7	91.19
I plan to continue the changes I made during the pandemic that improved the social and emotional development and learning of my students.	1.3	6.3	57.2	35.2	92.45
I have the administrative support to continue the changes I made as an educator during the pandemic.	1.9	11.3	59.1	27.7	86.79

Figure 3.2. Ed K. S. Wang, *Pandemic Positives Support Students' Mental Wellness*, 2023

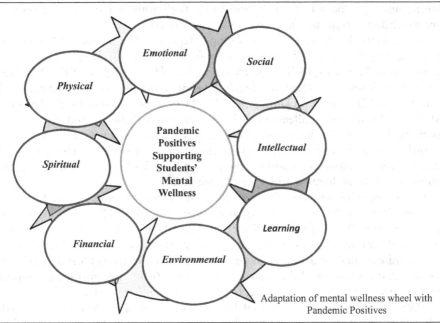

Adaptation of mental wellness wheel with
Pandemic Positives

and Wellness and Resilience in Children and Communities. The curricula offer professional development in behavioral health and human services, education, and youth programs. Both use the growth mindset of strength and resilience, focusing on understanding children's age-appropriate social and emotional milestones, and applied SEL strategies enable remediation for those who are experiencing delays. Trauma-Informed Care further focuses on the impact of ACEs, toxic stress and trauma, and social and emotional dysregulation and contains in-depth, trauma-responsive strategies. Demand for the training is high; it meets a need further confirmed by our survey responses.

The country has invested in two separate tracks aimed at student mental wellness: the SEL curriculum and trauma-responsive schools, both in existence years before the pandemic. The integrated vision and expansion of the two separate tracks need to be boosted, a theme developed more fully in Part III.[23]

The preceding discussion is captured in Figure 3.2, which combines the features of mental wellness with the pandemic positives.

LITERATURE SCAN

We reviewed books, reports, and articles pertaining to what occurred in education during the pandemic. To be sure, much of the content centered on the harms and losses students went through. But positive stories have crept into books and the wider media, revealing strategies that improved the lives of students who were learning online, in person, or in hybrid form. Both authors have written on this topic too, offering hope to educators in the midst of crisis.

Several helpful sources are worth noting: Gregory C. Hutchings and Douglas S. Reed's *Getting Into Good Trouble at School: A Guide to Building an Antiracist School System*, Wayne Journell's *Post-Pandemic Social Studies: How COVID-19 Has Changed the World and How We Teach*, Stéphan Vincent-Lancrin's "Educational Innovation and Digitalisation During the COVID-19 Crisis: Lessons for the Future," and David Osher and colleagues' "Trauma-Sensitive Schools and Social and Emotional Learning: An Integration." These texts are focused principally on areas in which positive change has occurred—antiracism, social studies, technology, and trauma-sensitive schools. By contrast, the present book looks across disciplines and learning spaces to highlight a wider set of positives.[24]

We have been influenced by the architecture and content of another text, Emiliana Vegas and Rebecca Winthrop's "Beyond Reopening Schools: How Education Can Emerge Stronger Than Before COVID-19." Despite the considerable value of this report, its publication predates sizable developments during and after COVID, something we address here in detail, including the installation of hybrid learning and the upheaval that accompanied the return to in-person attendance. Further, the report does not cover concrete examples that educators can replicate and scale.[25]

Many of the positive articles that have been published are loosely connected, in that they reveal certain in-the-trenches actions, activities, and approaches that teachers and leaders implemented. For a subset of educators from prekindergarten through adult learning, the pandemic brought an awareness of the need for change, new ways to address old problems. For example, teachers in Colorado were so motivated that they formed a group and issued a report on lessons learned from the pandemic. Among these is the need to think differently about assessment. They saw the benefits of suspending standardized testing, which occurred during the pandemic, a topic we take up in Part II. These educators sought to bring about different types of assessments, including those that measure "soft skills," often regarded as less important but that were critical during the pandemic and remain critical for work, family, and community success. Their report noted that some of the skills the educators wanted to measure were students' ability to work independently, to explain and show work in different ways, to manage time, and to advocate for themselves.[26]

In essence, while teachers might already have questioned standardized testing, the pandemic gave them the opportunity to think differently about assessment rather than simply following the prescribed norms. In a world where rules were bent or abandoned, there was the air to reenvision assessment. Doing so emerged from a powerful insight, and it is one of many that educators had as a result of the pandemic.[27]

We also were influenced by articles outside the field of education but that have an impact on how we see students and educators. One, in fact, was written by a coauthor of the present book; in his text "A Journey of Public Stewardship on Asian American and Pacific Islander Mental Health: Massachusetts's Approach to Addressing Disparities," he describes game-changing events and positive game changers that have transformed mental health care for Asian American and Pacific Islander communities across the country and that can transform education as well.[28]

TEACHER VOICES

From the onset our goal has been to include teacher voices. We often speak about the importance of listening to teachers in the trenches, but we fail to ask for their views, and even when we ask, we do not take those views into account in policy-making and decision-making. In this book, we seek to right those wrongs.

One of the authors learned the hard way when at an open meeting he addressed a planning group on developing supported education and employment services for young adults. After the planning members were introduced, a young Latina, who was not a planning member, stood up and stated, "Nothing about us without us." She represented the age group of users of this program. Our coauthor was embarrassed, and since that day, he has carried a slip of paper on which he had written the young woman's statement, to remind himself that representation has to be fully inclusive. Such inclusion brings relevancy to and ownership of the program. To that end, we have listened to teachers in various ways.

First, throughout the pandemic we conducted webinars on how trauma impacted the educational system. Often labeling the webinars "conversations," we provided key moments in which to get attendee feedback. We listened and took notes. We circulated the notes to attendees, so they could reflect on the topics discussed. Add to this that both of us taught online and in person during the pandemic, again opportunities not only to share information but also to learn from the participating adult students.

Second, during the pandemic, we, together with two additional educators, formed and ran the Virtual Teachers' Lounge (VTL), an online forum through which we continue to serve educators. Initially we had a consistent cohort but given the needs of educators, we went to an open enrollment approach. Every month (and sometimes more frequently), we have had an online dialogue with educators about their experiences. Some were new to the field, and their struggles were real and poignant, particularly in the absence of quality mentoring. Seasoned educators shared their thoughts about how education was changing. Retired educators—many of whom were still involved in education through substitute teaching, mentoring, writing, and assisting their own children and grandchildren—also expressed their thoughts and concerns. Over the years of VTL, we have listened to the voices— often repeated voices from the same individuals—of several dozen educators.

Third, during and after the pandemic, we visited schools and organizations, virtually and in person, to conduct seminars and programs and engage with teachers and counselors. All were opportunities to participate with those working day-to-day with students of all ages and at all stages. In addition, both of us have taught continuing education courses, which provide opportunities to hear the voices of enrolled participants.

Fourth, we both had independent, unique opportunities to engage with educators. One of us had call-in hours at various times with different schools and organizations to help individuals employed in these institutions who were struggling with the trauma of events. These one-on-one sessions were a chance to learn about what was most troubling to educators and to ponder with them how to move forward more effectively. The other author spent 6 months living in China, comparing cultures, considering the views of a wider group of educators, and experiencing different educational settings and pandemic protocols.

The amalgam of all this exposure to listening encouraged us to check our own biases and compare our own reflections with the reflections of those with whom we were engaging.

SURVEY

To ensure the presence of educator voice, the authors conducted an online survey over a 2-week period in June 2023 to gather the views of educators across the K–12 pipeline. We have preserved the anonymity of our respondents. Both of us had experience conducting surveys previously.[29]

The survey has 159 total valid responses. To participate in the survey, educators needed at least 2 years of teaching experience to provide a basis for trying out strategies and comparing classrooms. Standard demographic data were collected to indicate the diversity of respondents, with additional information on years of service, geographic location, educational setting, and use of online tools during the pandemic. Respondents had an option not to provide any of the requested information. It was voluntary for respondents to offer their email addresses. Respondents then could receive a gift card and entry into a grand prize drawing.

As reflected in Tables A and B, available through the QR code at the end of the book, we had marked diversity across a wide range of demographic categories; we also observed the substantially different educational settings in which the respondents were working and the length of their service. These data enable us to have comfort in the strength of the responses received. They are well worth reviewing in detail, even with a sampling limitation, because most respondents learned about the survey from the coauthors' webinars, VTL, and educational networks.[30]

The survey gathers information from educators on how they responded at the heart of the pandemic. We sought to determine what knowledge educators considered to enhance a positive school climate for learning and working during the pandemic and thereafter. We wanted to assess whether the educators would maintain changes they made in their practice postpandemic, and we queried whether school resources were available to support their efforts.

The focus areas are grounded in evidence-based education, mental health practice, and lessons learned from VTL. They are the following: understanding of the students as whole persons and in the context of their families, students' engagement and trust, social and emotional learning, online and hybrid teaching, school and community partnerships, alternative discipline strategies to substitute for classroom removal, sensory activation, creativity as a needed tool for teaching and learning, staff development, and hope as a motivator for improved teaching and working in schools during the pandemic.

The survey contained 33 closed-ended questions that used a four-point Likert scale of agreement and disagreement ratings. Each topic addressed had three similar questions related to knowledge, continued implementation, and resource availability. Table C, available through the QR code, presents an example, to familiarize readers with the format we continually use.

The respondents first rated the knowledge statement of each of the focus areas. The authors have incorporated relevant data results into this book.

There were two open-ended questions that followed completion of all closed-ended questions. We reviewed the open-ended responses, reading and analyzing for critical phrases and themes. The questions were opportunities for educators to write in their voices, and we have included their responses where applicable throughout the book.

The survey questions are available through the QR code at the end of this book.

METHODOLOGICAL COMFORT LEVEL

Between theory, research studies, news media articles, books, teacher voices, our experiences, the experiences of other educators, and our survey results (vetted to the extent possible to eliminate bots), we are comfortable that this book reflects what occurred during the pandemic in classrooms across the country. The survey met our goals, namely, gathering, listening to, and sharing the real voices and experiences of educators from 30 states working in the trenches. Our purpose was not to design a survey using sample representation, sample frame, and sampling types to minimize response bias. A census-based survey by design would lead to a higher level of confidence in generalizability. We reported the frequency of responses to each Likert item. That said, we did not intend to nor did we focus on statistical analysis of frequency distribution, central tendency, and variability of degree of dispersion. We welcome a more robust research design and its accompanying findings. Given all the sources we used as a whole, we believe that the pandemic positives we identify in fact were seen and tried by a sizable number of educators. We believe, then, that the approaches we suggest for replicating and scaling the pandemic positives will yield benefits to our educational system.

We are keenly aware of the differences between qualitative data (which constitute a sizable portion of the data we gathered) and quantitative data (also used here from studies conducted on trauma and mental wellness). In the context of the pandemic positives, the combination of both qualitative and quantitative data reinforces our approaches, including in the stickiness of solutions we proffer.

Of course, all data can be questioned and massaged by different scholars, and we recognize that no single source of data is outcome determinative, just as no single educational assessment of a child's learning is definitive. With caution we can say that here some data are better than no data, and we encourage readers to consider our findings through their own lens and to push back as needed, but to accept, too, the voices of many as powerful indicators of trends, ideas, and innovations.[31]

We conclude Part I with a voice from one of the open-ended questions we asked of educators. And then we turn to Part II, starting with the most dramatic change experienced in education in decades: schools and colleges shutting their doors.

> *Before the pandemic, my role as an educator was as a classroom teacher. I delivered instruction, supported my students in as many ways possible to guide them to educational successes. However, once the pandemic started, my role shifted into that of an educator also tasked as a community support person. We checked in weekly with all of our school families to ensure they had supplies, food, funds, internet, a computer, and time to do schoolwork. Coming out of the pandemic, we have continued many of our wraparound supports and it has taught me to engage my students in many ways; not just academically but to get to know them as a whole person. This shift has been instrumental in being a more effective educator.*

FINDING AND EXPLORING THE PANDEMIC POSITIVES

Part II

FINDING AND EXPLORING THE
PANDEMIC POSITIVES

CHAPTER 4

Closed Doesn't Mean Closed

THE COMPLEX CLOSURE TIMELINE

The impact of COVID on the educational system writ large was experienced at many levels and presents layers of complexity, even in developing a timeline for what occurred in terms of school closings and reopenings across the United States. While initially a chart seemed the best approach, we realized—and want our readers to realize—that there is no single timeline. Different states—and within those states different districts, and within those districts different schools—closed, offered online learning and hybrid learning, and then reopened at different times. Reread that sentence—difference abounds, and then you can add colleges and universities into the mix for added complexities.

What follows is a general sense of what happened and when within educational institutions, recognizing that readers will need to situate themselves based on their own locations, educational institutions, and COVID levels.[1]

Educational institutions began shuttering in February 2020, with the majority closing completely in March. The ramp-up to online learning varied dramatically among institutions, for reasons detailed later in Part II. Some were able to ramp up in as quickly as days; others took weeks or months, in some cases many months. In that gap between closure and online implementation, some institutions used alternative approaches, such as videoconferencing through the Zoom and FaceTime programs, to allow learning to continue. Some systems brought into the school building the students with the greatest educational needs for in-person learning. Others kept older children out of in-person schooling for longer periods when in-person learning was reinstated. To place this in a larger, international context, in 2020, schools were closed across the globe for an average of 79 school days, virtually half a school year.[2]

Starting in fall 2020, a limited number of institutions began in-person learning for some students (including in hybrid form, where some students were in school and others were learning online at home at the same time). But at most institutions, online learning was the norm until or through spring 2021. In-person learning (sometimes with an online component) returned in earnest in fall 2021, with some short-term temporary closures during that academic year. This meant that for some students entering 1st grade, it was their first year in a school building. And for some sophomores in college, it was their first year living on a campus. Academic year 2022–2023 was largely in person, with some continued use of online learning for some students or hybrid learning in some localities. By fall 2023, in-person learning was the new normal, though "normal" as we knew it never returned. There remained, and still remains, the risk of short-term closures, given spikes in COVID or outbreaks of other illnesses among staff or students.

To summarize, most schools were shuttered in March 2020 and many operated with online learning for the following 12 to 18 months; large-scale reopening for in-person learning did not return until late spring or fall 2021. It is also worth reflecting on how our memories have conflated these years—the COVID years—and collapsed our sense of time. The confinement, closures, and distancing all melded into one lump of time—without the usual precision with which we view time. You can test yourself: Come up with a relatively ordinary event that occurred during the pandemic (good or bad or in between, such as going to a movie, going out to dinner, having friends over, or going to the dentist) and try to remember the date, month, and year when the event last occurred. This is beautifully captured in a photograph by Andrea Frazzetta of a sculpture of a hippo suspended from a high ceiling: Time was suspended during COVID. Figure 4.1 shows one of our own renditions of COVID's

Figure 4.1. Karen Gross, *Time Confused*, 2023

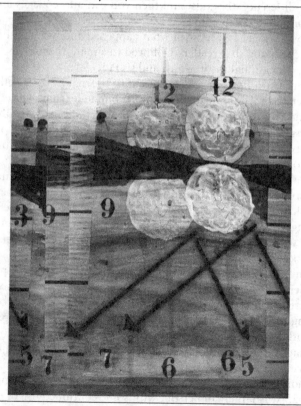

impact on our sense of time. It does have a title, but you can create your own title for it (a good activity for students as well).[3]

ADDED FACTORS AFFECTING CONTEXT

This chapter focuses on a time period when schools, colleges, and universities were closed and online programs were not yet operational or being used. It's worth observing that not all institutions closed. Some private and charter schools never shuttered. And for the record, it was often the elite institutions that did not close. And yes, there was homeschooling before the pandemic, some of which included online learning, presenting a set of issues we won't address here.[4]

We need to contextualize the timing of these closures too—not only the pandemic, but also social unrest disrupted education. In 2020, as closures occurred, the Pew Research Center reported that many Black and Asian Americans experienced increased discriminatory behavior. With the media reporting that COVID originated in China, there was increased anti-Chinese sentiment, with a considerable increase in physical and verbal violence and subtle discrimination toward all Asian Americans as if they were homogeneous. Surveying 16 major American cities, the Center for the Study of Hate and Extremism at California State University, San Bernardino, found an alarming increase in hate crimes against Asian Americans in 2020. Although the overall rate of hate crime reports fell by 7% during the pandemic, anti–Asian American hate crimes rose by almost 150%. This led to President Joe Biden, with the support of both chambers of Congress, signing the COVID-19 Hate Crimes Act.[5]

The increase in Asian hate crimes impelled Asian families to choose online learning or homeschooling rather than send their children to in-person school. Black and Hispanic families, too, increasingly turned to the use of homeschooling.[6]

One of the coauthors developed a frequently used poster with the assistance of the artist Shengqi Li, shown in Figure 4.2, to reach out to Asian Americans who needed to talk about their situation; the poster aimed to encourage Asian Americans to reestablish their sense of psychological and emotional balance.

At the start of school closures and moving forward in time, the data reveal, as noted earlier, that administrators and parents reported a growing youth mental health crisis.

When schools closed, working parents and caregivers were in a very real jam. As an aside, online learning did not cure this problem completely either. Their school-age children were home, and for frontline workers, work still called. For many, since house payments, rent, or bills did not cease, stopping work was not an option. And for those whose work could be done remotely, the presence of young and older students (including college students who returned home) created unanticipated challenges, among them the need for quiet space, development of learning opportunities for children, work requirements whether in person or remote, and caregiving for babies. The already complex balance of work and parenting became harder almost overnight. And the risk of illness to family members, friends, and the wider community was omnipresent.[7]

Figure 4.2. Ed K. S. Wang, *Wellness Under the Cloud of Racism*, 2021

A REAL NEGATIVE

Before turning to the positives that these closures generated (and yes, education continued in creative ways in some settings), there is one negative that merits attention if we are to retain some of the positives: Data reveal that school closures affected people of color and low-income families more severely, widening an already unacceptable equity gap. For parents and caregivers with resources and access to educators or who were college graduates, solutions were implemented more readily, including with children in different grades across the educational landscape. For those with limited resources before the pandemic or whose financial hardships were exacerbated by it or who struggled with English or did not have a high school degree, the difficulties mounted. And for those without a computer and internet access, it was even more challenging.[8]

School closures weren't easy even for families with money and education. We are not suggesting otherwise by a long shot. But families who lacked resources and education and were not proficient in English found school closures especially debilitating. These barriers are unacceptable when we consider future positives. Absent removing or at least lessening the harm of these root causes of disparate outcomes, school closures will continue to damage the most vulnerable. So any positives that ameliorated the impact of school closures through expenditures or access to key nonmonetary resources (personal connections, educational advantages) will require sufficient funding before they are suitable for replication and scalability.

HOME DELIVERY

The closure of schools did not impede all educators from educating. Some of them, perhaps more than we know, just did it differently. Some educators hand-delivered materials to their students' homes. This meant locating where students lived and leaving materials on a doorstep or outside an apartment door or in shelters. And these educators had to create the materials, often without access to their school building's copying machine and other resources.

To connect with their students, without online-learning programs, a few teachers actually provided learning at students' homes through living room windows, on driveways, and on lawns, using a whiteboard to explain how to do math problems. Usually this was done one on one, but some educators met with groups of students in parks and other open areas during the closures. For these students, just seeing their teacher—even if the teacher could not enter their home because of COVID risks—gave them a sense of continuity and engagement.[9]

Then, some teachers took to texting, calling, and teleconferencing students, helping them with work that they had left for them and encouraging them and telling them how much they looked forward to seeing them again soon. These educators were still educating students, just differently.[10]

School librarians read books to and with a child on the phone or via FaceTime. Harnessing what was being used in workplaces, educators turned to videoconferencing to teach students who had access to it. This was not online learning that came through the school system; it was use of technology personalized by educators to reach students. Add to this that librarians helped students access books and resources online during (and after) this period of closure. It was a role that led some librarians to define themselves as the glue that allowed education to continue. Book drop-offs by drone happened, although one has to suppose they were a rarity![11]

On a more personal level, one of us read our children's books to an isolated family, and both of us independently created YouTube stories on the subject of social distancing, in English, Spanish, and Chinese, making them available online for free, and promoted them through social media and our networks. Massachusetts's Quincy public library included links to *Key-Key the Monkey and the Coronavirus Intruder* on their online Home for Kids webpage. Many of the library's patrons are Chinese children and their families. The *Wrinkles Doesn't Like Social Distancing* YouTubes in English and Spanish appeared as online teacher resources and were featured in the *Today Show*'s online parenting resource site as well as through *BBN Times*, an online news source in the United Kingdom.[12]

A pandemic positive is that we all recognized the power of connectedness, however it is created. And that connectedness can be a focus moving forward when schools operate in person; educators who took extra steps saw the benefits of connectivity, and there are ways that it can be continued for students ill at home or students who are struggling. In a sense, the glue analogy mentioned earlier has broader implications: We need to be glued together.

For an image of how confusing school closures were for students, see Figure 4.3, taken from the coauthors' book *The Feeling Alphabet Activity Set*. Note that the image mentions both right- and left-brain functions referred to in Part I.[13]

EDUCATOR APPRECIATION

Parents and caregivers trying to provide education to their children on their own came to see how hard it is to be a teacher. These parents, perhaps without openly acknowledging it, comprehended the challenges in educating 20 to 30 students at once. The parents were struggling simply to educate their own children or grandchildren. Teaching is not easy, they learned. Even managing one's own children for 7 hours—with or without formalized content—was a challenge. Parental and caregiver appreciation for the skills, energy, creativity, and patience that teaching requires became evident.[14]

Figure 4.3. From Karen Gross and Ed Wang, *The Feeling Alphabet Activity Set*, 2022

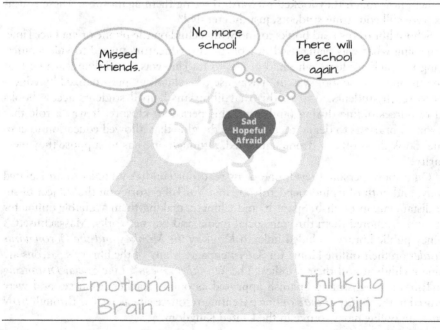

What also became clearer to parents was the role that schools played in the lives of their children and the many things children learned there, such as teamwork, structure, art, and music. And schools offered supports beyond the classroom, from a nurse, to a librarian, to a social worker, to a counselor, to all the caring adults who understood child development and were dedicated to students who were not their own. Most of that was missing when schools were closed and parents and caregivers couldn't fill the gaps.[15]

This is a remarkable pandemic positive. Some parents and caregivers, perhaps many more parents than we realize, came to understand and appreciate the role schools and educators played in the lives of their children and the difficulty of the tasks these educators performed daily. It is easy to forget that newfound realization now that schools have returned to in-person learning, but it is a lesson that should be remembered. As one parent tweeted when schools were closed, "Been homeschooling a 6-year old and 8-year old for one hour and 11 minutes. Teachers deserve to make a billion dollars a year. Or a week."[16]

We can support this appreciation for educators through perpetual reminders. For example, there could be the installation of some regularized teacher appreciation—notes, cards, calls, visits to school. What if once a month, parents made breakfast for teachers to enjoy at school or provided a precooked dinner the teachers could bring home to their families, to save them from cooking after a long day of work? What if there was one afternoon a month when teachers could leave early and different parents could come in and provide activities? To be sure, some schools across the nation already had teacher appreciation efforts in place, including through parent–teacher associations, but the goal here is to make this a more universal practice.

They say that respect is hard to gain and easy to lose. A study in 2020 showed that 80% of responding parents had "much more respect" for teachers than they had had before the pandemic. With a host of teachers gaining respect during the pandemic, it is our responsibility to ensure that respect remains intact to the greatest extent possible. We have already seen inroads to reversing the trend.[17]

PODS AND OUTDOOR LEARNING

In the absence of pre-K–12 schools, some parents and caregivers created pod learning, in which families gathered small groups of children, largely similar in age, and then either hired an educator or used a volunteer parent or two or three to provide these young people with educational options. The pods varied across neighborhoods. In communities where neighbors had preexisting relationships, it was an easier transition, as families had already engaged with one another. Pods were more common in wealthier neighborhoods, where parents had a college degree. In vertical communities, that is, neighborhoods with apartment buildings, where the groups could not be held in people's homes because of space constraints, organizations, community groups, and housing authority personnel had to create both space and pods for children. This was much harder to do than what was possible in more well-to-do communities, though it was far from easy there.[18]

Beyond their being the equivalent of small classes, what made these pods interesting was the amount of time spent outside and on play, as opposed to formalized learning, and the presence of engagement and joy. This harks back to an era when outdoor educational settings were common, including in times of threat from disease. In communities where pods were largely voluntarily formed groups, they functioned remarkably well.[19]

For students who lived in unsafe neighborhoods and were kept indoors for protection, access to learning outdoors was liberating. Just breathing outdoor air—even city air—was refreshing. An organization called Trust for Public Land developed math programs for use in playgrounds and for educating teachers and provided needed supplies, something that had begun before the pandemic. The programs could have been used by students when schools were closed, with parents acting as teachers, and they surely could continue after the pandemic. When schools become part of the community ecosystem, an excellent opportunity arises to mobilize community resources to support student learning. By viewing schools more broadly as key community assets, we help all learners in the community succeed.[20]

Where educators were hired (college students filled this role at times as their institutions closed, as did out-of-work educators), the pods involved learning. But it was not traditional classroom learning. Educators chose and put together materials on their own, although some used lessons prepared and delivered by school systems. And because much happened out of doors, learning through nature and activities outside became more commonplace. Outdoor games like hide-and-seek abounded. So did study of trees, plants, and water. Drawing flourished and tactile experiences grew, all activating the senses, which is critical for trauma amelioration.

Consider the many benefits of outdoor learning—even in the rain—for all learners, children and adults. Students use their bodies; they exercise; there's an outlet for anxiety and pent-up emotions; it allows for social interaction. Abundant

Table 4.1. Frequency of Responses on "Seeing Schools as Community Resources"

Statement	Strongly disagree (%)	Disagree (%)	Agree (%)	Strongly agree (%)	Agree or strongly agree (%)
Schools are an integral part of community solutions to meet the needs of students and families.	0.6	6.3	50.9	42.1	93.08
I support my school being an ongoing part of a community solution to meet student and family needs.	2.5	6.9	44.7	45.9	90.57
I have the administrative and community support to deliver on such an approach.	2.5	6.9	44.7	45.9	90.57

studies show that outdoor learning enhances attentiveness, adds new vocabulary, and improves memory. Exposure to sunlight has health benefits too.[21]

Outdoor learning was a way to reduce the risks of virus transmission in schools and other closed spaces. It was not a perk but a necessity, and even when schools reopened with social distancing, outdoor learning took on new prominence.[22]

Add to this that there were some differences in ages among the students gathered in pods, something rarely seen in school classrooms, where we perpetually are tied to age-based grade levels (even if we subgroup in a class based on performance and grade levels). The pods were similar to a one-room schoolhouse, where children learned together and helped one another. And some of the best of in-school education could be transported to the pods, making some wonder whether micro-learning should be the wave of the future.[23]

Stronger students had the chance to help younger or weaker students, an approach in some learning environments before the pandemic. Struggling students could join in activities where the age differential did not play out negatively. For all students, engagement and role modeling were part of the process. And it led to discovery, experimentation, and new ways of capturing knowledge. Drawing and other art forms, such as dance and music, could flourish, and without restraint. Food was plentiful in some settings. And given the way some pods were constructed, students did not all have to be involved in the same activity at the same time. If students needed a break, they could take one. If a student wanted to simply watch, that student could. Structure existed, with set start and end times and even time for specific content learning, but within the structure there was plentiful opportunity for personalization.

There are several pandemic positives here that have remarkable value. Outdoor learning for all learners (adults and children) can become a regular part of our educational system, whatever the climate, engaging students in hands-on, project-based learning. Combining classes—even for a brief duration—has enormous value, helping both stronger and weaker students. Add to this that helping others learn activates mirror neurons—our empathy engines—which are trauma ameliorating. Finally, pod learning—small-group engagement—has tangible benefits that could be re-created in schools, with students working in small groups on various projects across time.

SCHOOL STAFF STILL WORKED

In the midst of school closures, some may have assumed that school personnel simply stopped working and remained with their own families. But once we look more closely at what happened in practice, we see remarkable new activities among school nurses, counselors, social workers, psychologists, athletic coaches, and others employed by schools and colleges. What emerges from a sampling of their activities is a set of new roles, expanded understandings of the families they served, and the capacity to exhibit flexibility in the face of crises. The result is that these professionals acted in ways that created pandemic positives that should be retained and replicated in a post-COVID era. They recognized the need for wellness in all its dimensions.

One added observation: School bus drivers played a key role in learning, by shepherding school buses fitted with an Internet connection, referred to later in Part II, to where students were located. Further, we cannot forget leaders; we focus on them in Part III.

There is an added spoken and unspoken message to all: These professionals have a key role in future crises, and their voices should not be ignored (as they sometimes were) and the respect they need to be accorded should be recognized in the schools and colleges where they work daily. As one commentator observed quite pointedly, it took a pandemic to recognize the value of school nurses.[24]

NURSES

Even when schools were closed, school nurses worked on many projects (though, sadly and erroneously, they often were not consulted sufficiently, if at all, about school reopening plans). They worked on tracing student health; they focused on mitigation strategies schools could implement. Some had an increased communication role about COVID and strategies for testing and treatment of students and families as well as educators. They helped families understand the risks of COVID and the best wellness protocols. In essence, the function of school nurses evolved, from giving in-person treatment to students to playing a public health role in the school community. Some school nurses made referrals to outside medical professionals when they saw the need.[25]

Some school nurses also worked on getting food deliveries to students, quickly recognizing the high value for students of food in schools and the risks of its absence. And they helped to ensure that delivery rules were expanded so that food could be picked up by families other than in lunchrooms and cafeterias—at places of worship, drive-throughs, community centers, even school bus stops. Some nurses played a key role by emphasizing the importance of youth physical fitness to curb obesity and worked on ensuring that medications were delivered.[26]

One school nurse discovered that the family of a student at the nurse's school was stricken by COVID and needed formula for their baby. They intended to go out to get the formula despite everyone in the family having tested positive. With the help of a local community social service agency, the nurse arranged for a case of formula to be delivered to the family within a day, thus inhibiting the spread of the virus and greatly assisting the student's family.[27]

COUNSELORS

In some ways, school counselors worked on issues similar to those addressed by school nurses. They focused on needed policy changes and developed mechanisms for connecting with students that did not involve learning platforms. For example, they used texts, emails, and FaceTime.

They recognized familial mental health needs as well as physical needs for food. Telemeetings began and counselors found other ways to connect with their students. They continued to help students develop healthy mindsets to overcome social and emotional challenges and assisted with self-motivated and self-directed learning, time management, and study habits. They counseled junior and senior students on educational and vocational plans after graduation. They assisted with college applications. They reached out in person and virtually to students with poor attendance during the pandemic to reengage them in learning.[28]

In one district, several counselors coordinated their efforts to create an online resource for students called the Calming Room. This site, which still exists, is remarkable. It has interactive art opportunities, links to animal cams, and virtual tours of museums, the NASA research center, botanical gardens, and other locations. Like the Virtual Teachers' Lounge, it used the opportunities of the online arena to create safe and beneficial spaces.[29]

In some districts, school counselors created weekly check-ins with students. Some revamped their websites to make them interactive and engaging. Still others created online tools like Boredom Busters, developed by Wisconsin School Counselors, which continues to this day.[30]

We would be remiss if we did not recognize the role of school social workers in many school systems; not unlike counselors, they continued to support students and their families as well as the educators. Whether online or through calls or texts, they found ways to work to reduce the constant stresses the pandemic imposed. As expressed by the School Social Work Association of America in a resolution statement released in 2020, "We must prioritize mental health support if we expect our students to truly recover and regain skills from the lost in-class instruction time."[31]

PSYCHOLOGISTS

School psychologists continued to offer services to students when schools were closed, but the challenges were great and their focus was forced to change. Part of the shift came after the federal and state education departments and the Association of School Psychologists lifted certain regulations that permitted school psychologists to delay initial testing and reevaluations according to prescribed timetables. An added aspect of this shift was that these professionals could no longer provide special education assessments in person and could not administer learning assessments online. So their work shifted from doing large-scale testing to providing increased mental health consultation and collaboration.[32]

School psychologists were now needed more than ever to help students cope with increasing social and emotional issues, including stress and trauma, driven by the pandemic. Even before the pandemic, mental health resources had been scarce and many families had to wait for long periods to get psychological help for their children. It was an added challenge to impart needed help, as was true for other school professionals, when students and families had no computers or connection to the internet.

The pandemic was not the only driver of an increased need for psychological support. When educational institutions closed, disruptions continued outside schools. During periods of closure, violence; social and political unrest; unemployment and underemployment; and family dysfunction, including from addiction, negatively affected the mental health of many. Not only did students suffer from the grief of losing loved ones—in many cases, but not all, because of the pandemic—some also experienced adjustment disorders, acute stress, and PTSD. Educators also experienced anxiety and distress and needed support from psychologists. A National Association of School Psychologists survey showed that school psychologists, even before the pandemic, did not have enough time to provide mental and behavioral health support, to consult on student and teacher mental wellness, and to provide crisis intervention in communities.[33]

A pandemic positive is the recognition of school psychologists' critical roles and the previously untapped skills they were able to use when schools were closed. A related positive has been the recognition of the need to address, not skip over, mental wellness. This realization helped schools prepare for increased mental health needs when they reopened. This can be fully realized only if there is sufficient funding to improve staffing/student ratios (and this issue applies to counselors and social workers as well).

As noted by one of the respondents to our survey, *"Leaders can get help into the buildings for student mental health and to help students learn how to regulate their emotions and behaviors."*

ATHLETIC COACHES

To contextualize the role of athletic coaches, start with this reality, referred to earlier: Documented depression set in among high school and college athletes who were not engaging with their teammates and coaches when schools were shuttered. Some coaches continued to stay in touch with their athletes through online mechanisms (not learning platforms): They used phone blasts, Instamessaging, Facebook, and their own websites to do outreach. They also established regular communication schedules, as in "You will hear from me every Thursday morning with updates." This allowed for continuity and structure in the midst of disruption. Some coaches held team meetings online through Zoom or other platforms, replete with agendas.[34]

In California, coaches coalesced as a group to lift tight restrictions on in-person play. Some schools permitted outdoor conditioning sessions—no touching, prescribed social distancing, no high-fives, no spitting. Other coaches arranged reviews of films as part of their connection with students; watching sports and sports movies together also occurred. The goal for many coaches was to remain in the lives of their students. Some arranged a virtual signing day for those of their athletes going on to college Division 1 schools.[35]

The pandemic positive evidenced is twofold: Coaches found ways to connect with students that could be continued after the pandemic and they played a role in improving student mental wellness, one that was always suspected but now was clear. Indeed, a pandemic positive was the realization among educators and parents that coaches were more than sports leaders concerned with wins and losses; they were significant student mentors.

FOOD SERVICE WORKERS

Remarkably, when schools closed, the federal government allowed them to provide free lunches to all students, regardless of families' ability to pay. To contextualize this, from March 9 to May 1, 2020, more than 1.5 billion students did not receive their lunch in schools. It wasn't so easy to fill the food gaps as food workers dealt with food shortages and mandates for menus that were impossible to meet; meals had to be delivered in school parking lots and libraries. In some locations home delivery was provided. When the mandates for menus could not be met because of massive logistical issues in getting food to educational institutions, the food service workers collaborated across schools in their districts and beyond. They traded food among themselves, as they often had an excess of particular items and a shortage of others. And they had to be creative cooks, using the ingredients they had when there were shortages.[36]

The health of food service workers was a critical issue, as their work feeding students was vital to the community. These front-line workers needed protection, which should not end with the pandemic.[37]

There are multiple pandemic positives here: The value of food service workers in meeting the needs of students and families struggling with food scarcity was reinforced; the provision of regular, healthy meals to all students was visible; the respect due to these workers was recognized; opportunities arose for these individuals to work outside the confines of their own institutions as they helped one another; and the risks of mandated menus in times of crisis were discovered.

ADDED INSIGHTS

These positives can be brought into in-person educational environments, rather than being tossed aside, and continue in the prime learning environment. To summarize what we learned from school closures: Students need connection and they can get it in many ways from a range of educational professionals and workers. It was important for students to catch up not only on academic learning but also on social and emotional learning and mental wellness when they returned to school in person. The need for food is central in the lives of students and their families, and schools can be closely involved in flexible new ways to meet this need in the community. Already we have seen changes based on the pandemic's impact on school food: Several states have installed universal free school meals for public school students and more are expected to do the same. We have long lamented that educators are disrespected and the work they do is not appreciated by parents; that's changed at least in part. And we have commented on the negative impacts of silos—both in and across institutions. In schools and colleges, many folks who assist students are not in classrooms; their roles need to be recognized and emphasized and their voices included.

One other group whose role brought about positives when schools closed was leaders. Leadership during COVID—from educational institution closures to online learning to reopenings—was multifaceted and complex. We focus expressly on leadership in regard to the pandemic positives and the lessons moving forward in Part III. Our leaders needed a new set of capacities to navigate all aspects of the crisis, many of which have utility in a noncrisis environment. We haven't forgotten them; they will be addressed.

We want to make one added point about school closures and the claims that it ruined student progress, as allegedly did online learning (addressed in following chapters). We were struck by a lengthy article in the *Boston Globe*, "Lost in a World of Words," concerning poor—below-grade-level—reading scores in Massachusetts. According to the state's Department of Elementary and Secondary Education's testing results in 2023, fewer than one half of 3rd-graders were reading proficiently at grade level. This wasn't a new finding. Deficits in reading go back years, particularly among minority and low-income students. We can debate the quality of testing but we cannot deny that we are failing our students and that education needs to improve. The pandemic positives are surely not the only way to improve educational outcomes but they are one path forward. They are changes we can implement now.[38]

We now turn to online learning, which followed the shuttering of educational institutions in almost all contexts. With the closures, rules had changed; attitudes had changed; and we had already been living for extended periods with uncertainty, fear, and anxiety. It is in this context that the world of education saw a seismic shift from brick-and-mortar learning to remote, online learning. It is as if the tectonic plates undergirding education suddenly moved.

CHAPTER 5

Leaping Into Change

THE GIANT LEAP INTO ONLINE LEARNING

When many schools, colleges, and universities turned to online learning during the pandemic amid the closure of school buildings, this modality was often new territory. Yes, some institutions in higher education had a major online presence; others were in only the nascent stages of offering online courses in select areas or master's programs. Online learning was not prevalent in K–12 schools, and in some instances, it was downright avoided. Schools even confiscated cell phones. For many schools, colleges, and universities, online education was viewed as far inferior to in-person learning.

It is in this context that there was widespread implementation of online classes on, so to speak, the fly. Faculty and staff development for implementing and running online programs rarely existed. Instead, educators had to transfer what they did in the physical school environment to the online world quickly—in weeks or days. And it was surely a challenge for many to do so, as what worked well (or at least passably) in classrooms was not fully transferable to online learning, which many had guessed and subsequently discovered was the case. And online learners ranged from kindergartners to adults and included students at all stages with varying learning styles, languages spoken, and degrees of willingness to shift modalities without discussion or choice.[1]

Add to this novel transformation for institutions, students, and educators that families and caregivers were unprepared for the online launch, and online learning was new to them. Some families did not have computers. Some lacked online skills. Some lacked the internet. In families with more than one child and working parents, the demand for online time and computer access exceeded capacity. Not only was online learning new to schools and universities; it was new to accreditation bodies and governing boards as well as state and national educational oversight bodies.[2]

And there we were, building online learning in real time without sufficient support systems. As many teachers commented, it was like building an airplane while you were in the air. Tricky business to stay in the air. It would be like flying a plane without a fully developed flight plan, air traffic controllers, and mechanics on the ground.[3]

We acknowledge that despite the positives we now describe, there were downsides to the online environment. Some students did not learn well or at all; some floundered and lost social skills. The preexisting equity gap associated with race, ethnicity, language, class, and health, among other factors, grew. Some teachers were burned out and were out of their element, unable to adjust to virtual learning.[4]

There were missed in-person events and activities, from athletics to the performing arts, fieldtrips, proms, and graduations. Some aspects of learning, such as science lab experiments and art, were harder to convert to virtual learning because they are experiential. There were absences from class and from class participation. Whole aspects of what schools provided in addition to classroom learning—break; lunch; snacks; and some in-school supports, such as social workers, guidance counselors, and medical professionals—became inaccessible, although some were made available online. All these negatives are well documented and appeared and still regularly appear in the media and in ongoing discussions about the future of education.[5]

We can discuss ad nauseam the kinks in online learning and the failures in certain areas, some caused by technological shortcomings. We can recognize lower test scores when standardized testing was reinstated a year or two down the road. We know there were learning failures that most affected vulnerable populations.[6]

But here's the remarkable thing: Education—flaws and all—did happen online, and in many situations it worked remarkably well. We benefit from looking at what necessity made happen; we learned both as we went along and learn now with the benefit of 20/20 hindsight. The pandemic created an unprecedented opportunity to reenvision the online delivery of education without strong support systems; we are relying on educators (and students and families) to figure it out. Educators know that the well-being of students is crucial to learning, and the classroom climate, including online, needed to support students' mental wellness. Many educators did figure things out. This and the following chapters focus on what we did in that online conversion and what positive lessons—large and small—we can take from it as we move back to brick-and-mortar learning. We add in this reality: The move back to in-person learning often involved online groups and in-person groups working together; where relevant, we have added lessons learned from this transitional hybrid format.[7]

We begin our focus on online schooling in this chapter with the most critical realizations that occurred in education. In the chapters that follow, we look at both widespread and more specific changes that online learning produced in school systems, institutions, and classrooms. Taking the chapters as a whole, we can see positive changes that can and should endure postpandemic based on what occurred when we moved from brick-and-mortar to online learning during the pandemic.

We begin with the most basic, elemental pandemic positives learned.

THE NEED FOR NECESSITIES

Three fundamental technology pieces are needed to enable the functioning of online learning: available working *hardware* for students and educators; available usable *software* for students and educators, with access to technology assistance when glitches occur; and access to stable, reliable, and affordable *internet access*.

The numbers are startling. The Federal Communications Commission (FCC) estimated that in excess of 15 million public school children lacked internet access or connected devices when schools closed and online learning became the norm by necessity. Others peg the number at more than 9 million; still others say it is closer to 17 million. To contextualize these numbers, there are approximately 50 million public and private school students in the United States. Schools today are still providing home internet in some areas (45%, down from 70% in 2021) through hot spots and reduced rates, but the number is declining along with pandemic-era revenue sources. And these numbers do not include older students in colleges, universities, and technical programs. It is not only for in-class instruction that we need internet access; the internet is a critical communication infrastructure that affects families, workplaces, commerce, and health care, including through telehealth and teletherapy.[8]

In short, before the pandemic, there was a digital divide; the pandemic exacerbated it.[9]

For online learning to work, there needs to be school and educator access to working hardware for delivery of information in real time. Access can take many forms: computers, laptops, tablets, and smartphones. All the hardware has to have internet access (more on that in a moment). And before the pandemic, many families shared their hardware, making individual access for online learning a problem. Previously, similar hardware among students had not been mandated; some students had Macs; others, PCs.[10]

Yes, some schools had Chromebooks and other computers that students used while in the building, in the classroom and school library. Bringing the devices home was often not permitted. And even when purchases were made during the pandemic by school systems or by families, there wasn't abundant time to buy needed computers and plan and arrange distribution and training.[11]

Access to hardware was only part of the problem. The existing and new devices had to be loaded with the appropriate software for online learning, software that did not exist in many locations. Moreover, both educators and students had to download the software, on different types of devices, and enable it to function, often without the assistance of technology experts, who had been available in schools (though not all). Not everyone is adept at or comfortable with downloading programs and getting them to operate effectively. Access codes alone can be a barrier, not to mention that since instructions are typically in English only, the language barrier can be a challenge for those with limited English proficiency. Thus, during the pandemic, learning, as with hardware, happened before all students had their software packages fully loaded and ready to function.[12]

The decisions about optimal platforms were made quickly and frequently without robust, or any, discussion among the educators who would be using these programs daily, an absence experienced in many pandemic contexts, as we observe. The reality was this: "Deal. This is the platform we've adopted; figure out how to use it as effectively as you can."

Then there is the largest issue in some senses: internet access. We have known about the challenges of internet access for years. Much has been written about the disparate access to this service, with poorer and rural areas struggling with needed access points. There were locations where students resided that had a weak signal or none at all. This major infrastructure problem, something that now came under, but wasn't originally within, the purview of educational institutions, required solutions: If educators needed or were forced to reach their students in all locations, then they had to ensure the presence of strong enough internet to enable learning.[13]

As noted, some students and their families could not access internet services before the pandemic. Even when access existed, some families did not have the financial means to pay for it. Some relied on schools, workplaces, and public spaces for internet service, and most of these options were out of reach during lockdown at the height of the pandemic. Such obstacles existed at a higher rate among the most vulnerable populations.

WE RESPONDED ADMIRABLY

With all this, online learning did happen. Yes, it was not all smooth sailing and it was not uniform, but consider what occurred. Some private companies reached out to provide computers to students and families in need, free of charge. Consider those platform providers who worked to enable quick installation and operation of online systems. Funding was increased at the local, state, and federal levels to provide hardware and software. Educators learned how to manage online, even when training was lacking. Public spaces opened their doors to those needing internet access (as they had before the pandemic), even if with restrictions for health and safety reasons. There is much praise to go around for those who stepped up to enable online learning to happen—albeit not rapidly enough in some locations.[14]

Now consider a remarkable innovation during the crisis of the pandemic, one that is emblematic of all the pandemic positives gathered in this book: Schools organized buses and vans to go to internet-deprived areas and brought not only online access but also computers fitted with software for students to use. Some of these vehicles carried educators who worked with students on the computers. In 2020, in Austin, TX, the effort began with 100 school buses loaded with internet access.[15]

During the pandemic, the FCC adopted rules that funded buses through an emergency connectivity measure. The funds also covered hot spots and additional routers. As a senior vice president at the Wi-Fi provider Kajeet noted, "During the height of the pandemic, many school transportation departments used their school busses to deliver food, instructional materials and Wi-Fi to students in need."[16]

The concept of educational internet-accessible buses, or simply put, educational buses, is worth exploring in more detail, because it can be replicated and scaled with stickiness, whereas corporate philanthropy is more amorphous and often a response only to crises, not to quotidian educational deficits, although the opportunity for quality programmatic development, experimentation, and pilot programs is cross-sectored.

To that end, imagine the possibility of educational buses in both urban and rural environments. The buses would provide students with the computers and internet missing from their homes. Perhaps for other students, especially if the buses supplied snacks, they would offer a safe place to learn (before or after in-person school or even instead of school) with a trusted adult and peer engagement. And why not launch school satellites in buses that go to where they are needed, providing small classes and safety and mental wellness support? If we had a national service corps in full operation, this could be one of the potential employment opportunities. Retired educators could be present in the buses. So could recent college graduates. So could other adults looking for mentoring opportunities.[17]

In the United States, buses with internet access existed before the pandemic, the best known having been launched by the Coachella Valley Unified School District in California in 2014. Nevertheless, we can learn a lot about educational buses from what has been happening for decades in less developed countries. In India, Malaysia, Tunisia, and Zimbabwe, for example, buses offering internet access have become portable classrooms, with mixed motivations, to be sure, ranging from the political to public relations. By contrast, the idea did not really catch on in the United States—until the pandemic. And to foreshadow the future, the buses did not remain active beyond the pandemic in many places.[18]

Educational buses are akin to the example in medicine of proning (turning patients on their stomachs), which we share in Part III. Before the pandemic, educational buses were deployed in some locations in some situations; there was hardly uniform implementation. But given the urgent need for online learning during the pandemic (in an analogy to the urgency of saving lives), shortages led to innovation and implementation. With the absence of sufficient ventilators and with rising death rates, proning found a role. Because of the lack of internet and sufficient hardware, educational buses likewise found a role. And like proning, the buses do not need to disappear in the pandemic's aftermath. It is a pandemic positive that has staying power—if we have the will to see it and implement it.

The educational-bus concept has not met with universal approval and has brought controversy. Sadly, these buses also have become politicized. Some within and outside the education field think that if we make buses Wi-Fi accessible or continue their accessibility (at reasonable, low rates), students will use them to play games or surf the net for indecent or inappropriate materials instead of doing school-related work. And the unspoken assumption is that what these students will be doing online, if it is not schoolwork, is useless or detrimental to their well-being. We disagree.

OK, that's a risk and filters can be added to block certain sites deemed offensive. But consider the pluses: For students spending lots of time on buses to get to and from school, athletic events, and fieldtrips, buses with internet offer opportunities for learning, particularly if we expand our notion of learning to include shared communication, problem solving through puzzles and games, and writing messages, perhaps replete with acronyms. And educational buses, as we see them, are far more than vehicles for getting students to and from educational settings at the start and end of each day. The buses can stay in students' neighborhoods during school hours that are not in person, to help students who are learning at home. They also can stay in neighborhoods after school to provide needed support and a safe space.

They can make stable internet available for many families as well, while allowing students to complete their schoolwork and use the internet in creative ways that encourage learning.[19]

We can't help but reflect on the idle buses we see to this very day parked during school days that could be mobilized to foster education in addition to supplying internet access. Yes, it is not free of cost. But the lack of internet access and of engaged education is costly too. It is time to roll out fleets of educational buses, with endless opportunities of what can occur on them. They are a pandemic positive that is being discarded.

Creative solutions were deployed by educators on and for the buses, and those educational buses themselves are a creative idea, which can be replicated. The community stepped up to stock the buses and ensure their internet accessibility, and the value of their doing so should not be lost as education has returned to the school building.

Let's now turn to additional positives learned in the context of online education.

CHAPTER 6

Change Abounds Through
Larger Lessons

OPPORTUNITIES APLENTY

The pandemic positives occurred in education, on a large scale in broad policy changes and on a smaller scale in classroom practices. All the positive changes matter, including those that initially are not visible or articulated. When we view the pandemic positives collectively, we can harness their power.

We start with the large-scale changes that the move to online learning brought about. Before we do so, it is worth considering how the pandemic's tectonic shift in education forced us to deal with change and made us ask different questions, as we were confronted with an entirely new set of circumstances, questions that led to some of the changes that occurred.

Some students became aware of how they learned best and whether they benefited from an in-person guide. Other students saw opportunities to declutter their lives and then managed to fill them with activities that they previously would not have pursued. Educators realized their capacity to change and flex in new ways. The coauthors, too, asked ourselves and others how to manage in a world we had never anticipated, with the omnipresence of illness; death; and financial, emotional, professional, and household uncertainty. *USA Today* published a series in which students and educators revealed how they felt at that time, from school closures to the beginnings of online or hybrid learning. The authors note that we were "presented a set of real-world lessons too close and too fresh to be captured in textbooks." Ponder that observation, both its downsides and its upsides, including the opportunity to learn with fewer texts and more creativity.[1]

Often viewed as a negative, the move to total online was speedy—and we know how glacial change in education typically is. Again, instead of the usual committee reflection and incremental installation of newness within education, the pandemic wrought rapid change. But here's the key. The change was not only rapid but also repeated, and adjustments were made regularly. In others words, educators adapted and reflected as change occurred. *Adaptability* and *flexibility* became the watchwords. Real-time, in-the-trenches work allowed educators to shift and bend and try out new approaches. And what worked on day 1 of online learning might not have worked on day 2. So educators kept adapting what they did, asking questions of themselves and others and building success as they went.[2]

This is a different approach to educational change. Educators having to bend and twist with changing times made them explore new ways of teaching and enabled students to share through their successes, or lack of success, what was and was not working. In essence, there was an unspoken give-and-take, a seesawing movement as part of learning. With the novelty of online learning, educators and students shaped how education was carried out rather than being forced to fit themselves into a preexisting model. They made their model and reshaped it over time. And some students benefited remarkably. Leapfrog moments.[3]

This approach can prepare educators and students for future change, whether caused by a crisis or simply by a new program. Educators learned that instead of having to dot every *i* and cross every *t* when change is upon us, they can not only survive but also thrive. The experience and wisdom displayed by educators could be and was transported; they did not lose their capacity to educate. Instead, they discovered how to educate differently. We address this in Part III in the context of artificial intelligence and ChatGPT.

There are life lessons for students that will help them with their social and emotional development if we recognize what they are seeing modeled. Students are seeing that even with major, unplanned change, one can adapt, adjust, and find ways forward. Students can experience a range of feelings, even contradictory ones. This is very different from feeling that one is stuck in the midst of a storm or one must adhere to what was despite changing circumstances. In short, the brain's capacity to navigate new terrain is a lesson well worth learning.

Ironically, at the heart of a difficult learning modality—online—we witnessed our capacities. That's a pandemic positive for sure. Hear the voice of a respondent to our survey:

> Prepandemic being an educator meant facilitating academic needs with an on site only perspective. Now, there are multiple ways to meet the needs of the learner that expand far beyond the walls of the classroom. I continue to see myself as a learner and resilient individual. My learning never stops because teaching doesn't ever stop.

In reflecting on the questions and changing answers as we moved into unknown space, we were struck by the similarity of what occurred in education to what happens in a musical composition by Marc-André Hamelin, *Four Perspectives for Cello and Piano*. In this 2016 piece, the two instruments engage in a conversation and ask each other questions. It starts with an invitation to engage by the cello, to which the piano, hesitantly at first, responds, and then the instruments "speak" to each other.[4]

What follows are some of the specific larger-scale pandemic positives we've encountered in the online context.

CHANGES IN ASSESSMENT APPROACHES

A central question on which all education rests is, not surprisingly, whether the system is accomplishing desired ends. And to be sure, unlike in the case of public companies, whose degree of success we measure by, among other things, the value of their stock, we are not all in agreement on what outcomes are optimal in public or private education, making it unclear how we assess success. We cannot even agree on what should be taught. We cannot agree on what books should be allowed in classroom and school libraries. Educational success isn't gauged by dollars-and-cents measures, except perhaps when we look at the value of high school technical training programs and undergraduate or graduate degree programs.[5]

Despite the assessment gaps and differences, we already have some answers—perhaps by default. We accredit educational institutions and deploy assessment devices to measure achievement and student and institutional benchmarks. Accreditors at all levels measure prescribed indicators, including seat time; they visit schools and campuses; they measure institutional financial stability. In addition, state and national assessment tests frequently are given in public schools.[6]

The quantity of student testing varies from state to state. Some states mandate testing on key subjects at specific grade levels. In others there is multiple yearly testing. Some tests are state or federally mandated assessments; others are run by private entities and deployed by schools at the behest of school boards and other local overseers. The average public school student in the United States takes eight standardized tests in a year; from prekindergarten to 12th grade the student takes 100.[7]

The debates surrounding the benefits and detriments of student assessment are long-standing. We have pondered whether the tests are fair; whether they cover the correct content as well as noncontent learning such as social and emotional development, problem solving, and analytical processing; whether they are anxiety provoking; whether they should measure progress as well as content acquisition. We have looked at various forms of assessment, from multiple-choice questions, to verbal tests, to individual portfolios, to personalized feedback. We have critiqued the time educators spend on testing in their classrooms and the time they spend preparing students to perform well, particularly if educator performance is linked to student test performance. Educators recognize that time is lost before and after tests as students anticipate testing and wind down from it. And then there are the political and governmental forces pushing testing and test results, from local school boards to state departments of education, along with federal oversight.[8]

Testing was one of the many disruptions of pandemic learning, and some localities suspended it altogether. The states and the federal government suspended previously mandated testing. Now for the first time educators were freed up to assess students in the ways they saw fit. Without the constraints of standardized tests, they tried different assessment modalities, including personal feedback loops and progress reports. In some cases, content ceased being king (or queen). The absence of testing was a relief for many educators, who felt they could use the time dedicated to testing more effectively. That's a remarkable change that impacted all of education as we knew it. That's a pandemic positive—a new pathway into something that was entrenched.[9]

Consider this voice from a survey respondent:

In the period between the pandemic and today, I began to pay more attention to students' developmental comprehensiveness and practical application. I also realized that education is not only a process of imparting knowledge, but also a process of self-discovery and personality development. Therefore, I am trying new teaching methods and strategies to meet students' personalized needs and learning interests, and encourage students to innovate and explore.

Now, it is fair to recognize that student test results on standardized tests fell off when students returned to in-school learning. True enough. But perhaps instead of using that finding to damn all that happened, we need to see that there was learning of a different sort during the online pandemic experience that is not measured in the usual ways. Rather than say that learning did not happen, we need to determine what learning did happen. And we could do that if we shifted what and how we are testing. It would be hard to go back now to assess pandemic learning using different tools, but we most assuredly can use different and additional tools moving forward, enabling broader and more robust assessment in what is assessed and how we assess. While we are doing this reevaluation of evaluation, it is worth pondering the new research on the length of tests. Currently, we set time limits on tests that don't actually test skills, information, or processes. This is because test times can be too short for the amount of material. If students were given less material or more time, they could show what they had learned more accurately.[10]

What the pandemic forced was a rethinking of assessment and assignments, when educators were freer to assess and assign as they saw fit. Operating within the online environment and its risks, they created new forms of assessing and providing assignments; these are pandemic positives that can inform how we test and provide homework on a go-forward basis to measure better and differently.

We are educating, or have the potential to educate, the larger community of stakeholders on the many ways in which education can be measured, of which standardized testing is but one. And we certainly can look to employers to measure whether students are ready and able to succeed in jobs, a form of assessment we have avoided. The educational elements of success in life and contributions to society are far more than what we currently assess. Students will spend more than 50 years working, even if they decide to attend college.

As was done in *Trauma Doesn't Stop at the School Door*, consider this sports analogy to illuminate the foregoing issues of assessment and data interpretation. We measure the quality of an NFL quarterback based on, among other statistics, the number of interceptions he throws (although some more subtle team statistics are being employed). The higher the number, the lower the quarterback is ranked. However, and this is key, we do not take into account how many of those interceptions resulted from a failed catch by the intended receiver or other non-quarterback-related failures such as tipped balls. It doesn't take into account throws made while being sacked. It doesn't take into account poor offensive play calling. For some quarterbacks, the statistics, absent contextualization, make them appear worse at their position than they are. If a quarterback has 15 interceptions over several games but 10 of them resulted from a receiver's failing to catch the ball or dropping or fumbling, then the number 15 doesn't tell the full story.

The same problem exists with students: If we measure their competencies based on standardized multiple-choice tests, we don't factor in the many possible reasons for students' low scores: socioeconomic status; racial, ethnic, or gender bias in the tests; poor educational preparation, including because of weak school systems or weak educators; or the presence of trauma in the home or on the way to school before the test.

In short, the data we collect don't always tell a full story.

DISCIPLINING DIFFERENTLY

Before the pandemic, there was plenty of research suggesting that the common punitive approach, as in suspension or removal from school, was ineffective at helping students reregulate. Disconnection, something that occurs in the context of trauma, is exacerbated by punishment that removes students from their educational setting. In some institutions, new approaches, referred to earlier, were tried, while other institutions ignored or downplayed the new research. Data collected by the U.S. Department of Education's Civil Rights Data Collection Project show that discipline in schools was and still is not handed out evenly. Some regions of the country had more disciplinary issues, and subgroups of students, including racially and ethnically diverse students, were more adversely subjected to discipline. This motivated the U.S. Department of Education and civil rights groups to look more closely at disciplinary practices across the country. Further data come from states, and, as with the federal data, their results are far from comforting in terms of who is disciplined and why.[11]

Studies, data, and reports on school discipline did generate change before the pandemic. Some elementary school students were sent to the principal to get a break from the classroom, not just to receive a reprimand. In fact, some students were so pleased to have a break that they acted out to get some one-on-one time with administrators. Some schools had started in-school suspension and peer conversations as alternatives to punishment, recognizing of course that no one's physical safety should be put at risk, whether students or teachers. Restorative circles, with historic roots in the behaviors of other cultures and their dispute-resolution mechanisms, came into being.[12]

When the pandemic hit and online learning took over, students who acted out online had to be handled differently, rather than the traditional disciplinary approaches enacted previously being imposed on them. They were already home. Cutting them off from internet engagement meant they might not return that day or on future days.

In fact, the internet allowed educators to exercise different options. Younger acting-out students could be spoken to right then and there by the teacher, who could suggest that the students take a break, mute themselves on their computer, and draw something and share it. For older students, the educator could suggest they engage for a few minutes in an alternative activity such as a breathing or balance exercise and then return to the class. Educators could assess whether the problems had originated in hunger or a lack of sleep. And educators did use the private chat room feature in Zoom that allowed connection over the negative incident in real time as the class was proceeding. Yes, educators were multitasking.[13]

Educators found that many struggling students who took breaks reregulated themselves. If they did not, the teacher could do outreach after that class period or later in the day, for example, asking parents or community members to work with students who had presented problems, providing food or needed services. Educators created a kind of processing in place, rather than disconnecting students when connection was what they needed. Educators recognized the importance of social and emotional learning—for the acting-out student and for other students, who got to observe reregulation in action. These are trauma-responsive approaches (see Table 6.1).[14]

But here are two cautionary flags. Some schools have decided to impose discipline by sending students home to learn online. With this approach, it is unclear whether such learning is synchronous or for how long the student is relegated to online learning. It puts a negative connotation on online learning as if it were punishment, and thus we fail to capture its positives. Add to this that there a movement back to punishment-based approaches because more students are misbehaving in in-person classes. This reversion reveals our willingness to discard what we learned during the pandemic and our preference to return to what was familiar, rather than ask why so many students are acting out and what can be done about it that is responsive and restorative, not punitive.

MENTAL HEALTH ACCESSIBILITY AND ITS SIGNIFICANCE

During the pandemic, with the curbing of in-person contact, the federal government declared a public health emergency and instituted temporary health care–delivery

Table 6.1. Frequency of Responses on "Doing Discipline Differently Using Social and Emotional Learning"

Statement	Strongly disagree (%)	Disagree (%)	Agree (%)	Strongly agree (%)	Agree or strongly agree (%)
It is vital to students' social and emotional development and learning not to remove them from class activities as a form of discipline or behavior management (absent a threat to safety).	2.5	11.9	52.8	32.7	85.53
I will continue such practices as an integral part of being an educator.	1.9	5.0	56.6	36.5	93.08
I have the resources to deliver such an approach to discipline.	6.3	13.8	56.0	23.9	79.87

rules for telehealth. Teletherapy became available without the requirement that patients go to a clinic or private office. Whether they were school based or located in the community, psychologists, social workers, psychiatrists, counselors, and others licensed to practice mental health care adjusted quickly to meet the changes. The government made it financially viable for non-school-based professionals to be reimbursed, with HIPAA flexibility.[15]

The new health care rules not only reduced the risk of COVID infections but also saved on traveling time and expense to see therapists. As with online learning, students could dial in or videoconference their therapists. For students in distress who did not have a therapist, school psychologists, counselors, and social workers reached out and provided telecounseling to them.

Inevitably, there were technological barriers like those in online learning—limited broadband access, unreliable Wi-Fi and videoconferencing platforms, lack of home computers, and lack of private space. Moreover, adolescents were wary about parents listening in to their therapy sessions.[16]

Many therapists were concerned that doing therapy via a screen led to a psychological distance that affected engagement and connection with their patients; they worried about not seeing body language and that not all mental health conditions were suitable for online treatment. Current and future research on the efficacy and outcomes of online treatment has to guide its expansion, but teletherapy is here to stay, whether carried out exclusively or combined with in-person appointments. In education, teletherapy or telecounseling will continue to be an additional resource for developing or enlarging school-based mental health services, something that grows out of the pandemic positives.[17]

Listen to the voice of this respondent to our survey:

The pandemic made me feel like a first year teacher—so much that was new and different in how I had to teach. I feel very accomplished, but teaching has changed. But the biggest change is student mental health and behavior regulation.

Three further benefits should be mentioned. First, there was partnering with community mental health providers, which was vital in enabling some students to get needed services. In the crisis of the pandemic, this effort in some localities was seamless, more integrated, coordinated, and comprehensive than it had been before the pandemic. In essence, the mental health crisis of the pandemic activated partnerships.[18]

Second, during the pandemic, the federal government provided increased resources to help students recover from the pandemic's effect on their mental health. The American Rescue Act funded the development or expansion of school-based mental health services and connections between schools and existing community programs and services to address the development and well-being of the whole child.[19]

Third, consideration of mental wellness moved from the periphery to the center, with the growing realization in education that mental health was key to successful learning, as educators noted a marked decline in how students were managing psychologically. The push for social and emotional learning, while politically charged, can now be seen and evaluated through a pandemic lens. Adoption of social and emotional learning may help prevent more severe mental distress, which can lead to serious social, emotional, and behavioral disorders. While we can debate whether social and emotional learning is "core," we do know that its inclusion is vital if student success is to be achieved, as noted earlier. We can disagree about many things, but the pandemic made mental wellness a recognized central concern for educators, parents, and communities.[20]

Mentally healthy students are more likely to succeed in school, an observation we have repeated and that grows from our individual and collective experiences in education and mental wellness. Students with good mental health go to school with enhanced readiness to engage actively in learning. They connect well with others, teachers and peers alike. Positive social interactions, nonaggressive behaviors, and problem-solving skills contribute to both student learning and a positive school climate.[21]

The pandemic highlighted the need for better mental health services for students. The online-learning environment crystallized that need and opened doors, through more personalized learning approaches and increased flex time, to augment services.

SUPPORTIVE SETTINGS

Some of the positive lessons we learned are from absence, not presence. We had known before the pandemic that for some students, school was a safe place—safer than home, safer than their streets, safer than their community. For students who experienced food scarcity, schools provided food—often several meals, including breakfast. Even the best reading teachers cannot teach a hungry 1st-grader to read.[22]

For students who were homeless and living in shelters, schools supplied structure, stability, and even privacy. For students with family dysfunction, schools were a place to see quality role modeling and ways to address problems without hitting or yelling. For students with caregivers suffering with addiction, schools were a place without parentification, where play was encouraged. For some students, after-school programs were a safe place to spend time, keeping them off the streets and out of empty homes. School and after-school programs were safe havens in addition to learning environments. With the pandemic, sadly, many students missed what school had provided—everything from safety to structure to stability. School provided caring adults who believed in students and their capacity to succeed and critical space where safety was paramount.[23]

The results of students' missing the expanded role of schools are plain. We know that the pandemic produced a decline in mental health and a rise in trauma. In-person learning in schools could not have prevented or ameliorated all that happened, but schools had a broader role than we had acknowledged and perhaps understood, and it mattered. For many students, school was not just about learning; it was about surviving and even thriving.

One of the coauthors is reminded of a school she visited before the pandemic to read some of her children's books with the students. While there, she noticed that in each class, one or more students were asleep. "Odd," she thought. "Shouldn't the teacher try to engage that student?" When she asked the principal, his response was direct and telling: "The students who are sleeping are not sleeping at home because they have no bed or it is unsafe or they are caretaking younger siblings. They can sleep safely in school and you can't learn anyway if you are exhausted." Revelatory.

The expanded role of schools has many aspects that need to be addressed. For starters, the role of educators is also expanded—in both their time commitment and their engagement with students. Not all educators see themselves as having obligations outside the classroom; they don't want to be parents to their students. This is particularly true as one progresses up the grade levels to college and graduate school. There is a cost of expanded schools, including the need for additional personnel.[24]

Our survey shows that many educators did see a change in their role, whether welcomed or not. As one respondent observed:

> Before the pandemic, my role as an educator was as a classroom teacher. I delivered instruction, supported my students in as many ways possible to guide them to educational successes. However, once the pandemic started, my role shifted into that of an educator also tasked as a community support person. We checked in weekly with all of our school families to ensure they had supplies, food, funds, internet, a computer, and time to do schoolwork. Coming out of the pandemic, we have continued many of our wraparound supports and it has taught me to engage my students in many ways; not just academically but to get to know them as a whole person. This shift has been instrumental in being a more effective educator.

The larger group of respondents reinforced the importance of the whole-child approach—and seeing the whole child—when working with their students.

An argument exists that the expanded role of schools highlighted by the pandemic and online learning is not the problem of schools; it is a societal problem that landed in schools and that we can now see more clearly (although many saw it before the shift to online learning). We can argue that society needs to step up to provide what expanded schools offer and that we should let schools be places for learning. But the pandemic made visible what we may not have wanted to see before: the essential role schools can and do play in the lives of many students. School is more than an institution for reading and writing. It is a place where students can grow up in safety with supports and structure, assisted by adults who are role models.[25]

The pandemic positives push us to accept the broad role of schools in our communities. We need students to have the chance to connect with educators who are critical role models for their development; we need creative approaches to ameliorate food scarcity, lack of sleep, and the absence of structure; and we need the resources of communities to support wraparound services in health care, social supports, and therapy to promote mental wellness and provide early intervention.[26]

Table 6.2. Frequency of Responses on "Seeing Students as a Whole Person"

Statement	Strongly disagree (%)	Disagree (%)	Agree (%)	Strongly agree (%)	Agree or strongly agree (%)
Knowledge of students as a "whole person" and not only about their academic achievement is necessary to help them to learn and socialize in and outside of school.	3.1	4.4	43.4	49.1	92.45
I will continue such a belief as a regular part of being an educator.	1.3	5.0	42.1	51.6	93.71
I have the resources to obtain information about the student as a "whole person."	1.9	9.4	66.0	22.6	88.68

If we accept the broader role of schools, we can recognize these institutions as integral to the community—they are not separate silos. Community partnerships can meet the needs of educators, students, and families by maximizing partnership resources to improve learning, working, and living for all.[27]

The key role of community was recognized by respondents to our survey, as revealed in Table 4.1. It also is reflected in the voices of respondents. As one wrote:

> Before the pandemic I thought I was student centered and whole child focused, but as a result of the pandemic, I am even more so now. I fully believe that Maslow's hierarchy is more important now than ever. We need to ensure that our student's [sic] basic needs are met before they can learn well. Schools which have taken a school and community-wide approach to ensure that their students are successful no doubt will benefit.

ONLINE ACTUALLY ISN'T ALL BAD

Before the pandemic, students in public schools and many colleges and universities did not have a choice—learning happened in person. We assumed that when students are gathered together in a space in person, they are able to learn in a classroom setting. We too infrequently differentiated between learning styles and types of intelligence. And we did not have an abundance of choices in learning venues. Many educators and parents and caregivers alike—and students too—viewed online learning as a lesser form of education; it was not quality education for good students. In short, we believed that in-person learning was the sine qua non of excellence in education.

One of the positive features of the online model is that it allowed students and their families to see what would be possible if they had different learning options, including some they had never considered. It allowed students to understand more fully how they learned and whether online learning had benefits for them.[28]

Further, educators could see how each student functioned in each environment, especially students who moved from in-person to online learning. Teachers were noticing improvement in some students and failures in others. Whether consciously or not, educators could personalize education more easily, allowing those who needed more time online to go into breakout rooms and permitting those who wanted in-person contact and affirmation to get them. Educators witnessed some students who were silent in the classroom engaging actively. And there were some students whose grades rose.

To be sure, some student outcomes were unchanged by online learning. Some excellent students continued to do well and some less successful students continued to languish. Some successful students did slump and some previously unsuccessful students found stronger footing. However, for educators who saw windows for engagement opening for some previously silenced or nonparticipating students, there were benefits that could be captured and encouraged. Educators could ask students who had not participated to share their thoughts and encourage their active participation. Further, educators could identify why certain students were more willing to learn in the online world, where they had space, food, and a personal, safe learning "bubble."[29]

As with students and their families, online learning offered educators an unexpected opportunity to learn about themselves and where they were most comfortable, personally and as educators. Some educators who had never taught online saw its value and discovered that they had technological skills that benefited students. For all these groups, the stigma of online learning diminished, even if there was a desire to return to in-person learning. Stated another way, we had a change of mind and heart about online learning's potential, recognizing that it did, like most things, have downsides.[30]

With this new openness to online learning, some educators saw the opportunity to take the good parts of online learning and transpose them to in-person education. As indicated in Table 6.3, our survey respondents saw the possible upsides of online learning.

Myriad options arose when in-person learning returned. Some districts preserved entirely online learning for a subgroup of students or increased their use of online strategies in the in-person environment for some or all students. For educators with long commutes and a paucity of reliable public transit, teaching from home saved both time and money and allowed them, with the extra time, to create lessons that worked. Some educators with health risks could mitigate those concerns if permitted to do online-only teaching. We recognize that this added option, one that benefited some educators and some students, surely adds to the complexities of staffing and planning that educational institutions face, but it is worth recognizing that we have more good options for some students and educators than we previously knew we had and it behooves us to ponder how to embrace these choices.

Table 6.3. Frequency of Responses on "Unzipping Zoom and Online Resources"

Statement	Strongly disagree (%)	Disagree (%)	Agree (%)	Strongly agree (%)	Agree or strongly agree (%)
Lessons learned from virtual and hybrid teaching during the pandemic are transferable to in-person instruction.	3.8	8.8	56.6	30.8	87.42
Online resources will be integral to my ongoing work as an educator.	3.1	6.3	52.8	37.7	90.57
I have the resources to deliver such an approach.	1.3	9.4	59.7	29.6	89.31

ADVANCE PREPARATION

Experts tell us that COVID is likely not the last pandemic to afflict our nation and the world. In addition to medical calamities, there are likely natural and human-made disasters that will force schools, colleges, and universities to close for short and perhaps long periods. Schools have been closed during floods, wildfires, and hurricanes and after earthquakes. School shootings in Colorado, Connecticut, Florida, Texas, and other states closed schools, as did the disaster of 9/11.[31]

Radar and satellites work moderately well to forecast storms and identify broad areas that will be affected, although meteorologists can fail to forecast narrow geographic locales accurately. We learned from the pandemic that we need public health warning systems to forecast global disease outbreaks. Indeed, the government has funded satellites to assess public health risks. Our educational institutions must be prepared before the next danger arrives. Based on what we learn from the pandemic positives, we can be better prepared for the next emergency.[32]

One of the pandemic positives is that we got online systems to work. Converting from in person to online in the future, if the need arises, is imperative. We often talk about creating strategic plans, but many of them sit on shelves collecting dust because they are too cumbersome or are outdated by the time they are completed. We do drills to prepare for fires, earthquakes, and shootings, but their effectiveness has been challenged and their traumatic impact on both students and educators noted.[33]

If we are to be ready for future mass school shutdowns, we must use the time now to reflect on how we can implement online learning quickly and successfully. That would be time well spent. We need to at least establish spending priorities or allocate savings and human resources that are forward looking, particularly in the event of a crisis or disaster when circumstances dictate changes. We should reflect on best practices we need for readiness; we should have technological training; we should work on hardware, software, and internet shortages now. We should pilot-test launches for online learning improvements. For example, we could have a school day each year when the entire school system goes to total online learning. Call it the internet equivalent of a fire drill but with advance notice, with discussion and follow-on debriefing among all of education's constituencies, curbing its traumatic potential. In sum, we could be better prepared than we were for the pandemic. We can build on the foundation of the positives of online learning.

But the need for preparedness does not make us prepared. Nor does simply saying we need to be better prepared based on our pandemic experience. Much has been written about how medically unprepared we are for another pandemic, despite all we have learned from the COVID experience. Articles have emphasized the need to plan now and warned of the dire consequences of failure to do so. Health organizations have issued directives for ways to prepare. We have trouble planning, in part because it reminds us of what frightens us and because we need a break from everything we recently have encountered. Further, it takes time, resources, and determination to be ready for the next crisis. But our reluctance to plan does not eliminate the need to do so.[34]

Think about it this way. The military spends its time on what we could call defense—being prepared for offensive action by others. It prepares for war in times of peace. It spends hours training soldiers, sailors, and air force personnel for what is to come, not what is happening now. There are lessons embedded there. We are reminded of the motto of the Army War College (the name of which is troubling): "Not to promote war but to preserve peace."[35]

As with preventive medicine, mental health services, and the military, we can be proactive in the educational sphere. Further, with the benefit of time and the diminishing of the pandemic, we can include the voices of many of, if not all, the stakeholders in education.

Based on efforts to advance preparation in other arenas as well as education, here is a partial list of what can be done in the educational system to prepare for the next disaster. Institutions can add further elements and create a checklist of what has been done, what still needs to be done, and what should be updated continually.[36]

- Obtaining and maintaining quality contact information for all families, having learned the critical importance of communication
- Collecting and regularly updating necessary information about services students receive outside school, with the sole intention of helping students succeed through better coordination, the data gathered voluntarily and privacy and confidentiality upheld
- Developing and trying out new assessments ready for implementation, including those focused on social and emotional learning and assessing the whole child
- Listening to and planning with many diverse voices, including those of educators in classrooms, school nurses, school counselors, social workers, families, caregivers, and community leaders, these individuals being able to employ their understanding and in-the-trenches experiences, following the saying "Nothing about us without us"

- Making forecasts, even if there is a risk of error, on what improving education will require down the road, including continued use of online programming in brick-and-mortar educational settings
- Curbing negative information and disinformation about education and its outcomes and focusing on the positives, which rarely get the needed attention
- Developing trust among varied constituencies, including between leaders and classroom educators, families and educators, students and educators, and schools and communities
- Learning promising lessons from other schools, districts, states, and countries that have experienced crises
- Creating advisory groups with diverse membership and heterogeneous perspectives that produce realistic, actionable outcomes, one example being the Massachusetts COVID-19 Health Equity Advisory Group, a diverse group of individuals who enabled high-level uptake of vaccines across the state
- Studying in schools, colleges, and universities about pandemics and the spread of disease and ways to stop it, employing advanced technology, and using research, so we are equipped with information and ready to process new information
- Identifying how to ameliorate the psychological toll of toxic stress and trauma on educational outcomes and mental wellness before crises occur, including by integrating trauma-responsive school strategies and social and emotional learning that focus on whole-child development

The positives identified here have concrete applicability in education now. We can improve our online capacities, assess in new ways, discipline differently, acknowledge and accept the expanded role of schools, and prepare for the future. These pandemic positives improve education in a nonpandemic world, and they all use connectedness, creativity, and community partnerships to achieve implementation.

Nonetheless, we can't stop here. There were other pandemic positives that, while not as broad in scope, appeared across the educational landscape, improving education in the places where they landed.

CHAPTER 7

Unanticipated Gifts From the Cloud

SEEMINGLY SMALL BUT CRITICAL PRACTICES

It was inevitable that as educators moved from classrooms to cyberspace, changes occurred in how teaching was conducted. Whether one was teaching a group of kindergartners, teenagers, or adults, here was a totally new way of engaging with students, transmitting information, and developing trust. This had an impact on students and their parents and caregivers. Think about online learning as increasing our line of sight—we could see more, and that added vision enhanced learning for some students and brought insight to some educators and parents and caregivers.

What follows is a sampling of these classroom-based changes that some educators in some localities tried, refined, and altered over the course of full-time online learning. A number are applicable to students of all ages, whereas others are geared to younger students, although they can be adapted for learners at other ages and stages. The identified small or practice strategies, having been applied and verified in the trenches, offer powerful lessons that can improve in-person learning.

We want to emphasize that the word *small* does not connote a lack of value but rather focuses on where the changes occurred, namely, in the trenches. We acknowledge that further lessons were tried by educators during the pandemic that have not been described here, but we hope that those we have identified and that we name below in the headings will encourage readers to share the additional positives they discovered with us and with one another. They have value for sure.

KNOWING OUR STUDENTS

A long-standing lament in education is that educators do not actually know their students. Although we tend to know them more the younger they are, even kindergarten teachers miss understanding the out-of-school life of children they teach every day. The shift to internet learning changed that.[1]

First, we saw students in their own environments—in their homes or in hotels or other locations when they became unhoused. We saw what was on the walls and where their learning materials were located. We heard and saw the people with whom they were engaging: siblings and parents or caregivers. We heard fights and debates and efforts to push students away from computers as their time was up and others needed the computers. We saw parents dressed in nightclothes, some skimpy and inappropriate for a teacher to see.

Educators saw students with greater fullness, as though in an unsanitized moving photo, capturing the environment in which they were learning. It wasn't always pretty. We recall one educator's saying to a student's mother: "I dress for school; it would be good if your child did too. And you might want to put on some clothing as well, as the day of learning begins." These observations are supported by respondents' recognition of the value of knowing their students' families, as reflected in Table 7.1.[2]

One respondent's comment typifies this point:

I don't think the meaning of being an educator changed during the pandemic. I do think that it gave us more of a glimpse into students' homes and gave us more recognition of some gaps we need to adjust.

What is also true is that students saw their educators in a nonclassroom setting as well. Some educators created mock classrooms in their homes with backdrops that resembled the school environment: whiteboards, posters, letters of the alphabet, and announcements. The idea was to create familiarity while online with what would have existed in reality.[3]

By contrast, other educators, particularly those with older students, shared what was on their own walls and in their hallways. They had interruptions, from pets and people, which would be out of the ordinary in school buildings. While that was perhaps annoying at times, it was also humanizing. The barking dog, the cat running across the room, the young child crawling on the floor—these all allowed students to peer into the lives of their educators. If they were embarrassing on first occurrence, they became normalized, part of the ambiance of online learning.[4]

Such opportunities offered by online learning have value. Educators could appreciate the real-time challenges of their students, the complex lives they led that

Table 7.1. Frequency of Responses on "Knowing Families of Students"

Statement	Strongly disagree (%)	Disagree (%)	Agree (%)	Strongly agree (%)	Agree or strongly agree (%)
Knowledge of students' families is helpful information to develop suitable approaches to help students to succeed in school.	1.9	4.4	51.6	42.1	93.71
I will continue such a belief as a regular part of being an educator.	0.6	4.4	52.8	42.1	94.97
I have the opportunity to obtain such information about students' families.	0.6	14.5	62.9	22.0	84.91

were masked when children were in school. In turn, students saw educators as real people with real lives for whom teaching was but one facet of their existence.[5]

One of us recalls that years ago, a group of students saw her at an after-school party where there was swimming. They kept staring at her, until one said: "You have legs. We've never seen your legs, because you always wear pants or long skirts." This same educator remembers when she brought her young son to her graduate class (something she did for years), and he pulled down her skirt from behind the podium where she was standing. As she struggled to pull up the skirt with a modicum of both grace and modesty, smiles and quiet laughter filled the classroom; students saw that she was real. That's the significance of both examples.

The benefits of the *real* are worth observing and carrying forward into classrooms: Students and their teachers and professors saw the value in knowing more about each other, and barriers and boundaries broke down. This could be facilitated by asking questions, sharing photos, or simply being more candid. Ponder the "ask me anything" exercise where students can ask their educator any question about anything—within the realm of decency. And suppose educators met one on one with students to share stories about their lives and homes. Suppose educators asked students, "What do you have or would like to put on your living room wall?" Recognizing that some students don't have a living room, discretion should be used in this exercise.[6]

In one school system during the pandemic, educators, wearing masks, went to each student's home, aiming to introduce themselves before the school year started online and to establish rapport and trust. With rare exceptions, they were invited in. During the visits, educators learned a lot about their students that in-school meet-and-greets did not provide. They could see where students slept, ate, and studied and the home environment. The power of their observations has been so great that the educators have been continuing these home visits following the pandemic, believing that understanding who their students are makes them better educators of the students.

If we can see students as teachers or professors, and teachers or professors as students, we enhance learning, something many espoused before the pandemic; students are not unknowing, and teachers and professors are not all-knowing. A shift in balance occurred online that has value for engagement in classrooms.

One educator who visited students' homes noted that the visits enhanced connections; the educator stated, in the context of online learning, "I want to ensure that I am continuing to build intentional relationships with students."[7]

SEEING LEARNING HAPPEN

When school buildings were closed, some parents who stayed home and had the time were able to watch how their children engaged with teachers and classmates and learned online, and some overtly helped their children. In these instances, education was alive at home! Online learning gave parents and caregivers an unanticipated opportunity to experience their children's education.

When teaching happened in schools, family members were privy to neither how their child learned nor how educators taught. One of the authors watched his grandchildren on video as their teachers enabled online access in Shanghai. Watching how his grandchildren engaged with their teachers and classmates in their unique ways of learning and socializing was instructive and opened a previously closed universe.

Think about how most families had learned about children's educational performance before the pandemic. They read report cards or met with teachers in person. Actually seeing what previously was only shown on a report card is very different from relying solely on reading and hearing about children's progress. Parents and caregivers could see their children's approach to learning, working on executive-function skills, engaging with their teachers, and interacting with their peers in an educational setting—all in real time. Some parents and caregivers as a result became more supportive of their children's learning. Some helped them get online and get settled; some helped them with homework and independent projects, depending on how the children understood their teacher's assignments and, in turn, families' ability to understand and assist with the assignments. With assignments being clarified, students could spend more time on the projects, avoiding the frustration of not understanding their teachers and having hosts of unanswered questions. Families could fill in gaps, something that enabled clarification and repetition, often needed to process tasks to be done.[8]

Families reported that they saw both the joy and the frustration of learning in their children. They also understood more about the teachers' challenges and, for children with special needs, how critical a good individualized education program, or IEP, is to learning and socializing for their children. This helped teachers and parents trust each other, have a less adversarial relationship, and work together inside and outside school. Respect was generated, a critical aspect of enabling educators to feel appreciated for the work they do.

CONNECTIVITY OF PEOPLE

Before the pandemic, some teachers used ClassDojo and other apps to provide supplemental information to family members, enabling a constructive partnership with them. This was amplified by necessity during the pandemic. Education technology regarded as marginal moved to the center and could be there to stay. Stimulated by increased parental understanding and involvement brought about during online learning, educational partnerships can be expanded and sustained with children back in school.

Consider the boosted levels of parent and caregiver contact with educators during the pandemic. For family members who struggled to get to a school building for meetings and conferences because of burdens of work, childcare, transportation, and perhaps discomfort with the process, online communication was beneficial. Existing gaps were closed and a process was created that enabled engagement—a process that can continue postpandemic.

With all the logistics of online learning, educators had to communicate effectively with one another and with parents and caregivers, as well as with students. Historically, there were not only disengaged students but also disengaged parents and caregivers.

We learned to communicate in real time more effectively online and through texts, and there was greater parental and guardian participation. The copious notes home and forms to be signed evaporated. Some educators spoke to parents they had not engaged with previously. And some parents and caregivers became working partners with educators in ways that did not always exist before the pandemic. We can take this as a true pandemic positive and replicate it in school buildings into the future.[9]

Consider this respondent's comment:

> The pandemic changed my practice as an educator. I now provide parents/students with my personal cell phone number, I maintain contact with students and families more consistently and frequently throughout the school year, and I self-reflect and evaluate my professional practice constantly so that I can be an effective, caring, knowledgable [sic] educator for my students.

We were taken aback by an article in the *Atlantic* suggesting that there is now too much communication between parents and teachers as well as increased tension between them. The article's intended audience, given its source, seems to be well-heeled families. While its observations may be true in some cases, they don't comport with our experiences, including in institutions serving low-income families, and our survey results. Moreover, we suspect that the increased tension might not be related to communication overload. Rather, it may result from parents being buffeted by the stressors of a changing world or their playing out undisclosed political agendas or feeling superior to the educators or not being in need of engagement with them. For us, quality communication remains key; it is what gets truncated by trauma and it is what is needed to create trust.[10]

Yes, communication needs to be reciprocal, but parental contact with teachers does not make all teachers insecure; some appreciate that parents reach out. The *Atlantic* article correctly points out that communication between parents and teachers changes as students age and that communication about (and, we would add, with) a student should not always be about a student's failings. Some communication from educators in a positive vein is beneficial, as in their sending a note saying, for example, "John did a terrific presentation today and I was very proud of him."

In treating increased communication as a pandemic positive, we have considered the socioeconomic-political-technological conditions that have shaped our educational system and led to disparities. We know that students, parents, and educators wear their particular lenses. With that in mind, pandemic positives reflect a sensitivity to the individualized needs of students, families, and communities because they are diverse and because we are paying close attention to the equity gap.

STUDENT INTEREST

Another valuable insight educators gained by teaching online, as noted earlier, was that for some students, the online environment was beneficial. Educators found that some students who were silent in the classroom engaged actively when online, and some students' grades rose. This encouraged many educators to reflect on how to engage all students more effectively.

They discovered that during online teaching, it was possible for students to participate at their own pace; educators could be more flexible in giving instructions, by using text and visual cues in addition to verbal directions. Educators could encourage students to deploy their own learning styles, whether through chat or breakout room work, and they could offer a greater selection of assignments and activities, with students responding in a wider range of ways, instead of just verbally presenting a report to their class. Different uses of the chat feature benefited students who preferred this more private way of participating. More-varied cues from educators—through writing or oral and auditory means—helped some students find a way to participate more actively. One of us paused periodically online and asked students, "Are you with me? Wave or something." This all motivated some students to learn and be more productive, and their educational outcomes improved.[11]

These insights can reap benefits in brick-and-mortar education. For example, why do we need to completely abandon online learning? Could we use a hybrid approach, temporarily allowing students to attend classes online, while ensuring that we were not stigmatizing students who benefited from online learning? Could certain days or subjects have online components that enabled some students to learn effectively? Could we identify how to protect students who felt vulnerable attending school in person, by recognizing teasing and harassment and addressing them more directly or by giving students a way of sharing, in ways that were safe, what was happening to them? Could we have dividers in classrooms that allowed for learning bubbles for some students who wanted and needed the protective walls that online learning provided? Could we also have dividers in cafeterias, to diminish tensions? Could we have more specialists engage with our students because they could appear online? Could we use a hybrid learning model throughout the school year when there were weather- or illness-related school closings?[12]

The answer to all these questions is yes. We can do these things if we transport the pandemic positives to in-person learning. Perhaps, too, we can eliminate the stigma that sees online learning as lesser for all students. For some students it is an easier and better way to learn, at least some of the time.

BEING ON THE SAME PAGE

With in-person learning, we often aimed for everyone to be on the same page. We assumed that students entered classrooms ready, willing, and able to learn. We further assumed that educators were ready, willing, and able to engage. We didn't just ask for this cohesive attentiveness; we demanded it.

We recall the story of a new educator who repeatedly was criticized during in-person pandemic learning because she couldn't manage to get all her 2nd-graders quieted down before the content lessons began. Imagine whether it is even possible to get 15 or 25 second-graders to all be engaged at the same time. In any case, a false premise was at work in many schools; all students had to be totally engaged for any student to learn.

The online learning environment from the get-go shattered the demand that we must be on the same page. First, some students signed on and showed their face but muted themselves. Other students did not show their face but stayed unmuted. Others were both muted and visually absent. Students could come and go; it was not like a classroom, where educators could control who was engaged and who was not (as if that were the sine qua non of excellence in classroom management and subsequent learning).

This led some educators to reflect on strategies to employ before starting substantive teaching; the aim was to begin the content teaching when almost everyone was attentive. Some educators required visual presence and unmuting. But some realized that they needed to jump-start the class with an activity or opportunity for expression that gave more of the students time to connect with them online.

Consider this exercise that some educators tried online. They asked students to write down one positive and one negative feeling they had right then. Then they asked whether there were students who wanted to share what they had written. The educators shared too. In another exercise, educators asked students to name a song that mirrored how the students were feeling at that moment. In yet another, educators encouraged students to draw a picture of how the students were feeling. Even young students can do emoji faces that display their feelings. Even scribbles count.

Some educators realized, too, that different students were in different psychological states and suggested they display online red, green, and yellow blocks to communicate readiness to engage: red for unwilling, green for ready, and yellow for on the fence. By displaying these blocks, students were empowered to situate themselves in their learning capacity on a given day or part of a day. Educators were able to identify which students were ready to learn and which were habitually unsettled and needed personal attention and intervention, whether during or after class.

During the pandemic, teachers and professors came to see that they had to prepare and organize differently before they started class—for students of all ages. A newfound, increased unpredictability in student engagement and behavior could affect the entire day's learning. If students acted unpredictably and educators were unprepared for the behavior, that set the tone for the day, even when educators were well prepared for the day's substantive learning.

This realization led one of us to begin all workshops and classes with their conclusions, in case students faded during the online session. That way, she observed, students got what mattered while she had their attention, recognizing that online, some would not be on the same page for the whole class or workshop. The approach was an acknowledgment of how hard it was for many students to concentrate online for long periods, a realization that led to the use of "chunking," discussed later in this chapter.

Educators who embraced the need to prepare for unpredictability turned to various techniques, not all of which needed to be deployed each day. Teachers stepped back from the substance and instituted a feeling-thermometer exercise, where students determined how they were doing emotionally at the start of a particular lesson. If educators saw there was unrest, they would institute "four-square breathing" (online or in person) to help regulate the autonomic nervous system, which could be activated in some students, particularly those whose home experiences were disruptive or whose trip to school had been uneasy. Educators who had the same students over the course of a day did periodic check-ins to ensure that students were paying attention. Some educators also did end-of-the-day check-outs.[13]

Reflect on the voice of this respondent:

During the pandemic, I was more concerned with making connections online than academic progress because I knew the isolation was taking a toll on my students. I see myself as a teacher who takes care of the whole child, and sometimes that means social–emotional development and sense of belonging comes before academics.

Through monitoring student feelings online during a class or a day, a different tone and atmosphere were created. Students sensed that educators actually were listening to and hearing them. Even those who didn't experience distress benefited from knowing that if they did have disruptive feelings, there was a method for handling them. All students gained from knowing that a responsible person was there for them, giving them the space to reregulate. In other words, students felt welcomed online even if they were not fully ready to learn. The pauses that teachers created were brief but the benefits were lasting. The learning process was smoother, and in the absence of the pauses, less learning would have occurred. All this provided a different facet of learning: how to regulate and engage in times of stress. For educators worried about loss of content coverage, one lesson learned during the pandemic was that brief pauses and attention to emotional balance enabled better learning.

Bottom line, online educators recognized what they may have missed or not concretely identified in classrooms: Feelings were encroaching on learning during the pandemic, and until a student was all there, learning could not effectively happen. Educators saw firsthand in the online learning environment that social and emotional balance and readiness were key. All the content learning one wanted to impart would not happen if students were not on the same page as their educators.

Such recognition is this pandemic positive; not all students will likely be ready, willing, and able at exactly the same time, and some students have to be folded into learning as it progresses, as in folding in ingredients in baking, where the mixture is not smooth and time is needed to mix the ingredients together.

Reflect on this strategy employed by one of us using an imagery exercise, whose novelty made it quite a hit during the pandemic. The coauthor invited students and adults to ponder a picture of purple shamrocks with four Chinese characters and a meditating Buddha (see Figure 7.1). They were asked to silently describe the image to themselves. After a few minutes, the group shared their descriptions.

Figure 7.1. Ed K. S. Wang, *Quiet, Heart, Health, and Peace,* 2020

First, many previously had not seen a purple shamrock with flowers. Second, the coauthor translated the four Chinese words, which have strong personal meaning to the coauthor. The words are *quiet, heart, health,* and *peace.* Each word has an independent meaning; when two words are combined, the combination has another meaning. If the same two words are placed in a different order, a different meaning is generated. When three words are combined or placed in a different order, a different meaning emerges. Participants came up with their own combinations and order of words, in English or other languages, that were meaningful to them. The exercise prompted a discussion among the participants about mental wellness as a central theme in everything we do. As an important aside, when in-person training resumed, the real pot of shamrocks with the attendant words became a prop for the coauthor's workshops on mindfulness. A positive transportable pandemic lesson.

STUDENTS AND EDUCATORS BEING IN THIS TOGETHER

It matters that students believe that their educators have the knowledge and capacity to lead them forward, even in difficult times. Students look to their educators for messages telling them they are safe and that the teachers or professors are able to engage with them effectively.

But online learning was new, and some educators openly acknowledged a benefit to sharing that both students and teachers and professors were in a new space together, discovering new ways of learning. Rather than hide that reality, they spoke about it and accepted suggestions about what was and wasn't working. Educators divulged to students that they could teach each other. After all, the pandemic was a shared experience, with masks, social distancing, and the risks of illness. Through their navigating the experience together, an opportunity for increased trust and openness to express what was and wasn't working pedagogically arose for students and their educators. Some educators said to students, "I get how hard this is. I understand that online learning is not easy. I understand that not being with your peers is hard. Share with me what would make it better."[14]

The recognition of the centrality of trust between educators and students during and after the pandemic is reflected in Table 7.2. The significance of trust reappears in Part III in the context of stickiness.

Consider this respondent's voice, emphasizing the importance of trust:

As a counselor, I needed to know the student[s] and understand who they were as learners. Trust was integral to building lasting relationships with students and what carried me during the pandemic. When other's [sic] struggled with attendance, I held seminar sessions. I continued to provide high-quality support because I had established a rapport with the student[s], and they trusted me enough to let me in during this difficult time. I will continue working on relationships and trust as I continue [in] this profession.

Here's the point and the pandemic positive, using the analogy of Hurricane Katrina. In the aftermath of the hurricane, the relationship between therapists and their patients changed; there was value in shared recognition of a crisis situation. During Katrina, it was a shared understanding of the loss of one's home and community, including among therapists and their patients. During COVID, it was a shared understanding of the risks of illness, the isolation of people, and the need to find new ways to connect students and educators. The point is that following online learning, there is no need to discard this newfound appreciation for shared experiences and listening to the voices and suggestions of others. These approaches don't damage boundaries; they encourage understanding and trust.[15]

Table 7.2. Frequency of Responses on "Trust: Connecting and Engaging"

Statement	Strongly disagree (%)	Disagree (%)	Agree (%)	Strongly agree (%)	Agree or strongly agree (%)
Trust was indispensable between the educator and the student during the pandemic.	2.5	5.7	46.5	45.3	91.82
I will make time to develop trusting relationships with the students I serve.	1.3	4.4	37.7	56.6	94.34
I have the resources to deliver such an approach.	0.6	6.9	63.5	28.9	92.45

The removal of artificial barriers between teacher or professor and learner is an enormous pandemic positive that we can carry forward.

STRATEGIES TO ENGAGE STUDENTS

One of the most difficult tasks for educators teaching online was to engage students. Online learning can facilitate disengagement through its very technology, as in the options to mute oneself and remove one's image from the screen, alluded to earlier. A student could be doing something completely unrelated to the education being offered, with teachers and classmates being unaware of what the student was doing; for example, the student may have been playing video games, eating, or enjoying other activities. Without being seen or heard, students could be doing just about anything during class.

There is another way of pondering disengagement, namely, by asking the question, Why are students disengaging? We need to ask, What is behind the behavior and does the answer lie in far more than technology?

When we are traumatized or experience toxic stress, it is reflected in our behavior, and a known symptom of trauma is disconnection. Trauma truncates neural connections, so it is unsurprising that students can be hindered from engaging online. Their behavior evidences their feelings. To be clear, disconnection or dissociation is not intentional, although it may appear so to educators on its receiving end. As with dysregulation, students are not trying to tick off the teacher; rather, their actions betray what they are feeling inside.[16]

To address this—and both authors spent considerable time with educators on this very topic—students need to have their senses activated and they need the seven *d*'s referenced earlier: delight, dance, distract, dazzle, demonstrate, dignify, and donate. Educators need to give students tasks in which the students can engage apart from those of content learning.[17]

Our respondents recognized the importance of activating the senses, something encompassed by the seven *d*'s. And it was a practice they wanted to maintain moving forward. The recognition of how the senses can be mobilized to activate the brain is reflected in Table 7.3.

Examples of what can be tried include the following:

- Consider true/false questions, where *true* is the screen off and *false* is the screen on; then reverse the process, where *true* is the screen on and *false* is the screen off. Then add in some joy and play, which trauma takes away.
- Consider an online game that can be played, such as connecting dots, finding hidden words, or filling in blanks in a phrase.
- Consider having educators wear costumes and ask their students to do the same. (Some educators have created a "hat day" or a "green day," where everyone wore a hat or wore green.)
- Consider civic engagement projects that encourage students to help others, activating the students' mirror neurons.

- Consider turning to dance or other kinds of movement and to music to get students active and employing their bodies, not just their brains. This activity calms students down and allows them to reconnect.

These engagement strategies can be implemented in brick-and-mortar classrooms, where we should not cease asking the question, How can we engage students and keep them engaged (both those who are disengaged and those who are already engaged)? Many of the strategies tried online during the pandemic can and should be transported to the classroom. For example, instead of launching into subject matter content the moment class begins, why not spend 5 to 10 minutes doing some connecting exercise that allows students to ready themselves for engagement? Sure, it takes away from strictly learning time but if students aren't ready, willing, and able to learn, even more classroom time is wasted. If at a certain point in the class students seem disengaged, stop. Switch up what you are doing; take a break; do a balance exercise where students stand on one foot without holding on for a minute.[18]

Online learning was disruptive for some students but for other students who had struggled before the pandemic with transitions during the school day, online learning was better, as no movement was entailed. To be sure, for other students, online learning enabled more movement—and in some instances unnecessary movement because of noise and other family disruption.

Recognizing that moving from class to class and place to place was disruptive for some students is beneficial. Now, the reasons for disliking disruption vary; they include separation issues, emotional challenges, fear of harassment and other loss of personal safety in the hallways, or severe traumatic experiences. Fewer transitions, as well as better preparation before a change of space occurs, and smaller classes may help reduce the level of student distress. Another lesson from online.[19]

Table 7.3. Frequency of Responses on "Connecting Senses to Activate the Brain"

Statement	Strongly disagree (%)	Disagree (%)	Agree (%)	Strongly agree (%)	Agree or strongly agree (%)
The mobilization of senses to activate brain functions was essential to student learning during the pandemic.	0.6	6.3	47.2	45.9	93.08
I believe continuing such practices is integral to my work as an educator.	1.9	1.9	57.9	38.4	96.23
I have the resources to deliver such an approach.	4.4	12.6	62.9	20.1	83.02

FLEXING

As educators became more familiar with the capacities of the online learning platforms, they saw there was flexibility not commonly deployed in brick-and-mortar classrooms before the pandemic. For some, this seemed odd, since online learning initially appeared more confining than learning in school buildings.

Here's what some educators tried when teaching online. Students were broken up into small groups to work together in breakout rooms without outside noise. The educator could drop in and provide feedback as needed or could choose to let the students manage on their own for a bit. Students posted questions, answers, and thoughts into a chat that ran simultaneously with the class, and the educator periodically stopped to comment on or address what was in the chat. Some students were directed to work with the teacher in the main online room, while others were in smaller rooms working on a separate activity or on different projects. Educators might meet one on one with a student in a breakout room while the remainder of the students worked on a project together or individually.[20]

In short, online platforms allowed educators to introduce space flexibility into their teaching. And a lesson to take from their approach is the emphasis on the value of small-group work and collaboration. Not all students learn well in large groups, and we know that different students learn differently. The online environment permitted all these factors to be accommodated through the technology options that presented differently from what is offered in brick-and-mortar classrooms.

Space flexing is a pandemic positive that can be transported into classrooms, albeit not easily, given space constraints, noise levels, and restrictions on the movement of educators from chat to breakout room to the whole classroom. Nevertheless, with some ingenuity, classrooms could mimic some of what online learning provides, recognizing that retaining online learning in some settings for some flexing of space makes real sense. Ponder the use of movable dividers in classrooms as opposed to what we do now, with students at different tables. Imagine students' conducting the equivalent of a chat using a whiteboard or an interactive screen. Picture an educator with a more private place to meet with a student individually where it would not be embarrassing, cause shame, or be isolating.

Another space-flexing example to consider is the change in lunch procedures. When students returned to school, lunches were eaten in classrooms as part of social distancing. This benefited students and teachers, beyond being a precaution against spreading the coronavirus. It improved time management and team building; saved time for creative activities during lunch, such as a class check-in or mindfulness exercises; and resulted in less fighting and harassment. Let's reconsider the value of eating outside the cafeteria for some of the time or even dividing the cafeteria into smaller spaces.

The pandemic positive is the power of space flexing and the important role it can have in learning. An additional positive, not explored here but worth pondering, is time flexing. Online learning changed our notion of seat time and activity-learning time. In addition to chunking, discussed in the following section, it is worth exploring how much time should be spent in school and in doing home-work and assignments. Already some schools and colleges are turning to shortened schedules—via the 4-day week. The pandemic primed the pump for discussing and implementing such changes.

CHUNKING

Before the pandemic and ubiquitous online learning, we tended to have extended seat time. Students in classrooms had periods lasting from 30 minutes to 2 hours. Even with breaks in classes that ran over an hour, seat time was long.

With online learning, some educators quickly appreciated that seat time had to be reduced, even if the online learning was for an extended time. There is only so long one can look at a screen and engage productively. Educators who saw that online learning was time delimited turned to *chunking*—breaking material to be learned into manageable, small segments.

What these educators found is that chunking material strengthened learning, facilitating the incremental building up of knowledge. If a particular chunk was difficult, an educator could stop and begin again, offering it differently. Students therefore would not be behind on entire topics but only a chunk or two behind.

For educators, chunking and thinking in chunks were not necessarily intui-tive. But for many learners of all ages, chunking was comfortable. They were used to television programs with commercials—breaks between chunks. Programs built around learning, such as *Sesame Street* and *Mr. Rogers' Neighborhood*, used chunk-ing all the time. Lessons were short; things shifted from one setting to another; char-acters changed. The concept of educating in chunks is made visual in the depiction of squares, made of paint and fabric, shown in Figure 7.2.

Online learning enabled us to capture how students were engaging online in their own time outside school. Think about learning chunks as a time-limited video game. Students are familiar with short virtual games and using word-limited online platforms. Those of us who were educated without technology had a steeper learn-ing curve during the pandemic.[21]

Studies suggest that we cannot sit and learn for more than 45 minutes at a time. In the online arena, we don't need to be seated to learn. We can be standing or lying down. We can pause learning by muting ourselves if we are overwhelmed and we can fidget or eat with the screen off.[22]

These online capacities have been recognized by some educators, and when used, they can enhance student learning. One of the authors of this book never sits to write. She writes whole books (including this one) standing at a countertop and has for decades. Imagine if we allowed students to read or write standing in class-rooms; imagine if we let students use the floor to read lying on their back or their side. Chairs and tables became less important in the online world.

So here's the pandemic positive captured by some educators that is transferable to classrooms: Less material may be more, and less time at each learning session on a new subject may enhance student uptake of material.

Figure 7.2. Karen Gross, *4Squared*, 2021

DECLUTTERING

Online learning had an additional powerful and unexpected benefit. Before the pandemic, students' schedules were lengthy and jam-packed. Students arrived at school early, often for breakfast, and stayed late into the afternoon, participating in after-school programs. With the pandemic, students who had participated in athletics, music, or other extracurricular programs—whether tied to or independent of their school—found these programs were truncated or abandoned. For some, this was a major loss; these students were deprived of not only activities that had held their interest but also mentors whom they cared about and from whom they received support. Yet other students lost fewer positive things; taken away were enforced tutoring; required homework support; or mandated lessons in a language, religion, or other subject that did not appeal to them. Some of these activities were not creative and in some cases marginally productive.[23]

With online learning, students saw the opportunity to better allocate their time. They had less structured lives and could meet their needs in new ways. Without being scheduled every minute of every day, some students had more time to engage in play, including outdoors, since it was safer to be outdoors during the pandemic. Some of this play was unstructured, allowing for creativity.

With the altered schedules, less seat time, and students being online, educators had the chance to rethink what homework made sense. Instead of just assigning rote activities that teachers copied and handed out, they could assign projects and research activities that employed online resources. Imagine instead of being given a math sheet with repetitive geometry problems, students were urged to build structures using geometric shapes, with their work then being shared online. Imagine students being asked to research the individuals who had developed the geometric principles being taught.[24]

Once educators changed up how they thought about homework, they saw opportunities to try untapped activities. Imagine an educator who was working on writing having students critique other students' essays in Google Docs or on other platforms. Thinking through online learning enabled educators to consider new ways to use artificial intelligence and ChatGPT, a topic we discuss in Part III. For homework, students could take polls and then learn how to read the data in class, with an online program providing pie and bar charts. In certain material ways, online learning loosened or removed constraints, and in the freedom and space created by necessity, educators and students got creative.

A crisis created time and unstructured space, which became positives for many students, freeing them from activities they did not want or did not fully enjoy and allowing them to engage in creative thought or play. We'd call that a pandemic positive that can inform how we structure both school and free time moving forward. The overprogrammed childhood may end, if we see the benefits of its absence.

The pandemic positives identified in Part II, including in this chapter, can, when taken together, enable us to see that online learning was not an abject failure. As important as the larger lessons described in Chapter 6 are, the smaller lessons detailed in this chapter have power too. When the larger and smaller changes are combined, their power increases exponentially. We can do with some of each, but it is much better to have all the larger and smaller pandemic positives if we want to improve education in meaningful ways that can be scaled and replicated with stickiness.

It is true that online learning, and its positives, did not work for every student and every educator. We know that. But in the interstices of failure are things that were positive that can inform educational delivery for our students in a nonpandemic situation. The pandemic positives, as demonstrated here, are mechanisms not just for surviving a crisis; they are strategies that can inform educational offerings into the future. With that in mind, we turn to how to make the pandemic positives game changers in education.

CHAPTER 8

Brick-and-Mortar Education Wasn't Prepandemic Redux

THE RETURN

The return to in-person learning, which was staggered throughout the country, as noted in the timeline in Part I, was not a return to education as we had known it before the pandemic. When schools and colleges reopened, there were new health and safety requirements, among them air filtration systems (in those schools where they were ready to use), wider space between desks, and changes to playgrounds. Masks and social distancing were implemented in classrooms, lunchrooms, hallways, and athletic facilities.[1]

As a preliminary matter, it is worth noting that some students did not return to school or college. In-person enrollments declined, as was made stark by Stanford University professor Thomas Dee's estimate that 230,000 students from 21 states were absent from public schools and we don't have reasons why. One reason for absences from brick-and-mortar schools has been documented, however. With the rise in bullying and other harassment in schools, many Asian American families chose to have their children continue with remote learning. Data from the Institute of Education Sciences showed that 78% of Asian American 8th-graders attended school virtually in February 2021, compared with 59% of Black students, 59% of Hispanic students, and 29% of White students—numbers vastly different from the respective enrollment percentages. Absenteeism and fear of in-person attendance are obviously not pandemic positives. That said, since some of the causes for absenteeism may be related to student or familial mental health issues, the recognition of mental health issues is a pandemic positive.[2]

One overarching problem for those who returned to in-person learning was the failed expectation that things were going to revert to the way they were before the pandemic. Somehow, in the push to get back to learning, we failed to appreciate the effects of the pandemic and acknowledge the profound impact of all the disruptions and changes in families, the educational system, and communities, as well as other issues, including violence, natural disasters, and political upheaval.[3]

Thus, there were disappointments on the return to brick-and-mortar education from the get-go. Normal as we knew it, despite our fantasies and desires, no longer existed. This reality was hard for many to accept, although there was a growing recognition that what had existed previously was far from perfect. Reflecting on the pandemic positives as schools reopened, one of the first hurdles was recognition of the need for a new normal.

Beyond the new health requirements inserted into many aspects of life, the pandemic had changed all of us, often in ways we did not recognize or acknowledge. The uncertainty of our world, the unaccustomed omnipresence of illness and death, joblessness and changed workplaces, and changed families had their effects. This is the VUCA world referenced in Part I, the world of volatility, uncertainty, complexity, and ambiguity. As individuals, the absence of engagement with others had affected our social skills. We were restricted from being in groups. We had not been in structured environments. We had not navigated the needs of those outside our family. Our behaviors had been changed by the fear in which we were living.[4]

There was an added dimension to the return to schools. Students and educators kept getting sick, and that sometimes meant that whole classes were canceled for days at a time and some schools even closed for short periods. When educators were ill, substitute teachers were needed, and they were in short supply. Then there were students who did not know they were ill and showed up at school, exposing others to COVID, only to be sent home. Further, especially among certain age groups, there was shared drinking and eating, all of which added to the risks of disease. On top of all this, there were teacher shortages, as not all educators returned to classrooms. Some had retired and others had decided that being in school buildings was too risky or difficult. Still others wanted to teach online only, having seen its benefits, for both them and some of their students.[5]

One more dimension of the return to school is worth mentioning. When both students and educators were wearing masks in school, communication was different. First, it was hard to understand everyone. Mumbling and masks don't go together. And singing was prohibited. Facial expressions are hidden by masks, so it was hard to gauge the dynamics of a classroom. Along with their faces, students' emotions were masked. Add to this that social distancing, especially among certain age groups, was unnatural. Students were used to playing together and having physical contact, which was forbidden or at least filled with risk.[6]

What also happened is that students began to exhibit trauma symptomology, which frequently went unrecognized as caused by trauma. Most of us had experienced collective stress and other, even more severe experiences during the pandemic. The out-of-school experience had stressed students, families, and educators, and they brought all that social and emotional baggage into schools and colleges.[7]

Student misbehavior was a shock to educators. Students who had been engaged were now disengaged. More students were dysregulated, overregulated, and dissociated than before the pandemic. Educators exposed to students' behavior started to be infected by the students' trauma, in a condition officially termed *secondary trauma*. Strategies that had worked previously to maintain class engagement, structure, and stability were failing. Even seasoned educators were struggling to adapt when schools reopened, and the student behavioral issues persist in many educational settings even with the passage of time. Some would say they are worsening.[8]

Add to all this the readiness problem. Mandates by certain states that childcare and prekindergarten facilities be closed reduced children's readiness for kindergarten. For students who attended kindergarten and 1st grade remotely for those school years, entry into the following grade was their first time in a formal school setting. Second-graders were coming to a school building for the first time. Some school principals told educators to disregard language (profanity and the like) that certain students were using, as those students had not been exposed to the school setting and were used to more indelicate conversations elsewhere, including at home or on social media.[9]

We underestimated the impact of learning lost in math and reading as well as in the social and emotional sphere. Students were not used to crowds. They were not used to structure. They were not used to rules. They were not used to physical play with others. They were not used to schedules. Teachers found that while assigned to teach 2nd or 3rd grade, they actually were teaching students who had missed lots of learning in kindergarten and 1st grade. Second-grade teachers remarked that they were like kindergarten teachers; kindergarten teachers observed that their students knew little about group engagement, rules, and social courtesies.[10]

Learning loss and the loss of social and emotional development were not evenly distributed in a single class or school district. High-poverty districts and districts with Black and Hispanic students had spent more time on remote learning and thus experienced greater loss and a more difficult transition to in-person learning. In addition, vulnerable populations experienced more health care disparities and worse health outcomes from the pandemic, meaning that students from these populations were struggling with illness and death in greater proportion. The data, although there is variation, show that more than a half million children lost one or more primary caregivers during the pandemic. This figure is an aggregation of loss of parents, grandparents, and other caregivers.[11]

Disparities in lives lost particularly impacted students from non-White families. The 2020 pandemic death rate for non-Hispanic Blacks was 29.7%, the second-highest mortality rate behind American Indian and Alaska Native populations, which had a mortality rate of 36.7%. The Black Lives Matter movement brought attention to the health disparities of and barriers to overall health care among minority populations. As a result, there were targeted efforts to disseminate information on COVID and conduct vaccination outreach in minority communities. Following that outreach, a study of 977,018 adults across the United States who died from COVID-19 did show a 60.3% decrease in mortality from the virus for non-Hispanic Black individuals between the initial waves of the pandemic and subsequent Omicron subvariant waves. To be sure, there are a number of complex variables that need to be assessed to ensure quality health care delivery to all.[12]

In short, in-person schooling was not what we expected. It was as if the world had rotated on its axis and we were in a new place with a whole new set of issues, but

we acted as if time had stood still. Educational approaches that had not been working were not working now. How could they work with so much death, fear, loss, and
change? As much as we wished for the past (even an imperfect one), it was long gone.
If we look at human resilience not as bouncing back but as moving forward with
new capacities, pandemic positives are evidence of human resiliency and lasticity.[13]

The repeated question among educators at all levels within education when
institutions reopened was, Now what?

STRATEGIES THAT WORKED

A host of educators, confronted with new guidelines for health and safety and students who had changed, found remarkable strategies to improve the educational experience. Some were creative ideas that educators tried; others were garnered from
webinars and group meetings among educators; others were simply from instinct,
from the need to try something new when what used to work had failed. Access to
a vast store of knowledge on the internet was available to support change as long as
those using the information were able to distinguish between good and bad information, a not-so-easy task under optimal circumstances.

Below we explore some of the remarkable strategies educators deployed, many
of which need to continue in a postpandemic world. Some of them appeared in different forms in online and hybrid learning and when schools were shuttered. We
have tried to indicate where they appeared before, recognizing that in-person learning presents a different context. Every strategy we name in the sections that follow
is a pandemic positive. All are drawn from in-the-trenches approaches that often
went unrecognized or unheralded.

These strategies are not temporary salves to be used until we return to where we
were—a place that no longer exists. Indeed, the approaches turn out to be trauma-
responsive strategies and recognized ways of improving mental wellness (often
without the labels or preexisting awareness that they functioned in this manner).
Virtually all have a place in education moving forward.

Two added notes: First, for those who believe that trauma responsiveness is
coddling or not useful to students who are not traumatized, that is simply not true.
Trauma responsiveness builds mental wellness, and its impact is not limited to traumatized students. A rising tide lifts all boats, not just those low in the water. The
same holds true for trauma-responsive strategies: They help all students.[14]

Second, our survey repeatedly showed the need for leaders to listen to and understand the educators with whom they are working. This suggests to us that many
educators felt that their leaders did not fully appreciate or understand the work
those on the ground were doing during the pandemic and that the leaders were not
cognizant of the depth of the in-the-trenches challenges. Consider this an opportunity for leaders reading this book (we address leadership in Part III) to absorb the
remarkable things that happened in their educational institutions, if they have not
already recognized, acknowledged, and praised these efforts. We now turn to the
strategies tried by educators.

Home Visits

As mentioned in Chapter 4, when schools shut down, some educators went to students' homes to deliver resources and even taught on the lawn before implementing online learning. The same happened in the context of online learning. Some educators, ahead of school reopenings, visited the students they would be teaching in the coming year, rather than relying on in-school meet-and-greets taking place. Most, though not all, families welcomed them in.

Because many students had not been in school for many months, the visits were an opportunity to meet their educators in advance and start adjusting to and feeling comfortable about the upcoming school experience. The meetings were personal. Educators learned a great deal about students and their families that could inform how they taught and responded to students and families moving forward, a lesson mentioned earlier. The lessons learned were so sizable that many of these educators have continued the process of home visits, with the expectation of making it a common practice.

Greeting Students

Some educators realized that they needed to greet students differently, long before they began the class or school day. They welcomed students at the door, greeting them by name, smiling, and encouraging them to enjoy being in class. These were new ways for some educators to start their class and their day, especially for those in upper grades and college or graduate school. More recently, this approach was adopted in Gloucester, MA, where students responded to questions posed on whiteboards as they entered school, allowing them to feel welcomed and valued.[15]

Charlotte Elementary teacher Barry White, Jr. personalized his handshakes in 2017 to greet each student in his class every day before the students entered his classroom. ABC broadcast a video of his handshakes during the pandemic to show how teachers needed to reengage students to make them enthusiastic about attending school. This relationship builder was even more critical when many students were disengaged from school because of the pandemic. We acknowledge that this approach had to be modified to eliminate touching, given the concerns about social distancing during the pandemic.[16]

Students needed to feel welcomed. They needed to feel they were recognized, and such recognition was optimized if there was personalization. Educators had to change the way they received students into the learning environment. Indeed, in higher education before the pandemic, professors often entered class after all the students had arrived. After the pandemic, that strategy was not effective, as students did not jump to attention when their professor arrived.

One way of reflecting on this is to recall how many educators used to view the first day of class, particularly in elementary schools. They greeted students and welcomed them back after the summer vacation. They made an effort to create an environment that said, Come learn with me; it is safe here. Now that effort was required daily. And the "summer vacation" was months or years long during the pandemic and often was not a happy time (though vacation never was for some students). By the time schools reopened, students had directly experienced or witnessed dire events, dissatisfaction, having to move from one home to another, illness, and death—and the list continues.

As we move forward, we can expect ongoing crises, family disruptions, job losses, and job changes. With this as backdrop, students need help adjusting to a learning environment when they leave home—whether for the day or for college. That means educators and the institutions serving students need to change their culture based on what we learned through the pandemic positives.

Activities

As described in Chapter 7, some educators realized that as each day or class started, not all students were ready, willing, and able to learn. Some were distracted. Some had had a bad experience that morning or the previous evening. Some hadn't had breakfast. This situation led some educators to take the first few minutes of every class to do some type of exercise designed to help students reregulate and focus. The daily morning check-in, a midday check-in, and end-of-day check-out had tremendous benefits for individuals who needed it and provided a positive class and school climate for the entire school community. The activities varied, from writing down thoughts, discussing current events, listening to music, doing a balance exercise, coloring, or drawing. Educators who worried that the minutes given to these activities meant less time for content learning discovered that these were minutes that in fact enabled classroom learning. Losing a few minutes meant lots of gained minutes, a valuable trade-off.[17]

Some of the activities that worked for younger students could be adapted to older students, even college students. This concept often was met initially with skepticism, and educators saw some of the proposed engagement activities as juvenile, as did some older students who viewed themselves as more advanced.

But the literature and in-the-trenches experiences showed us that these activities, when tried using the right tone and attitude, worked across all age groups. For example, using open circles to engage students at the start of a class goes far beyond early elementary school grades. The use of fidgets and other stress relievers works with younger and older students. Pausing to reset and reflect works with younger and older students—including adults. Playing music works for all age groups, as do balance exercises where students, and educators, stand on one leg or balance a book on their head.[18]

Masks

When schools still required masks as students returned, some educators discerned learning opportunities directly tied to both masks and social distancing, demands that were difficult for students.

Students could discuss the function of masks in different cultures and address how masks hide or show feelings. This makes for a lesson in culture, history, and feelings, all wrapped into current events. Masks could be researched and examples displayed. One of the authors had a wall in her home hung with masks and mirrors that she described to educators so they could replicate it in classrooms: Masks hide; mirrors show. The students also could draw different masks, including those that students and educators were wearing. The other author used a drawing of COVID masks as a lead-in to a discussion of Bian Lian, an ancient Chinese operatic art form featuring masks (see Figure 8.1). The author incorporated the masks into lessons on culture, history, social and emotional experience, mechanical science, and art.

Lessons could be taught about the health benefits of masks and whether and why they work optimally. This is a science lesson, and rather than just telling students to wear masks and keep them on, why not share their underlying benefits and downsides? Students who were introduced to the differences between masks, from N95s to bandanas, came to see the issues around mask wearing in a different light. Rather than having masks foisted on them with the admonishment "This is the rule," why not help them understand what mask wearing is for? This latter approach shifts the locus of control from an externality—a school or local mandate—to the student.

As for social distancing, we could lament it or we could find ways to understand and even embrace it. We could see how to overcome its limitation. Social distancing stands in the way of connections, as do masks. The urge to connect is real. Trauma truncates neural pathways, as noted earlier, but they can be rebuilt with connections.

With creative solutions, we can form connections in space and between one another if we focus on the importance of this task and understand why it matters. For example, some teachers, including one of the authors, did exercises where students made paper clip chains and connected them to poles, desks, chairs, and one another. One of the authors did this exercise successfully with school counselors.

Figure 8.1. Ed K. S. Wang, *Feelings Behind Masks*, 2020

Other teachers did this with paper loops. Others used the opportunity to measure distance. Others looked at the science behind social distancing.[19]

In other words, the pandemic requirements themselves became learning opportunities. There is broader pedagogical value here that can carry forward. If we ground education in what matters and make what we learn matter in our lives, it is likely to have greater impact. This is not to suggest that history has no relevance. It is not to suggest we abandon math and science. Rather, we figure out how to make math, science, history, reading, and all school subjects relevant to life, for students of all ages. We contextualize learning.

Students' Concentration

To continue the theme of interestedness, educators became aware that students' levels of concentration were not what they had been. Various factors explain this, among them how learning occurred online, discussed in Chapter 7, before the return to school buildings. Students had had more freedom. They could move around, they could eat, they could dress as they pleased, and they could mute the class or turn off the video screen. These freedoms disappeared when in-person learning returned, but losing freedom is not like turning off a light switch. It takes time to adjust.

Some educators took the opportunity to chunk material, described earlier, teaching smaller segments of material and building in breaks. Others recognized that not all students had to be fully engaged every minute of every class, despite our desire to have everyone with us on the same page all the time. Educators had to flex.[20]

As mentioned in Chapter 7, some educators provided students with red, green, and yellow blocks. If students were willing to engage, they put a green block on their desk; if they were unwilling to participate, a red block; and if they were borderline ready, a yellow block. This gave educators a visual clue about what students were feeling—not just thinking. It allowed educators to see patterns in student behaviors, and if there were too many reds on too many days, they could talk to students about their reluctance to participate.[21]

Content

Some educators saw the need to provide different content and to present it in different ways. The usual curriculum was hard for some students, at the level of both interest and preparedness. If a student hadn't written an in-class essay or read from a textbook in 12 months, it wasn't an easy transition back. Some educators questioned whether a return to previous educational approaches even made sense in the new climate.

As a result, some educators turned away from textbooks and toward shorter material, online essays, videos, and other means of communicating material and assigned project-based learning in class that allowed students to work together and gather information. When educators believed that earlier approaches for content delivery did not work as well as they once had (arguably, to be sure), they adapted how and what they taught.[22]

Such adaptation had particular relevance as our world was experiencing major upheavals: natural and human-made disasters, political shocks, and increased nastiness among individuals. Rather than ignore these realities, educators, using lessons gained from online learning, presented activities and readings that encouraged engagement in current events. When athletes misbehaved, there were lessons there about why this happened and what caused people to use bad judgment. With well-known public figures succumbing to overdoses, the opportunity arose for discussion of opioids and fentanyl. Students are exposed to these and other issues, including war, through social media—why not link learning to contemporary events as a way to engage students?[23]

We can extend this point when thinking about books students could be reading. Yes, there are standard books that students read at different ages and stages. But why not mix things up and find books that have relevance to thoughts and feelings students are having now? Educators can use a layer cake approach to discussing ideas, themes, culture, and values beyond the actual story presented. This works in both children's stories and adult literature. To go further, students might be interested in the topic of book bans, those now and in the past. What is it about some books, one can have students consider, that makes them threatening, and if they are threatening, is banning the best approach?[24]

Feelings

One observation repeatedly noted by educators was that students were not just thinking but also feeling. Their feelings appeared, reappeared, and even interfered. A range of emotions, from anger, to sadness, to happiness, to discomfort, to fear, were evident. Students' feelings were not kept inside but leaked out.

Educators began to incorporate ways for students to express feelings—good and bad, and everything in between—before, during, and after class. Some educators developed "feeling trees." Some offered stickers on which students could put a name to a feeling, placing the sticker on a whiteboard. Other educators addressed students' mood swings and even shared actual sculptures of mood swings. In fact, one of the authors worked with the creators of miniature items to produce tiny models reflecting mood swings, as shown in Figure 8.2.[25]

The Feeling Alphabet Activity Set, mentioned in Chapter 3, was developed by the coauthors to assist educators in enabling students to express their feelings. The activity set is a collection of materials (available at little or no cost) through which educators can encourage the naming and regulating of feelings with students (see Figure 8.3). Although designed for younger students, many of the activities can be adjusted to work with older students and even willing adult learners. Social and emotional learning and behavioral self-regulation or coregulation are not content per se, but they can be integrated into content learning in and outside the classroom.[26]

It is easy to dismiss the role of feelings in education, viewing them as outside the purview of educators. Many educators are much more comfortable with content than with feelings. However, we are capable of both cognition and emotion, and

Figure 8.2. *Mood Swing,* **2022. Created by Ancientgnome From a Design**
by Karen Gross

one informs the other. A way to get at this is to help students understand how our brains work. There is a mitt that educators can and did wear that showed students how the brain is structured, where our feelings are situated, and where our cognition is located. Indeed, when wearing the mitt, the educator can show students what happens when the brain is stressed; it literally flips out.[27]

In addition to or in lieu of a mitt, we suggest Dan Siegel's Hand Model to show different brain areas and what each represents: thinking, feeling, and behavior. Students can learn how parts of the brain influence their social and emotional experiences and learning. The Hand Model also shows what happens during a flipping-the-lid moment, assisting educators in helping students bring their brain

Figure 8.3. *Emotions, Behaviors, and Thoughts,* from Karen Gross and Ed Wang, *The Feeling Alphabet,* 2022

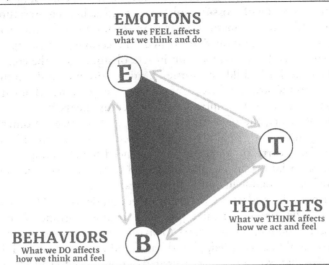

back under control. Educators can teach students to demonstrate their brain flip-out moment visually by showing a hand with fingers outstretched from a fist position (the brain position), for both their own benefit and that of the educator. It is as if the student were saying, without words, "I am flipping out and I need help." This works in the home setting too. As one parent noted to one of us, her child used the gesture because she needed a way to communicate without words what she was feeling. Understanding how we think and feel is a strategy for enabling us to better concentrate, process, remember, and learn.[28]

In short, identifying and owning feelings moves the locus of control from an externality to an internality, with students feeling able and empowered to share what they are feeling right in the moment.

Art

Some educators saw the value of paying more attention to music, visual art, and dance, via subjects that initially did not seem to mix with these. However, dance can be tied to geometry, and math can be found in literature, as aptly described in Sarah Hart's *Once Upon a Prime.* Singing, which was not allowed during the pandemic because of the risk of spreading COVID, can be listened to; many feelings are expressed in songs, with and without words, and students can identify what the feelings are. Visual art can be used not only for representing content but also for expressing feelings, as evidenced by the many works of art displayed in this book. Moreover, art can be two- or three-dimensional and use an assortment of materials, allowing the student artist to create mood and depth and experience engagement.[29]

We often learn in silos; thus, art frequently is separated from content learning, except in thematic learning programs. After the return to schools, however, educators discovered the value of cross-disciplinary activities, linking literature to art and linking music and dance to math. Rather than separate fields with their own time block, there was an integration that created connections, activating feelings and cognition. One of us did art online with in-school students in the context of reading one of the coauthor's children's stories. Students drew with the author and tied the drawings into the storyline, also an example of expanding what can happen in brick-and-mortar schools if we introduce online components.[30]

For some students, the opportunity to express themselves in different ways—through dance, music, or visual art—made the content more meaningful and understandable. The dearth of concentration, the need for chunking, and the health requirements of social distancing and masks led us to see new value in the workarounds, which are valuable in and of themselves.

Consider how these ideas could be expanded. Students could watch a video of the show *Stomp* or snippets of the tap dancing troupe Dorrance Dance. The students, in person or online, could then try to do one or more of the steps they had just seen. The steps could be recorded, played back, and improved on and the new version played. Rhythm, sound, and coordinated actions could yield fantastic results. The video could be shown in hospitals and nursing homes to bring joy and connection to others in the community.[31]

Some educators used trauma art and trauma writing as strategies to help students, often without specific mention of the word *trauma*. For example, art projects that let students showcase feelings helped. Building decorative wooden boards with holes in them through which students could throw beanbags was beneficial. Wall drawings done by students in stairwells and open spaces allowed for expressions of feelings and thoughts. So did writing and drawing with chalk on sidewalks and crosswalks and in entryways. One of the authors began to use buttons in her art, with the theme of everyone being buttoned up or unbuttoned, emotionally. An example is shown in Figure 8.4. The buttons were reminders that we were struggling with our emotions and trying hard to keep it together.

One other critical art initiative, mentioned in Chapter 12, was the use of Kintsugi and Ju Ci, two art forms. Students could break and mend pieces of pottery or piece together shards of broken items, creating peace from pieces. The authors shared their own art with educators, showing discarded objects turned into sculptures or large artworks derived from broken pieces. The piece shown in Figure 8.5 takes odd items—thread, paint, shards, sticks, and a host of other common materials—and puts them together. This is a different take on Kintsugi art.[32]

Play

Some educators perceived that one of the harms the pandemic wrought was an absence of play. In a world of hurt, play seems useless. Those who are traumatized often delete play from their lives. Play needs to be restored; it is part of who we are at every age. If we cannot play, we cannot feel joy and hope. It is hard for older

Figure 8.4. Karen Gross, *Buttoned Up or Not?* 2022

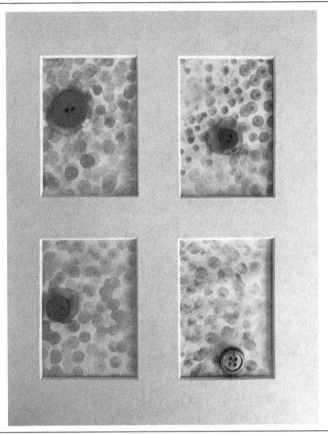

students who never played to learn to play as young adults. They see play as infantile, as one author observed while working with youth; they needed to appreciate the power of play. Indeed, LEGO has created sets of their famous interconnecting blocks for adults to use in the workplace.[33]

A group of educators—perhaps not thinking about psychological theory or neurobiology—introduced play into their classes. They wore costumes, created word games, and developed other ways to employ playful activity, including with fidgets and other stress-relieving toys that students could choose from a basket. Some educators saw that if students were using a fidget, they also could absorb information. One university professor convinced his department chair to reimburse him for fidgets he had purchased for his students, once he explained how they helped his teaching and showed the chair literature (that one of us actually had written) that supported their use. One of us found that mazes, constructed of marbles embedded in felt or cloth-threaded channels, helped students. The development of the trauma toolbox, better called a care kit or wellness box, was a direct outgrowth of the recognition of the need to play.[34]

Figure 8.5. Karen Gross, from *Making Peace of Pieces* series, 2021

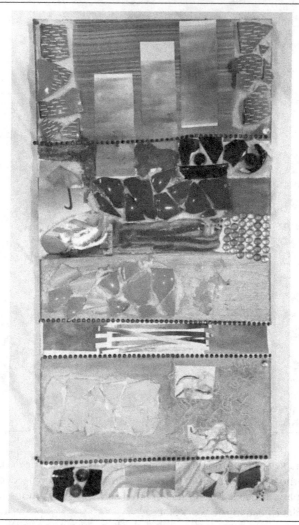

Younger students, deprived of childcare and prekindergarten during the pandemic, were not used to interacting with peers and learning from them. Learning rules, taking turns, and delaying gratification through play activities are critical for early learners, for their social and emotional development, regulation of behavior, and executive functioning skills. The children who missed the opportunity for this significant development struggled, and kindergarten teachers required more time to make up for the unfinished learning.

Many of these educators recognized the crucial role of play and the delay of content learning. Play reduces stress. Play is for all ages. Play involves both the mind and the body. Play is a recognized psychological benefit described in studies and in the training given to educators, although our focus has sadly not been as robust for the educators of older students.[35]

In his Wellness and Resilience in Children and Communities training curriculum for providers, one of the authors presents a dedicated workshop on play. In addition to including physical play and board games, he broadens the definition of play to movement and song games as well as quiet activities. These additional forms of play aim to promote auditory–visual and sensory–motor mindfulness, creativity, imagination, language, and reflection.[36]

Writing

Consider writing assignments that were given but not shared among students. The coauthors did this in Virtual Teachers' Lounge workshops and other locations. For example, an assignment might be to write three good feelings and three bad feelings you had today. Educators provided prompts such as "The worst thing that happened to me today was _____" or "The best thing that happened to me today was _____." Educators assigned students the task of making lists. Students could list six things they wanted to do that day or six things they wanted to change the following day. Writing prompts that enabled students to share feelings helped, even when the writing itself was not shared. Making lists tied into the rich literature on list making allowed students to see the ways in which lists were beneficial.[37]

Here's the point: These short writing exercises enabled students to express themselves—even if only to themselves—and that had value. They also helped with stress.

Managing stress is a vital wellness practice, especially for those living in a persistently stressful environment. An attendee at a training workshop run by one of the coauthors told the group that she had heard a gunshot in the neighborhood while waiting with her 1st-grader for the school bus in front of her house that morning. Her child had instantly grabbed her legs. Her experience taught the coauthor to include brief relaxation and mindfulness experiences at the beginning and end of all his trainings.

Empathy

Our brains have mirror neurons, noted earlier, and these can be used to good effect, which some educators have recognized, and the coauthors recommend taking advantage of this. In the presence of trauma, one pathway for amelioration is activation of our empathy engines, which seems counterintuitive when one is struggling. But helping others turns out to be beneficial to the person helping, because not only does one feel good helping others but also the benefit others receive reflects back to the giver, mirroring good feelings.[38]

Mirror neurons came into play when one of the coauthors received funding from the Massachusetts Cultural Council, which enabled students, school counselors, and educators to create "kindness rocks." In some cases these were rocks painted on canvas and in others were painted real rocks; the results were then shared, displayed, or placed in key locations where they could be taken. Baking or delivering food to seniors was another activity that activated mirror neurons. Visiting seniors was beneficial, and more than one student group performed at senior centers during the pandemic.[39]

These were all opportunities to mobilize folks to do for others and in so doing, to help themselves.

Traditions

Many educators came to see that traditions as we had known them had to be relinquished. This was a big loss across all races, ethnicities, and religious groups. Celebrating holidays with hugs, get-togethers, and singing were things of the past. Countering the loss of traditions across our different cultures provided opportunities to create new ones that could be embraced and carried forward—traditions that were inclusive of all. Moreover, we could be overt about what we were losing and what we were creating.[40]

Consider these examples of new holiday practices some educators installed in their institutions, with the possibility of their becoming traditions. (Families had opportunities to create new traditions too.) Instead of the usual singing of Christmas carols, recordings were played and students would sign the words, having learned sign language for this purpose. Giving secret presents across a neighborhood was another new event. Neighborhood residents placed lighted stars in their windows, so families walking down the street could see them. Shared holiday festivities in person not being possible, this was the creation of community in a different way. Instead of schools' convening in assemblies where everyone gathered for events and holidays, a class or two could make a video of a play or other activity and share it with other classes. A tradition could be invented of bringing in an author, artist, or athlete on Zoom who could share with everyone online, with discussions happening in separate spaces or classrooms.

Recognizing the importance of traditions, we can start new ones for our current world. Some that have been started are so poignant that they can survive.

Ventilation

The last in-person learning positive is in some sense the broadest of all, although it was not universally instituted, despite plenty of economic incentives. Regrettably it has not been carried forward by many educational institutions, which has been damaging to students, educators, and communities. At first blush, it appears quite different from all the other suggestions proffered in this book. The positive is summarized in two words: *good ventilation.*[41]

Before the pandemic, we knew that many school buildings were not in the best shape, with maintenance often deferred. Old school buildings with antiquated heating, cooling, and ventilation made classrooms too hot or too cold. We know that uncomfortable temperature is not conducive to productive learning and working for students and educators. Windows did not open or close properly and doors did not shut or lock easily, another issue for learning and also for safety.[42]

When schools reopened, despite existing building deficits that needed attention, a major push for improving ventilation took place. At the time, the focus was on improving air quality to inhibit the spread of COVID. The options went from the simple to the complex. There were the opening of doors and windows and the installation of fans, as well as of large, expensive ventilation systems, many of which included HEPA filters. In between these two extremes, there were room-by-room improvements in some schools, including through relatively inexpensive ventilation boxes that one could make oneself and were even put together by middle school students.[43]

Schools that installed ventilation systems had a lower spread of COVID, and indeed a moneymaking system developed almost overnight to transform school ventilation systems. Despite the availability of federal funding, many schools did not take advantage of it. It made a difference whether schools used more expensive or cheaper methods. The schools that installed higher-quality, more expensive devices saw a 48% decrease in the incidence of infection, whereas those with cheaper interventions saw a 35% reduction.[44]

Of K–12 schools, 33.9% reported replacements or improvements in ventilation systems, including air-conditioning. Twenty-eight percent reported in-classroom improvements, as opposed to system changes. Around 8% used ultraviolent systems to eradicate viruses. More than 50% failed to even report on this topic.[45]

As suggested earlier, improved ventilation does not just help curb the spread of COVID. Schools with quality ventilation see improved student learning, test scores, concentration, and educator wellness. With good ventilation, student and educator absences go down, which is also valuable for continuity of learning.[46]

And the benefits do not stop there. Quality ventilation cuts down on the spread of viruses other than the coronavirus. Schools often are viewed, quite rightly, as viral petri dishes, and students falling ill not only miss school but also bring illness home to family members, which then leads to spread in communities. Good ventilation cuts down on allergens and pollutants. Good air curbs asthma. If schools, which serve students from every walk of life, had better air, we would improve equity and wellness. Thus, if schools improved their ventilation, they would enhance the wellness of the larger community.[47]

Unlike many of the pandemic positives we've identified, ventilation improvements had a specific origin: The incentive for them came from the government. However, they were only partially implemented in some schools—and the uptake stopped. We would be well served to read a British study that sharply pointed out that quality air mattered during the pandemic, but we have since lost the opportunity to capitalize on this awareness. As the study observed, ventilation "garnered a lot of airtime over the pandemic but has, currently, dropped off the agenda slightly. . . . However, we would be remiss to ignore ventilation and its importance in schools."[48]

Lost opportunity here, and not just for schools and their students and educators. Lost opportunity also for community wellness.

MAINTAINING THE STRATEGIES

To be sure, some of the pandemic positives described here have been maintained in education, but, sadly, that has not been the universal result. These new approaches were seen as something for the pandemic and not something to improve education meaningfully moving forward.

There is no reason to discard some of these strategies that respond to trauma and create a sense of belonging and community, even when social distancing and masking are no longer necessary. Whether learning occurs at home, online, or in person, the approaches suggested here in Part II work to overcome distance and have relevance on an ongoing basis.

We have focused on the pandemic positives that some educators implemented during the pandemic, positives we think are worth replicating and scaling with stickiness. Therein lie the moving-forward issues. How do we enable change in education to take root for the future? How do we make sure that leaders, educators, and communities recognize the value of the pandemic positives? How do we engender hope for education and replicate the creativity that a crisis enabled? How do we ensure that the improvements made possible by the pandemic positives extend to all our students, regardless of age, race, gender, ethnicity, or social class? It is to these hard issues that we now turn in Part III.

STRIVING FOR STICKINESS

CHAPTER 9

Connectedness, Creativity, and Community Partnerships

POSITIVES WE IDENTIFIED

We, and others, have identified positives in education that, as noted in Parts I and II, rarely have been addressed fully and certainly have not been examined in depth in the context of trauma and mental wellness. The obvious question to ask is, What do we do next, now that we have named the pandemic positives?

We start by looking at the pandemic positives as a whole and cull the central themes that emerge from them. Taken together, the themes become a recipe for improving education in both the narrowest and the broadest senses. Next we seek to cook the recipe, turning the pandemic positives into a larger educational framework that leads into the future. The result is what we call *game changers*—pandemic positives with stickiness.

Before turning to the themes we have identified, let's review some the pandemic positives detailed in Part II:

- The value of online learning for a host of students and for some subgroups of students in particular
- The opportunity for educators to see their students in their home settings, through visiting or online, allowing educators to get a better understanding of their students
- Changes in homework, testing, and evaluation, necessitated by the online environment or social distancing
- A newfound appreciation for the critical role schools play in fostering students' social and emotional development
- The importance of educators' serving as role models for calming behavior in times of stress and engaging with students in difficult conversations
- The changes to more restorative and less punitive disciplinary practices
- The use of creativity to bring play, reregulation, and joy to students
- A sensitivity to the recurrence of trauma and the outsize responses that retriggering trauma brings, often unexpectedly
- The increased need for connection and communication among the many constituencies engaged in and affected by education

- The acknowledgment of the centrality of a sense of belonging for students, parents and caregivers, educators, and community members
- The reciprocal engagement of the wider community with educational institutions

Three themes emerge from and repeat in this list of positives: *connectedness*, *creativity*, and *community partnerships*—three terms that have appeared at various junctures throughout this book. To encapsulate the themes and help us and our readers to easily recollect them, we introduce the concept of a three-legged stool whose legs are connected. This visual representation can guide us in reflecting on how to make the pandemic positives stick and become game changers.

THE THREE-LEGGED STOOL

Using the metaphor of the three-legged stool is not new; it comes out of a rich history, and for a reason. First, three-legged stools are stable, more so than four-legged stools, since all three legs are on the same plane, to use basic geometry. Second, their stability means that they are stable on unstable ground, something farmers take advantage of, using three-legged stools to milk cows, as observed by one of us, seeing a grandparent milking the family cows. Third, the idea of three legs often has been used to metaphorically refer to needed posts for success in a number of fields of study. For example, the legs of the stool have referenced financial security in retirement (social security, pensions, and savings), business success (leadership, strategy, and management), and education (parents, students, and teachers).[1]

We expand on this common image. For us, in education postpandemic, the legs of the three-legged stool stand for the three themes: connectedness, creativity, and community partnerships. We see the three-legged stool as the furniture we must have in educational institutions at all levels. We can furnish schools with what is needed into the future by introducing changes that echo three-legged stools—changes that embody connectedness, creativity, and community partnerships. Readers can print out pictures of a stool or get a miniature stool as a reminder of how to improve education, something we have done in our own workspaces.

We also can use the stool as a rule of thumb for creating and evaluating priorities, large or small. Basically, any priority, any program or plan, as long as it has the three legs of connectedness, creativity, and community partnerships, is worth trying in educational settings today and tomorrow.

SPECIFIC DESIGN FEATURES

A three-legged stool can have different shapes and sizes and be constructed of different materials. However, all three-legged stools, regardless of their specific design, share features. And to these we add more in our educational stool.

Each stool has a top on which someone or something is placed. In our educational model, the top of the stool has the word *trust* etched into it, since no work on implementing positive change, such as toward physical and psychological safety, can proceed without trust. Trust must exist between students and educators; between educators and administrators; between parents and caregivers, educators, and administrators; and finally, between leadership and the local community, including governing boards and town government. Yes, if one or more elements of trust are missing or underdeveloped, positive change can still happen, but it will not be the fulsome change that will improve education over the long haul—and without the seat of the stool (which actually holds the legs together), the stool will fall apart.

Fostering and maintaining trust is not a simple task; just repeating the word doesn't do it. Actions and engagement are central features of producing trust. In a world with diminishing safety, trust is ever harder to maintain, and it is difficult to build but erodes easily. One school shooting, one lockdown, one incident of discrimination can undermine school safety, and it is not necessarily police or school resource officers who are able to restore trust.[2]

The necessity for trust and how it is developed are factors that appear throughout this book. All discussions about engagement, communication, connection, and community are reflective of trust. To highlight a core concept, we have no hope if we don't have trust.

We were struck by an interview with Dan Bauer, superintendent of the Danvers, MA, public school system, in which he said that, first, his goal was to focus on the district's positives, not the negatives. Next, he saw the need to establish trust before changes could be made. He asserted, "It's important to build that trust to start. The worst thing you can do is come in with lots of big changes before creating that sense of collaboration." Later in the interview, he added, "The way to do that [develop trust] is developing relationships."[3]

The words *trust* and *safety* appear in our survey respondents' answers to the open-ended question about key qualities required in a leader. One noted, *"A trusting, caring, and collaborate [sic] working relationship can help many schools tackle tough situations and prosper."* Another stated that leaders should *"trust their People."* Another asserted that the ideal leader *"builds trust, improves morale, and fosters a sense of belonging in the school community."* Yet another reiterated the importance of trust: *"Trust was integral to building lasting relationships with students and [trust is] what carried me during the pandemic."*

As described earlier, when it comes to the pandemic positives, the legs of this stool are connectedness, creativity, and community partnerships. Call them the three *c*'s. These three legs operate together simultaneously, and in our stool, they are connected in meaningful ways. This is a key design element: The legs are not freestanding, because each engages with and is related to the others—not just for stabilizing the stool, which cannot be stable without them, but to reinforce how intertwined the three *c*'s are and how each informs the others.

EXPLICATING THE THREE C'S

As reflected throughout this book, we are using the term *connectedness* broadly, to acknowledge that the many constituencies in the world of education need to engage more fully with one another: Connectedness is needed between students, between students and educators and administrators, between schools, between educators and parents and caregivers, between teachers and professors and administrators. In addition, connectedness is important between students, parents and caregivers, and educators and between educational leaders, teachers and professors, and communities. The connectedness can take many forms, including interactions in person, texting, and online chats.

Again, we turn to the voices of our respondents, here to reinforce the importance of connectedness. In referring to leaders, one stated, *"[Leaders] can create better community among staff members."* Another observed that leadership requires *"building strong relationships between parents, teachers, and the students themselves."* One respondent wanted leaders who do *"community outreach that actually inspires the community to be involved."* Another advised, *"School leaders can work with stakeholders such as teachers, parents, communities, and government."* We return to the challenges and concerns of educational leadership later.

Not only is connectedness vital; we also must recognize and encourage the second of the three *c*'s, creativity, and the development of new or reconstituted approaches toward it, in many contexts: classrooms, administrative decision-making, and responsiveness to upheaval or unusual behaviors. Such creativity can and should take many forms, including in the arts. Creativity can be discerned in choices made, or not made; in the presentation of physical space; and in novel approaches to new or difficult situations, whether involving students, families, or communities. Readers can refer to Table 2.2 in Part I to see evidence of the importance educators placed on creativity during the pandemic and in their work postpandemic.

We need to remember that, as described earlier, creativity can be linked to adversity. As Ben Orlin, a specialist in teaching math, stated, "Creativity is what happens when a mind encounters an obstacle. . . . No obstacle, no creativity." While we might not be that hyperbolic, we agree that creativity is central to educational success, particularly in a crisis situation.[4]

Regarding the third component of the three *c*'s, community partnerships, we urge that educational institutions not be islands. Community resources, including for food, mental health, and athletic teams such as Little League, need to be partnered with schools on a regular, not ad hoc, basis. Community organizations and local businesses can provide supports for students and educators, through internships, fieldtrips, and subject matter expertise. They can provide resources, both human and material.

Reciprocity can be developed to enhance community partnerships; it is not a one-way street where schools and universities get and communities give. Schools and universities help the community. Schools can be a community resource when community-based organizations lack the resources to hold large gatherings and run community-wide activities. Schools can be places where community members can create community gardens and where adult education and wellness programs are offered. They also can train individuals who can contribute to the workforce, whether through volunteering, internships, or paid apprenticeships.[5]

It is worth noting here Emily Lubin Woods's work on community engagement in schools and her book on community schools, *The Path to Successful Community School Policy Adoption: A Comparative Analysis of District-Level Policy Reform Processes*. As explained by the Coalition for Community Schools, "The community schools strategy transforms a school into a place where educators, local community members, families and students work together to strengthen conditions for student learning and healthy development."[6]

We concur wholeheartedly that the community should be involved, but we also emphasize reciprocity; in other words, community partners receive benefits too. From our perspective, community partnering is but one of three key approaches necessary in making the pandemic positives a sticky reality. A critical feature we add is hinted at in the coalition's statement, namely, *healthy development*.

We believe that where the three-legged stool is situated and what it is set down on matter in three central ways. First, the stool "furnishes" education in that it is what fills the decision-making space as we evaluate educational initiatives and priorities. Second, recall that a three-legged stool can stand with stability on unstable ground. What is that ground? One way to reflect on the ground is to consider social and emotional learning as the carpet on which the three-legged stool is situated. Third, while we can debate the centrality of social and emotional learning to school curricula, we do know that students cannot learn content material without being socially and emotionally ready to learn. So, for us, one aspect of the ground on which the three-legged educational stool sits is the needed carpet of social and emotional learning.

Viewed even more broadly, education itself is uneven ground for many reasons, the pandemic being only one. The uneven nature of education's ground results from a divisive social and political discourse surrounding education, marked disparities in educational outcomes across all levels of learning, achievement gaps, and the economic instability of institutions and of those in them—and the list goes on. The three-legged stool, as our educational model, is fundamentally stable even though the ground on which educational planning and implementation occur is not. The ground under education may shift because of public demands and politics, but the stool's stability and its three themes persist. This is illustrated in Figure 9.1 by a collage of a three-legged stool with interconnected legs sitting atop the sea of social and emotional learning in the educational landscape.

It is our belief, then, that prospectively and under the umbrellas of trauma responsiveness and mental wellness, our educational system will improve if it fosters and develops strategies for implementing connectedness, creativity, and community partnerships systemically and systematically, regardless of whether a crisis exists.

When an educator or school system evaluates changes, considers new programs, makes decisions, or prioritizes the sourcing and application of funding, it is useful to reflect on the three-legged stool, as it will foster wise prioritization, quality questions, and important framing. To use parlance from Brookings, the three-legged

Figure 9.1. Karen Gross, *Imagining*, **2023**

stool will "power up" education and support enduring change. Put another way, the three-legged stool, a representation of the pandemic positives, has the capacity to mend education.[7]

IT'S MORE THAN WORDS

Two words continually leap off the page for us in our work and in this book: *positives* and *pandemic*. The pandemic has been and in some senses still is a crisis that, by its very nature, was unexpected, unpredictable, and uncertain, engendering fear and insecurity. As noted in Parts I and II, we were all unprepared for the depth of its impact—its effects on our physical and mental health, our home life, our educational institutions, our work life, and our larger communities.

Although it is the negatives that have generated the most attention, there were positives. As we described in Part II, the pandemic crisis created opportunity for all of us as individuals and as members of communities, the workforce, and families. And we all had different reactions. The piece shown in Figure 9.2 demonstrates efforts to deal both seriously and with some humor with all that confronted us during the pandemic.

As we have stressed, the positives allowed us to move forward in education, not always with grace and equanimity, but with determination, as evidenced by successes that resulted. Education persisted and continued forward, albeit not in all localities and contexts. Education as a whole didn't get mired in the past with a refusal to adapt; it didn't stagnate by repeating what we had always done. It didn't regard masks and social distancing as insurmountable challenges. Educators exercised talents and skills that may not have been used before the pandemic. We return to this notion of forward progress later.

Figure 9.2. Karen Gross, *Masked Salad*, 2020

What has become clear, even through the pandemic's omnipresent fog of disaster, change, and confusion, is that those with a positive outlook did better. While as of yet difficult to prove, we sense that educators with hope did better than those without it. Yes, there was pessimism and sadness. Yes, there was death and illness. Yes, our world was changing before our very eyes. Nevertheless, we managed to move forward in education, in part, at least for many, because of a feeling that we were fighting for a brighter future. This made for a shift from short- to long-term thinking. We developed the pandemic positives not only for today but also for tomorrow: That shift was critical to forward progress.

LONG-TERM THINKING

The presence of the many educational pandemic positives identified in this book have power if they become game changers, and to make that transition, they need to have stickiness. Before we turn to approaches for developing stickiness, we must look at the value of long-term thinking, something that is challenging for us as individuals and also for the country generally. American culture is much too focused on immediate outcomes and rewards.[8]

Individually and collectively, we need to become good stewards of our planet and its inhabitants. To borrow from Roman Krznaric in *The Good Ancestor: A Radical Prescription for Long-Term Thinking*, which we will return to, we should be good ancestors for all those who follow us.[9]

In the gap we all experience between birth and death, in whatever work we do, whatever relationships we build, wherever we reside, and whatever communities we are part of, we have a chance to make that gap have meaning. Generations before and after us have dealt and will deal with crises. Current generations have an opportunity to demonstrate how we deal with crises, specifically in the context of this book, the pandemic crisis.

Education is our exemplar and a good one, because education does not happen just in schools and colleges. We continue to grow and learn throughout life, and ideally our experiences, both positive and negative, enrich us and those around us to give us hope that following generations will be wiser and happier than we have been.

For education to work well, we must be open to learning, willing to learn, able to take risks. We need to be creative, connected, and engaged in our communities. We need to put our hope in those we are educating now and in the generations to come. Above all, we need to take those two words, *pandemic* and *positives*, and understand that they will point us forward, make us better long-term thinkers and doers, if we give them stickiness so they become game changers. How to do that isn't easy, but it is possible. It is to that challenge that we now turn.

CHAPTER 10

Game Changers and How They Work

THE MEANING OF *GAME CHANGERS*

Thus far, we have focused on how the pandemic positives came into being and how they operate in practice, in the trenches. The ultimate goal is to make the pandemic positives game changers, something that occurs when they become sticky. We can make this determination only by looking back, assessing whether a change has become influential. When we look back and see the profound systemic and sustainable changes made by the pandemic positive game changers, then we can say the COVID pandemic that erupted in 2020 was a game changer in the history of education.

Now come the hardest questions, apart from those surrounding stickiness addressed in Chapter 11: How do we make the pandemic positives true game changers in education? What enables people and systems to transform? What enables game changers to produce profound systemic and sustainable change?

These questions are best addressed in three stages: (1) looking at game changers across U.S. history; (2) examining the concrete steps taken in the mental health field to create successful systemic game changers across time, described in *The System of Care Handbook*, "Cultural and Linguistic Competence and Eliminating Disparities," and "A Journey of Public Stewardship on Asian American and Pacific Islander Mental Health"; and (3) probing a recent game changer in education—artificial intelligence and associated technology, which emerged during and subsequent to the height of the pandemic.[1]

Several added observations:

We can learn critical lessons through using an analogy, and we use mental health as an exemplar and analogy because it can inform education, given that both mental health and education are large, complex public systems. Add to this that mental health is keyed to education; we can't educate students if they are not mentally well. So improvements in mental wellness have educational benefits in three ways: on their own, through their intersectionality, and by way of example. To these ends, in the context of stage 2 above, we actually identify for readers the transportable lessons from the mental health example to guide the application of these lessons into the educational system.

It is worth explaining how we arrived at the ordering of Chapters 10 and 11—beginning with game changers writ large and then turning to the stickiness of the pandemic positives in education. We considered reversing the order of these chapters, and perhaps some readers will want to read them in reverse order, but we need to understand the game-changing process, which is difficult and can be lengthy, and its success is measured with the passage of time. Once we understand the process, we can set about getting there—putting the pieces into place in education that will produce game changers now and down the road through stickiness.

We characterize *positive game changers*, combining various definitions, as a newly introduced factor or element or situation (whether introduced deliberately by an individual or organization or by an act of nature or without any agency or attribution) that positively alters an existing individual, situation, activity, behavior, organization, or social/cultural norm in a significant way. Yes, there are negative game changers, for example, nuclear weapons. In this book, we do not explore the negative game changers, leaving that task to others.[2]

Across time, we have witnessed, read about, or experienced many game changers. They are not new phenomena. We have had large-scale game changers since the beginning of time. Game changers can be massive or smaller in scope. And while we usually do not see them in advance, there are instances where we can anticipate catalytic events that create sustainable game changers. Often, game changers require extra effort to make stickiness happen. What is key to positive game changers, whether affecting people, things, or organizations, is their transformative power.[3]

Consider these examples. The discovery of electricity led to game changers such as lightbulbs, appliances, and computers, all of which improved our daily lives. The discovery of microbes led to game changers such as antibiotics, vaccines, assorted medications, and antiretroviral therapy that have improved health care. The use of proning (turning patients on their stomach) was a game changer, helping individuals suffering with COVID. The invention of artificial intelligence (AI) led to generative AI, including through ChatGPT and whatever new incarnations of AI may exist; these have changed and will continue to change our way of life.[4]

GAME CHANGING ACROSS TIME

Reflect momentarily on the introduction of the printing press. Or the automobile. Or cancer treatments. These all were game changers that altered how we managed our lives and work.

With the printing press, reading was no longer limited to a certain elite, those who could afford manuscripts written by hand; the invention was an educational equalizer. As the printed word spread, it exposed ever greater numbers of people to new ideas. It also made propaganda possible, but on balance, despite the negatives, the printing press moved society, and education, forward.[5]

The development of cars, trains, and planes allowed us to be with others who were far away and offered access to distant places. We could visit family and friends more easily and work and collaborate with those who were not geographically proximate. We could learn about and from different cultures, share ideas more widely, and deliver and receive products more quickly. Horses can't compete with cars, trains, and planes. And yes, transportation can lead to deaths and injuries, but the benefits outweigh the risks.[6]

More than a century ago, people with cancer carried the stigma of a disease associated with death. Some doctors did not give their patients the diagnosis because to do so seemed cruel and took away their patients' hope. Society's fatalistic attitude inflicted on cancer patients social isolation, shame, and discrimination. One of us distinctly remembers her surrogate father's getting cancer and asking him if it was all right to still sit on his lap and hug him. She was scared of catching his illness but was reassured that touch did not lead to its transmission. The other author's mother passed away in 1968 when he was 12. His family told him not to tell his classmates that his mother had died of cancer, for fear they might shun him. Sadly, this stigma still exists, and though it is diminishing, it still prevails in various cultures and for certain types of cancer.[7]

The discovery that cancerous tumors can be removed was a game changer; so was the development of new diagnostic tools and treatments, among them advanced imaging (including in DNA sequencing), targeted drugs, immunotherapy, bone marrow transplants, and increasingly precise radiation therapies. Through the increased openness and courage of patients (some of whom are famous) and public campaigns about treatment options, together with anti-stigma education, we have come to view cancer differently. It remains difficult, and death still results for far too many, but we celebrate survivors and the pathways to survival. This move away from stigmatization has been life altering for patients, families, workplaces, and communities.[8]

MENTAL ILLNESS DESTIGMATIZATION

Stigma is clearly not unique to cancer. People with mental illness carry stigma also. They are burdened with negative stereotypes intimating they are unstable, are violent, or have a weak character. "Just pick yourself up by your bootstraps" is the dismissive refrain. When school shootings or other horrific events occur, individuals say the perpetrators must be mentally ill, thus sidestepping (among other issues) the difficult Second Amendment debates.[9]

In the United States, with its broader narrative of rugged individualism and a lack of knowledge mixed with a misunderstanding of mental illness, those struggling with mental illness suffer discrimination, subtle and overt. This runs across individuals of all ages, genders, races, and ethnicities. But there has been progress. The discovery that mental illness actually can be treated or even eliminated in many instances was enabled by game changers like the Community Mental Health Act of 1963, medications, various psychotherapeutic treatments, and well-structured and informed recovery programs to improve mental health care. The public disclosures of mental illness and accompanying revelatory memoirs (including by famous, high-achieving individuals) and social media awareness have enabled increased destigmatization.[10]

Just think about Simone Biles and the "twisties" she encountered in the Olympics that led to her withdrawal from competition. Nevertheless, she returned, to greater success, and has not stayed out of the public view as she has worked to overcome her struggles, including from sexual abuse by a coach. Many individuals—ordinary folks—who struggle with mental illness live and function productively in our society without being confined to an institution. Yes, the challenges remain, including through historically insufficient funding for services and support (such as housing) from federal and state governments. And the path of public messaging of mental illness has not been easy, because of the ingrained social stigma within our society.[11]

In this context, let's look at the transformation of the public mental health system facilitated by one of the coauthors in the Commonwealth of Massachusetts. Generally speaking, public mental health aims to reduce stigma, disparities, and inequities in the mental health status and care of those served and underserved. Massachusetts's mental health system, like those of other states, was challenged in terms of access to and availability of services offering cultural and linguistic competence (CLC) and the needed funding. Transformation began in Massachusetts first through the creation of an organizational entity within the state mental health authority with the sole responsibility (the functional responsibility) of implementing CLC plans and actions in the service delivery system.[12]

Once the organizational entity (the structure) was established, a logic model, based on established theories of change, guided the removal of many of the barriers to those served or underserved. These actions were critical at the macro, meso, and micro levels, reflected in policies, programs, and practices. The annually operationalized CLC action plans identified focus areas through community partnership, leadership development, service standards, data and evaluation, workforce and professional development, and information dissemination (messaging). Implementing annual action plans, with a focus on the word *action*, was essential to enabling systemic transformation.[13]

Many other strategies were used during the transformation of the mental health system. They were developed from and grew out of the organizational entity. Specifically, the action steps in the CLC plans aimed to modify existing system operations with as few disruptions as possible. This benefited both users of the system and the providers of care.[14]

The centrality of the CLC focus remained unchanged and omnipresent as the key focus of the mental health system was and continues to be end users and their families. Changes that developed in one CLC focus area were often used to advance the goals of another. For example, community engagement was not limited to facilitating service outreach; it was used to increase buy-in and program relevancy for the people served. It also was used to recruit a diverse workforce and provide professional development, where attention was paid to cultural nuances, knowledge, and competency in the services offered.[15]

One reigning recognition throughout this process was that transformation is complex and takes time. The coauthor used road signs in speeches, meetings, and written materials to describe the omnipresent hurdles and changing realities on the road to the destination. A *stop* sign was displayed during the 2008 economic crisis when funding for some programs was cut. A *yield* sign was used to signify the need to slow down progress when other, more urgent demands needed attention. *Speed bumps* were used to represent the need to slow down progress because of pushbacks. The use of *detour* signs signified the extra time it took when there was no direct way to achieve an outcome.[16]

The role of time is key here. In describing this entire process and his work over 2 decades, the coauthor states that the following phrase both describes his modus operandi and is his frequent utterance: "It is a marathon, not a sprint." He keeps this message on a card with him to this day.

Attention and commitment waxed and waned because of competing public demands and the underfunding of day-to-day operations. Catalytic events brought mental health and the ongoing system transformation back to public attention. Examples sadly abounded. "No one who sees a disaster is untouched by it" was a repeated public mental health message that this coauthor used following September 11th, the Boston Marathon, and other human-made disasters, as well as natural ones. These disasters touched the hearts of many, and the experience of human losses, loss of control, fear, and uncertainty made the public pay more attention to their own mental health (or lack thereof) and the mental health of those around them. Community engagement was the top focus in these situations, leading to service development, staff training in trauma-informed care, and the tackling of inequitable distribution of services and of disparities in general.[17]

There were also non-disasters that caught the public's attention and served as catalysts for furthering change. Concrete examples are instructive. The White House Conference on Mental Health highlighted the importance of mental health and wellness. At the event, President Barack Obama delivered this message: "Too many Americans who struggle with mental health illnesses are still suffering in silence rather than seeking help, and we need to see [to] it that men and women who would never hesitate to go see a doctor if they had a broken arm or came down with the flu, that they have that same attitude when it comes to their mental health." The White House event in and of itself was not a game changer. But personal disclosures from movie stars and politicians attending or speaking at or in response to the event were powerful and heard, enabling many established game changers to again be visible and sticky.[18]

The impact of race experience, social determinants of mental health, and direct and indirect trauma on the individual mental health and well-being of African Americans, Hispanic Americans, and Asian Americans became the topic of 2-year-long community conversations in Boston following the White House conference. The Boston Marathon bombing of 2013 also brought about a strong community partnership in planning and participation. Among the witnesses and victims and their families were advocates who had lived through mental health crises. They spoke with strength, clarity, and effectiveness about their fear of social stigma and the dismissive reactions to their mental strains from families and friends, similar to what one of the authors heard at the White House conference. Their disclosure and sharing on a broad scale of their hope and recovery were truly incremental gains in reducing the stigma of mental illness that had started years ago.[19]

There were so many more catalytic drivers, among them the former surgeon general's report on mental health and supplemental report on race matters, the Institute of Medicine report on the quality chasm, and personal disclosures from actors and sports stars, all incrementally making game changers stick. During the 20 years of public stewardship over Massachusetts's public mental health system by the organizational entity, referred to earlier, the critical approach was to ensure that these key drivers to improve a public mental health system were on everyone's radar, inside and outside government. It takes a village to raise a child; this village is also transforming the public mental health system.[20]

Empirical work was tied into these reforms in mental health. With collaborators from the Harvard Program in Refugee Trauma and the Instituto Superiore di Sanità and other international partners, one of the coauthors conducted the Project One Billion Global Mental Health Survey. He adapted it for the Global Mental Health and Action Plan as a model of macro, meso, and micro mental health and trauma recovery planning and implementation for governments of postconflict countries worldwide. The survey also deeply informed the work he did on improving mental health in Massachusetts, as described here.[21]

IS EDUCATION SO DIFFERENT?

Many of the lessons from the just described improvement in the mental health system in Massachusetts have parallels to and lessons for education. And, in the context of education, COVID was an added factor that contributed to the possibility of change. The critical question, then, is what enables positive game changers to produce profound systemic and sustainable change in education and what lessons from the mental health care model can be transported into education.

While we believe that there are transportable lessons from mental health care into education, we recognize that there is not a perfect match between mental health care and educational systems. But we start with this premise: Students' mental health is crucial to learning; we can't educate students if they are not mentally well. The following is a summary of lessons for education that we can draw from the transformation of mental health—and they can all be seen as pandemic positives:

- The three-legged stool we employ to describe the approach to education is a necessary framework, similar to the structural framework for a dedicated organizational entity responsible for planning and implementing change in mental health systems.
- Implementation of one change within education can lead to other changes in the educational system, making it possible to see advances in more than a single arena from each advance.
- The intentional use of similar strategies across many different areas within the educational system in need of improvement can produce integrated and systemic change across the entire educational system.
- The presence of crises—the pandemic in this case—has an impact on our mental wellness, and the need to pay attention to its remediation to facilitate learning for all students has risen to the surface and can be felt and seen by many.

- The change in rhetoric matters, and messaging the importance of education to our society at large needs to be heralded. The key is listening to and hearing the many voices of those affected by and within the educational system, including those whose voices are often not given sufficient credence. Empiricism in the form of surveys informs policymaking and provides the needed data to support change. Transformation is deliberative and not a sprint.

The examples of and lessons gained from the profound, systematic, and sustainable change in the context of mental health took many years. It was a marathon. Yes, educational transformation will take a long time too, but we are hopeful and we have a catalyst that can speed up change: the pandemic. That makes the pandemic itself a positive, as it can serve as a catalyst for positive change, enabling us to pivot in ways that otherwise would not have been possible or would have taken decades.

The pandemic changed some (not all) systems and organizations for the better. In the field of education, though, sadly, the pandemic positives have been only a minor game changer thus far; they have not changed and are not changing the face of education in a positive direction—yet.

Because education involves many individuals negatively affected by the pandemic, in the sites where they are active—schools, colleges and universities, students' homes, and community groups—their organizations have struggled to make positive change.

One of the survey respondents delineated the difficulties:

And then there's the fact that we were all forced [by the pandemic] to grow up so fast. We lost our parents and our childhoods along with [the students]. We had to start taking care of ourselves and each other and that's not something you can just forget about or put behind you when things get better. It's still there inside you; it's part of who you are now, whether you want it to be or not.

We have seen evidence of losses caused by the pandemic: Many students and educators are no longer participating in education. Academic progress has slowed, at least as measured by current assessment devices. Also, students often do not complete assignments. We acknowledge the existence of negative outcomes. But we are focusing on what the pandemic positives taught us, to bring about beneficial educational transformations.

As other crises have done, the pandemic provoked anxiety, fear, lack of control, and emotional and psychological distress for many. The number of deaths and illnesses was shocking, and with long COVID, illness persists, as does the emergence of new viral variants. Seclusion and masking had profound effects, including on family functioning and communication skills such as reading emotional cues. Mental health needs rapidly rose among students, educators, health care providers, and families. Mental health challenges were widespread across all ages, genders, ethnicities, and races.

Nevertheless, the crux of the argument in this chapter, in Chapter 11, and throughout the book is that if the pandemic positives can be made to stick long term, they will be game changers that will transform education. Their replication and scalability will flow from their transformative power post-stickiness. So if we can understand game changers and use the transformation of mental health as an exemplar, we can push the change needle in education.

Our survey results give us hope, because they show that the pandemic positives we identify have the possibility of taking hold. In education, if there is traction for some teachers in some schools, the advances will be shared as more educators and parents become aware of the benefits of these adaptations. This observation is supported by the many tables from our survey, displayed throughout this book. They show that our respondents wanted to move the pandemic positives forward.

WHY SOME, NOT OTHERS?

For reasons that escape us still, not all negative events have become positive game changers, although one would have anticipated that they would be. Sandy Hook, Parkland, and Columbine should have been catalytic moments, with students and educators being shot at and killed in large numbers. A place once considered safe—an educational institution—became a site of potential calamity. These events, despite their repetition in other schools, did not sufficiently galvanize the population or policymakers in a positive direction. School shootings have continued, despite the damage they cause.

The failure of these shootings to become positive game changers is baffling. We can blame it on politics. We can blame it on deeply held beliefs about gun ownership or the inclination to assume that only mental illness could cause such catastrophic behavior. We can blame it on the argument that the shooters were not terrorists attacking the United States and thus were less heinous individuals. We can blame it on the perception that the deaths and injuries have been fewer than those from 9/11 or the Boston Marathon and as a result extreme measures are not required.[22]

THE ALL-IMPORTANT THREE M'S

For game changers to work, as noted earlier in the mental health context, we need to look at what we can call the *levels of stickiness*. These levels of change are identified throughout the other two books in this trilogy: *Breakaway Learners* and *Trauma Doesn't Stop at the School Door*. Changes can occur in individual classrooms, promoted by individual educators or a small group of educators working together. Call these *micro* changes. They surely matter but they are not broad in scale.[23]

Then we have *meso* changes. These occur at the institutional or district level. Meso changes are adopted when there is buy-in across an institution or a particular system. If a school district in Massachusetts adopts a theme for all its schools—such as a sense of belonging—and it is incorporated into all aspects of school life across the K–12 pipeline, that is a meso change. Cultural change across an institution has power.

When widespread state and national changes in policy are implemented, these are *macro* changes. Suppose we changed state requirements for testing students; that would be a macro change. Adopting social and emotional learning principles across institutions would be a macro change.

The pandemic positives, as identified and described in Part II, can operate at one or more of these levels—micro, meso, or macro (the three *m*'s). For lasting change to occur, there must be buy-in at all three levels. While limited buy-in does improve education, if we want systemic and replicable change that transforms the educational landscape, all three levels are needed.

The model of the three *m*'s is used across many disciplines—from sociology, to social work (which uses the term *mezzo* rather than *meso*), to health care, to psychology. To be sure, there are divergences in what a particular discipline seeks to impart to its students; for example, does a social work program want its students to be exposed to individual practice (micro), institutional work (mezzo), and policymaking (macro)? Sometimes, for various reasons, not all of which are positive, we shortchange students' exposure to macro changes, leaving the policymaking to others; at other times, we place a greater emphasis on policymaking, leaving a deep understanding of practice to the workplace, a not uncommon approach in law schools, which may strike some as odd. In medicine, we surely help students appreciate the micro and meso levels of being a doctor but often skip or ignore the deeper policies involving health care delivery, leaving that perspective to those involved in public health.[24]

In this book, with its focus on education and the desire for positive change, we seek implementation at all three levels—micro, meso, and macro. Otherwise, the change would not be systemic, replicable, and scalable. But as with the three-legged stool, it is not enough to have macro change if there is no buy-in at the micro and meso levels. Conversely, changes at the classroom or district level do not lead to systemic change, at least not easily, quickly, or uniformly. Further, all three levels of change do not need to occur simultaneously and synchronously.

The diagram shown in Figure 10.1, which originally was created prepandemic for mental health and has been adapted to relate to education and the pandemic positives, is a good visual indicator of how this works in practice. It reveals that the three *m*'s are interconnected. Not only do we need to implement all three, but each of the three informs the others.

In sum, if we want the pandemic positives to become game changers, they need to be implemented at the micro, meso, and macro levels. The challenge of that has not escaped us.

LET'S CHAT ABOUT CHATGPT

The technological advances we are seeing and that will be developed in the coming decades are here to stay in one form or another. Few would question whether they are game changers—they are. Early on, many people purchased computers,

Figure 10.1. Ed K. S. Wang, *Three M's and Three P's*, 2019

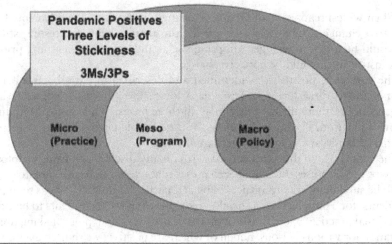

copiers, smartphones, and tablets. Remarkable advances have been made in AI and ChatGPT that have already had an impact across disciplines. Some of the latest changes arrived with unexpected speed and found their way into educational institutions—from kindergarten through higher education. We are changing what and how we teach and test.[25]

What interests us is the early adoption and acceptance of these AI-based technological advances even during the years we were wrestling with the pandemic across education. While some educators have been fighting the AI-related changes—and we don't deny the challenges—many have worked on creative ways to adopt them and to adapt their teaching and testing to the challenges these technological advances present. This has occurred despite educators' seeing the negatives. This is acceptance we have not seen with the pandemic positives, perhaps because for them to work, we need to keep remembering what we want to forget—the pandemic. It's like that sheet of plastic in the book *Poemotion*: Illustrations change and move only if the plastic paper is present in front of each image.[26]

With AI and ChatGPT, we are responding differently from how we historically have in education, which was to be negative and move slowly. Instead, we increasingly focus on the upsides (or is it the inevitability?) of ChatGPT in classrooms, in school systems, and in policy. This is despite the fact that, as Kevin Roose observed in the *New York Times*, ChatGPT made educators think they had been hit by an asteroid. They weren't prepared. That observation is akin to how educators had to manage the impact of the pandemic, when school closures and the shift to online learning also hit like an asteroid. But ChatGPT has now been adopted with much greater ease and is forcing us to both ask and answer difficult questions. Instead of fighting its presence, many educators are reflecting on how to adapt and flex because of it.[27]

With the creation of chatbots, some educators have already tried, and likely will continue to try, to find ways for students to do research and problem-solve despite the easy access to information (sometimes wrong) and solutions (sometimes wrong). Figuring out the AI-generated wrongs is educational in and of itself. Other educators have worked to develop novel questions that are not easily gamed by hired personnel or bots. These are questions based on in-class and online activities. Sometimes these questions are answered through putting together projects in teams of students working in virtual space with AI. Educators are using the students' chatbot essays as pathways to thinking about good and bad writing. Perhaps informed by the experience of the pandemic and the autonomy it offered to both educators and students, many educators, and their institutions, are working with students to determine what guidelines or rules they should institute about access to and use of online materials in assignments and tests.[28]

True, some schools and universities have banned ChatGPT and similar technology (at least as of 2024), suggesting that if it is detected, the student will fail or, worse, not graduate. Some educators have banned calculators too. Were we prognosticators (which we are not), we would suspect that these bans will be lifted over time. Add to this that we are aware of what AI cannot do, at least now in the educational sphere directly. It can't replace an educator's hand on the shoulder of a struggling student; it can't give a student the emotional capacity to feel the educator's sense of accomplishment that comes from students' finally understanding material or reading words for the first time or having trust that their educator can help them reregulate.[29]

Despite this just described negative knee-jerk rejection of AI by some educators, we think that there are other explanations for educators' non-knee-jerk acceptance of AI in educational settings. For us, we see a connection between the non-knee-jerk way some treated AI and the way some educators responded to the changes created by or caused in education by the pandemic. Our observations about a shared welcoming of change (AI and pandemic positives) could be mere coincidence, not necessarily correlation or causation. We still believe that the pandemic positives taught us, often without our being aware of it, that our prepandemic antipathy to change, often negative, did not serve us well.

Through the struggles of the pandemic, some educators actually worked with students, using cooperative approaches to navigating online learning. They flexed and adapted—despite themselves on occasion. They are now better prepared to consider helping students—and themselves—understand the pros and cons of ChatGPT and other AI developments. Like the pandemic, these are new challenges, but rather than letting them deter us or have us resort to prior approaches, we can let them empower us. Students and educators together can use the novelty to learn and grow. Together, they can probe the technology; they can consider its role in gathering information and misinformation and its impact on us as individuals and as a society. Educators can see what AI can do that humans cannot and the reverse: what humans can do and machines cannot.

We were struck by a professor's opinion piece in the *Washington Post* indicating what position the professor was taking with students concerning AI bots and

ChatGPT. His university had asked him to identify a policy for students. His policy, despite a lengthy essay suggesting he was not in favor of their use, was that he had no policy; he left it up to students whether, how, and when they used AI bots and ChatGPT.[30]

Here's our point on this professor's approach. Before the pandemic, but with the presence of the pandemic positives, we suspect that three things in this situation might *not* have occurred: (1) the university would not have left it to faculty to decide on a policy on AI and ChatGPT; a directive would have been sent from on high, perhaps without widespread faculty input; (2) a professor would have felt the need to do something because of being told to do something, even before knowing how AI bots and ChatGPT would play out; the decision to not have a policy is, then, a new choice; and (3) student empowerment would not have had the role it currently has in some regards, as educators and students partnered with respect during the pandemic and that respect and partnering is being carried forward. On the other hand, there might be no correlation or causation between a professor's choices and the pandemic; it could just be coincidental.

Perhaps the greatest lesson we can learn from the pandemic positives in the context of ChatGPT and other types of AI is to embrace change, to see its power and potential and how we can use it for good. As technology expert Paul Browning has written, educators shouldn't be scared of ChatGPT and issue warnings to students about its risks and downsides; instead, we should focus on what ChatGPT does well. This is precisely what the pandemic positives do: They teach us what educators did well. And that's a powerful lesson—focus on the positives, not the negatives.[31]

With the examples from mental health transformation and AI, we can now turn to how the pandemic positives we named here can be made to stick, remembering that without stickiness, they cannot be game changers.

CHAPTER 11

The Many Streets That Lead to Stickiness

GETTING TO STICKY

In Chapter 9, we recognized the overarching lessons from the pandemic positives—the three *c*'s represented by the three-legged stool. In Chapter 10, we saw how game changers operate outside the education field and in it in the context of ChatGPT. Now we need to address what will enable us to create stickiness for educational improvement from the pandemic positives.

What follows are some of the ways in which pandemic positives can have stickiness. What we provide is not a step-by-step progression, in that not all the approaches are required for forward progress; in some instances, we can deploy only several approaches because of lack of time, resources, or will or because of political barriers. That said, each of these approaches will further our ability to transform education, including in the relatively near term, something for which we have been aching for decades. The pandemic positives enable us to ponder long-term change too. Some of the roads to stickiness will sound familiar, as they have appeared in other guises in this book. That's fine: Approaches can be applied in different settings; not every road has to be new. One idea or strategy can serve several purposes, as we noted in the context of mental health transformation; we're not unintentionally being repetitious!

We view our sections listing factors for stickiness, set out below, as being like streets on a map, where the destination is change in education, recognizing that change is not a fixed place but an ongoing process. As with the adage "All roads lead to Rome," there are many paths to lasting educational change. Some paths are obvious, others less so. Some are wider than others, some have more bends and curves, and some can be driven on more quickly. Individually and collectively, they provide enduring improvement. Readers may see possibility in some and no capacity in others, and that's fine; stickiness isn't a single road. It is many roads headed in the same direction, but we don't all need to go down every single one of them.

INFORMING OUR THINKING

In our thinking about change in education, we have been enriched by the work of many writers on transformative change and by our own efforts to create change in the fields we work in, including through law and public policy. We are drawn in particular to the work of brothers Chip and Dan Heath, both educators, in *Made to Stick: Why Some Ideas Survive and Others Die*, released well before the pandemic, as well as to Malcolm Gladwell's *The Tipping Point: How Little Things Can Make a Big Difference.*[1]

The Heath brothers share a framework for how to make an idea stick—how to create a message with stickiness. They say that one needs to make listeners (in our case educators, policymakers, parents and caregivers, and students) pay attention, understand and remember the point being made, agree with or share belief in the idea, care about the idea, and act. It sounds simple enough and, yes, messaging and communicating are key. But in the real world, stickiness is far from simple and involves much more than messaging.

Gladwell's concept of a tipping point also has relevance here. After all, a pandemic can be a tipping point. Many of the pandemic positives and the thematic three *c*'s had roots in practices from before the pandemic but they did not have universality or scalability. Social and emotional learning was not invented because of the pandemic; it is just that its importance and the critical role of trauma and mental wellness moved its relevance from the sidelines to the stage.

Significant barriers influence the speed of adoption of educational change, among them divergent views on topics such as book choice, student punishment, and the role of content acquisition and assessment. We do not have universal accord on how to treat issues keyed to discrimination and harassment based on gender, race, ethnicity, religion, and national origin. Moving the needle on social norms, particularly in a country as divided as ours, is downright demanding. But even in the midst of these factors, it is our view that change can happen and education can be transformed, though we recognize that, to return to our adage, Rome does not mean the same thing for everyone and not everyone wants to go there. And for those who want to go, the voyage is not short.[2]

To add another observation on change: We tend to view change as a light switch going on or off—we either have it or we don't. We act as if we need to move the needle 180 degrees, but the truth is that moving the needle 10 degrees is better than not moving it at all. Think about it in terms of racial, ethnic, and gender discrimination, harassment, and abuse. Yes, we want to completely eradicate these practices, but if we make improvements and move the needle 15 degrees, that is better than zero degrees. Moreover, if we move the needle, resulting positive ripple effects can change minds and hearts, including in invisible, undetected ways.

One of the authors is reminded of a conversation she had when she worked for the government in Washington, DC. A friend, a senator, noticed her as the coauthor was exiting a meeting and asked, "So how's it going in DC?" to which the coauthor replied, "Like working in a swamp; it is hard to make forward progress." To this the friend replied, "The problem is that you want to move the needle 180 degrees; if you move it three or four or five degrees, that's OK; that's further than it was in the past and that's progress." Wise advice.

THE STREETS OF CHANGE

We have identified 10 factors for stickiness, which, as alluded to above, we see as streets of change. We elaborate on these in what follows.

Naming the Positives

One of the first steps in making change is recognizing it. Much of the change in education during the pandemic went unnoticed, unremarked on, and unlabeled. Teachers and educational leaders took steps to improve what was occurring in their classrooms and institutions. But since people were often not together, in either formal or informal ways, their improvements were not recognized. In short, the pandemic positives lacked visibility.

We've often said in this book that the act of naming is key to processing and progressing. For example, if we don't see trauma, if we don't name it, we can't tame it and then we can't frame it—as in recognizing its importance and creating an architecture that scaffolds it. These are repeated themes in *Trauma Doesn't Stop at the School Door*.[3]

We need to recognize what is occurring among our students and in our educational institutions before any replication and scaling can exist.

In Part II, we named the pandemic positives, or at least a goodly number of them. We have come to understand how and why they work, relying on trauma theory and mental wellness approaches as our framework, as well as on Part I's concepts of hope and crisis creativity. The aggregation of these elements is part of what makes them visible. There would be no need for Part III of this book if we hadn't identified what occurred during the pandemic in education that was positive.[4]

Two analogies can be drawn from medicine. First, for many patients, not knowing what is ailing them is immensely problematic. They have symptoms but no name for their ailment. This situation even has a name: the uncertainty of diagnosis. In such a situation, physicians need to be transparent about what they do and don't know, despite an urge to give a name to the ailment that might not be accurate, to ease a patient's disquiet. Recognizing and labeling the anxiety of uncertainty associated with assessment and treatment help patients understand what they are experiencing. Maintaining hope and motivating patients for further assessment and treatment that matches their affect are critical.[5]

Second, consider a primary care physician who had patients who were reluctant to take the COVID vaccine but were more than willing to take the weight loss drug Ozempic. Both injections were backed by research and development that got them to the end product; both rely on mRNA technology. But patients accept one with ease—despite its potential downsides long term—yet have antipathy toward the other. The physician was baffled by this. But staying far away from politics and our culture's obsession with thinness, here's a theory. Folks can't see COVID; the virus is minute in size (though not in impact). By contrast, weight loss is quickly visible. We are more willing to find stickiness in what we see, rather than in what is invisible and verified only by statistics (as in the numbers of people who have been vaccinated and are then less likely to die if infected with COVID).[6]

Both examples emphasize the importance of making the invisible visible—and that is what naming does. It concretizes what is amorphous and gives us a way to capture cause and effect more easily.

We believe that this book, if read and absorbed, brings about a naming of some of the positive changes that occurred in education during the pandemic. Once we see them, collected in one place, we can begin to form strategies for their replication, scalability, and stickiness.

Understanding Why and How These Pandemic Positives Work

Naming can be seen as labeling; it can give a descriptor to a set of similar items. But naming in and of itself does not necessarily explain why the collected items work. This latter point matters, because if we want replication and scalability, understanding is critical. Otherwise, we can't identify the drivers behind the changes we are concerned with here. We won't know when other, similar changes arise or need to be created.

In Part I, we addressed the reasons why the pandemic positives worked as well as they did, even if educators were unaware of why they were making the changes they made. The changes, adopted in the midst of an epic crisis, were trauma responsive and focused on mental wellness. They reside in hope and crisis creativity.

These explanations for change run counter to the many writings on how to make change occur, claiming that it needs preparation, planning, practice, performance, and repeated assessment. The pandemic positives had few, if any, of these formal steps. Yes, there was performance and perhaps there was subjective assessment in terms of determining increased student engagement and learning, but there was little planning, little preparation, and little opportunity to practice (as in pilot programs, and the like). Once the pandemic hit and education had to change immediately, the usual precursors identified in academic literature to enable change were rendered irrelevant.[7]

This book seeks to explain why the pandemic positives came into being and how they operated in practice during the pandemic itself. The positives happened because they were needed, and educators did what they could to navigate forward, filled with hope and crisis creativity. The absence of formality, hope, or crisis creativity may account for why some educators and their institutions made few changes. It also may account for why, in a postpandemic world, these pandemic positives were and are so easy to discard; they have not been embedded in the institutional culture, narrowly and broadly defined. Particular institutions and education writ large did not ask for, approve, or promote these pandemic positives. Change occurred differently. That means that stickiness has to come about differently.

By gathering, naming, and filling in the gaps surrounding the educational changes that were made in a crisis, we can ground what occurred. We make the invisible explanations visible and, in so doing, give rationale and voice to the pandemic positives and create a way for them to be integrated into our educational system rather than discarded. We animate the concept that crises create opportunities, and for these opportunities to endure, we need to understand them, even if we do so after the fact.[8]

The Role of Leadership

A host of variables attach to leadership in the context of change, and we use the term *leadership* broadly here to encompass institutional leaders as well as governing and school boards. We have referenced leadership elsewhere in the book; our focus here is on how educational leaders can contribute to the stickiness of the pandemic positives. As a useful aside, some of our suggestions extend to institutions and settings outside education. Folks interested in improving business, medicine, and government may find these suggestions on leadership transportable and thus helpful.[9]

Good Educational Leaders

Although it may appear self-evident, in education we need good leaders who can handle crises, embrace change, and shepherd the institution forward. And we need leaders to speak up and out to those with even greater power so these leaders can herald the need for and acknowledge the importance of change. Such individuals include members of governing boards and elected officials. We recognize that leaders have different styles and approaches, some that work better than others, and we recognize the challenges of leadership, with or without a pandemic.

We have seen the positives some educational leaders garnered in the pandemic—those pandemic positives we hope will endure. Many leaders recognized their changed role in a crisis and sought not only to model calm but also to be cheerleaders extraordinaire, empathetic navigators of deeply difficult familial issues and health concerns in their constituencies and artful and frequent communicators.[10]

But in terms of stickiness, we want to make another point about leaders and leadership. When leaders change, leave, retire, or are fired, institutions struggle, often with a dearth of candidates to fill in the holes. Consider for a moment Congress, the Supreme Court, and the executive branch of government. They are dominated by older individuals. So are some educational institutions. Since we ourselves are older, we are not dismissing the capacity of those who are older to lead.[11]

But . . .

We see a pressing need for the next generation of educational leaders to step up to lead. If we had a nickel for every person we've heard say, "Where are the new leaders?" we would be wealthy. Society seems to be struggling with a shortage of up-and-coming leaders. No shock as to why. Leadership is hard. Leaders are frequently criticized. They are vilified in social media. They are yelled at and disrespected. Their lives can even be threatened. Their physical health suffers. Just compare photographs of U.S. presidents before and after taking office. And we live in dangerous times, filled with natural disasters and the possibility of war, among other threats. In this climate, many university presidents have received votes of no-confidence from their faculties.[12]

Ouch.

Much has been written about how to improve leaders, but we want to examine this through a different lens, one generated by our instincts based on age and leadership, as we address the question, How do we cultivate quality new leaders? For us, this question is key to the stickiness of the pandemic positives and beyond, because, as we saw in Chapter 10, change and educational transformation are challenges that are not solved overnight. We need people with leadership potential to step up and become central to the changes we need in schools and universities, the country, and the world. We can't just sit back and await their arrival, if they do arrive. We need to find these leaders and help them.[13]

James Rosebush points out this irony: As the absence of leadership grows, the more we write about its absence. Wallowing (or researching) does not bring forth new leaders. Lamenting absence doesn't produce presence. And to be sure, complaints about leadership have a long history.[14]

Here's our suggestion. Find creative individuals—ideally already working in education—who are not scared, do not crave power, and in fact are not seeking leadership positions. Help them develop into educational leaders. Individuals who are in educational leadership for the right reasons—not power, not money—are more likely to lead well. Let's search for leaders who are amazing educators—yes, this might take them out of the classroom but the classroom lessons stay with them when they lead (and some leaders continue to teach as they lead, perhaps in classrooms or in different ways). And as Chris Minnich has observed in relation to emerging from the pandemic, we need strong leaders at such a time.[15]

Yes, we can turn to educational associations, webinars, and courses on educational leadership. But having a degree or certificate does not make someone a good leader. Sadly, we know too many well-educated individuals with degrees who repeatedly fail as leaders. And in education we recycle good leaders, some of whom return to the same institution for a second go-round after their first stint and a position at another institution.

So here's an idea for current leaders to carry out, one we have not tried enough but which we are now spurred to do. Identify a few individuals who would make excellent leaders, share that vision with them, and help them rise in the ranks so they can see themselves as leaders down the road. Identify them early. Look for creativity, compassion, empathy, and the ability to move people in one way or another. Lots of individuals can lead even if they don't know it; they lead through their work, their research, their contributions to the community, their perspicacity, their prescience. They lead because they are inventors and because they are willing to take risks to make their world better. These folks exist. We just have to find them. These future leaders, who must represent the racial and ethnic makeup of the community, can make the pandemic positives endure for generations to come. They will be models for our students, other educators, and parents and caregivers.

Increasing Institutional Hope

We see the need for educators during a crisis to communicate a culture of hope. And if we want educators to be creative—which is what is needed to bring about the pandemic positives and change—we would be wise to reflect on how leaders can contribute to building individual and institutional hope.[16]

To be sure, some individuals are by nature more hopeful than others. Some people have a doom-and-gloom approach to life. The glass-half-empty folks. Others envision the upsides of the world and see the road ahead rather than hurdles that block their way. The glass-half-full folks. And yet others are inclined to waver between hope and pessimism. One glass half empty and another half full look the same. That's an insight into the perspectives we bring to bear on a single situation.

While leaders can encourage positivity, they cannot change human nature. Hope cannot be forced on others, although individuals willing to change from a negative mindset can be helped to reframe how they see the world and themselves. For our purposes here, leaders cannot take the educator workforce and impose hope on them. Nevertheless, we encourage hopefulness in educators, because both physically and psychologically it is healthier than pessimism. And educators who have hope in their students are more likely to succeed in helping them grow and flourish.[17]

What we can do is focus on the creation by leadership of a culture of hope in institutions. This involves messaging from the top that imparts a belief in the capacities of the institution's educators and students to improve, make change, adapt, be flexible, be nimble, have agency and autonomy, and feel respected and encouraged. This we can do if we set our minds to it as leaders.

The concept of a culture of hope in educational institutions asks us to marry leadership and pandemic positives with the presence of hope. For some, constructing that marriage will be natural. For others, it is more forced, like the work of a matchmaker who sees ways to partner people who otherwise might not partner, and here it is partnering ideas that otherwise might not be partnered.

To create this marriage, recognize that institutions qua institutions obviously don't speak. Those who lead them do. And leaders who have optimism and hope can produce an environment where these qualities consistently are messaged. Indeed, the creation of institutional culture, while it involves everyone, can start at the top, and if it does, it can persist as long as it is institution dependent and not leader dependent.

While there is no one formula for building hope in an institution, we know from the abundant literature on leadership that certain steps are beneficial: high levels of communication, ready access to leadership, leadership's capacity to listen and adapt to the needs of employees, transparency, authenticity, asking for assistance, admitting errors, and requesting input that is then considered. The value of listening is reinforced by the voices of our survey respondents.[18]

To this list we can add treating people with genuine kindness and recognizing that the workforce is not a monolith, in that each person's life experiences outside the institution impact them daily. We can demonstrate respect, whether the employee cleans dishes and mops floors or makes financial decisions with institution-wide consequences.

A concrete example from the educational arena is instructive. If a principal believes that students in the school are deficient and will not succeed, that message trickles down to the educators who work directly with the students. When a leader lacks hope, educators become discouraged and lose hope themselves. Conversely, if a leader believes in the capacity of all students to make progress, to grow and flourish, that is more likely to happen. And if the institution's goals are based in progress, not arbitrary benchmarks, progress is more likely to happen, and with less stress and anxiety.[19]

Increasing Institutional Creativity

Along with a culture of hope, leaders need to foster and welcome creativity in their institution. Consider the difference between a principal who announces to the staff that all students must read within 5% of the nationally published norms for their age group and a leader who says, "I hope to see all students make progress of at least 5% ahead of where they were last year." A world of difference. And it is not dumbing down or catering to the weak; it is all about what enables learning to happen. It is creating a culture based on strengths, not deficits.[20]

As demonstrated in Part I, creativity can arise in the absence of hope—but it can thrive in the fertile soil of hope. So if institutions possess a culture of hope, leaders can work to develop creativity in educators—whether or not they are individually hopeful people. Indeed, both of us saw our own creativity rise during the pandemic, and in a sense, the art throughout this book is evidence of that: It was created during a crisis, that of education in a time of pandemic.[21]

Creativity requires agency and autonomy and involves risk taking, none of which is possible if institutional leaders are not supportive of creative endeavors. If everything has to be approved before being undertaken, if every new exercise, activity, or approach needs a committee's stamp of acceptability, creativity is slowed, if not halted.

How many times have we heard in the Virtual Teachers' Lounge that efforts by teachers were not undertaken because they were afraid that assigned mentors or school leaders would object? One coauthor remembers recommending to a teacher who was struggling to get her students' attention that the teacher bring in her violin and play for students before class began. The educator's response: "You can do that?" The other coauthor suggested that a new teacher in a diverse public school share the teacher's story of arriving in the United States not speaking English and being teased. Then the teacher could ask students where they were from and what languages they spoke and create a large map. Her response echoed that of the other teacher: "I can do that? It's allowed?" Yipes.

But leaders can do the opposite of discouraging creativity. They can encourage and reward it. They can message this in various ways. They can devise a fund for creative endeavors or introduce educator-generated creative ideas to the wider community. Leaders can be creative themselves, acting as role models to show how creativity works. Creativity also can be fostered through designing a physical environment that is open, welcoming, and filled with creative prompts that announce, This is a place where we can be creative; it is a creativity incubator in the school, designed for students and school staff.[22]

We have been in many classrooms, schools, and institutions in the course of our careers and know that an outsider can get a genuine sense right away of whether an institution is committed to creativity. Recently, one of us was in a high school where the hallways were empty of students during class periods. There was nothing on the walls. The lockers were traditional metal boxes. The floors were swept clean and there wasn't a piece of paper, a book, or a backpack anywhere in sight. When asked about this, one of the leaders said, "We run a tight ship."

Our reaction: Yes, you do, and there is nothing creative, engaging, or encouraging about the place. Where is the vitality? On the other hand, we have been in schools where artwork and decorations were on the walls and doors. Lockers were painted different vibrant colors. Between classes, students were seen rushing or ambling to and fro. Chalk drawings decorated the entryway. There was energy and excitement within those walls.

One of the founders of the Virtual Teachers' Lounge, an amazing teacher, described packing up her kindergarten classroom at the end of the school year as she prepared for a new administrative role. She indicated that she and her husband had several carloads of boxes of materials she had had in her classroom, including tons of items that had hung from walls or on whiteboards at different times of the year, as well as objects such as books, illustrations, and tactile items that had been sitting on her desk and on side tables. As she described this, many who were listening remarked, "We wish you had been our teacher in kindergarten." This leads us to two conclusions: This individual needs to become a leader in her institution (we are working on that) and she must have existed in a culture that encouraged creativity or at least did not stifle it or engender fear if it was manifested.

Fostering Community Engagement and Silo Busting

Educational institutions should not exist in isolation, though it often feels like that is just the way many currently are performing. The pandemic created opportunities for engagement across educational institutions, between educational institutions and faith-based and community service organizations, and between educational institutions and the private sector. Crisis-generated pathways for engagement and plenty of goodwill. Call it cross-pollination as a strategy for survival.[23]

The synergies, exemplified in Part II, were real and beneficial. But as the crisis of the pandemic receded, so did the engagement, as if its only utility was in a crisis. In the absence of necessity, we returned to the status quo ante. If we can determine why we retreated, perhaps we can figure out how to reverse the disengagement.

Cross-community engagement is difficult for leaders. It takes time, money, and energy. It is far easier to stay in one's lane, doing one's thing. Collaboration and collective action are not easy to sustain over long periods as personnel changes (particularly leaders) and the day-to-day exigencies of workplaces interfere and overtake us. The pressures of our work in our own organizations make cross-sector engagement cumbersome, despite the both tangible and intangible benefits.[24]

One of us remembers a four-college consortium that enabled a well-known lecturer to present to a large audience on each of the four campuses; to attend special dinners for faculty and students across the institutions; to offer a prelecture workshop, with students from all the institutions invited to participate (and with leadership participation); and to engage in extensive conversation with the four colleges' leaders and their staffs concerning content, promotion, and organization. It was, while it lasted, amazing, and it was funded largely, but not totally, by the wealthiest of the institutions. There was a remarkable, previously unknown sense of shared community. One of us remembers one of her students commenting after a workshop held at the coauthor's home, "I am not different from the students at the more prestigious institutions. I just haven't had the practice they have had speaking and engaging."

Sadly, when the leader of the wealthiest institution left, his successor did not see the value of the consortium and the attendant cost. The whole idea was abandoned. What a loss.

One of us remembers, too, the failed effort to get private colleges in Vermont (there were 18 at the time) to work together on sharing purchasing, health care costs, and HR resources. We couldn't even agree on the type of paper to purchase. We were reminded of Guido Calabrese's recounting in a speech at a meeting of college presidents how the Ivy League colleges refused to allow group purchases of electron microscopes even though it would save each institution $1 million. Why didn't it work? Well, no one campus would get credit for the scientific advance, and institutions would need to arrange and pay for delivery of their item to their campus (costing, of course, nowhere near $1 million). No one felt that savings of $1 million was enough to warrant the shared effort. Another yipes.[25]

If there is a rationale that will provide stickiness to community engagement, it has to be located in the benefits community engagement engenders. In other words, if we can show that community engagement is beneficial to all entities involved, in ways that siloed work is not, there is an opportunity for sustainability. Leaders can take it upon themselves to showcase these benefits—and often.

One way to show this is through financial benefit. If we can leverage costs and collaboration, we all get more and pay less. But the problem with this approach is that some gains are longer term and devalued for that reason. Or the savings are outweighed by other drivers or not deemed significant, as the microscope example demonstrates. We don't see the longer-term benefits for all; we see—sometimes— just the short-term, feel-good moment.

Suppose we upped the availability of grants that required collaboration and engagement. Suppose we created space and opportunity, as part of the workplace, for cross-sector engagement. It has to involve more than goodwill, as that can fade or gets ramped up only in a crisis. If we can throw out some of our rules on who can teach, educational institutions could welcome government and private-sector workers into their classrooms. Who doesn't want to impart knowledge, especially if it is within the confines of one's workload? Not extra work, but part of one's employment, it could be structured as a component of one's job, with the requisite hours accounted for in one's salary.[26]

Suppose that we allowed communities across sectors to problem-solve issues that had meaning for the community and there was a group effort to address the issues. An issue that immediately comes to mind is food scarcity. Surely we can agree that food scarcity, including in a first-world nation, is deeply troubling. Independently, many entities are working to address this problem—schools, faith-based organizations, social service agencies, and even the private sector. But what if there were deep connections between providers that allowed for collaboration and coordination? We did this during the pandemic and even before that time.

An instance of fostering collective community engagement and reducing silos took place in the field of mental wellness following the events of September 11, 2001. No one who sees or experiences such a disaster is untouched by it. The attack rocked the country's sense of security. All Americans felt vulnerable, unsafe, and helpless as individuals.

With this in mind, one of the coauthors developed the Massachusetts Initiative of Multicultural Community Outreach (MIMCO), created and funded through a federal grant formerly known as the Terrorism-Related Disaster Relief Grant from the Substance Abuse and Mental Health Services Administration and the Center for Mental Health Services. More than 20 local community organizations and schools across Massachusetts provided mental wellness outreach forums and generated locally relevant wellness projects to address the traumatic experiences and distress resulting from this atrocity.[27]

At the end of MIMCO, all the participating communities jointly shared the lessons learned with one another. The one consistent message from all of them was the value of community engagement. They wanted to continue such community actions during times of distress and celebration. Building on this enduring relationship, reflecting the metaphor of the three-legged stool with trust, community partnership is a true gem. It offers strengths and resilience at the grassroots level. This coauthor has continued to practice this "sticky" enduring collaboration for many initiatives of public stewardship in mental health in Massachusetts.

Here's another example from another location. Immediately after the 9/11 catastrophe and as soon as reopening was permitted, mental health professionals from wide-ranging settings offered their services without charge to educational institutions located near the site in New York City. These professionals came on site and stayed there for weeks, providing individual and group assistance to students, educators, and leaders. One of us was an educator at one of these institutions, and as she listened to hundreds of students over the weeks following reopening, she felt empowered to refer the students to the remarkable mental health professional newly situated in her institution.[28]

As valuable as it is, community partnering requires that we allow for a release of power and autonomy and see the collective good. That is a paradigm shift that started during and then halted after the pandemic. Most crises do facilitate a rise in collective action, but there isn't stickiness. And in a world containing divisiveness and dissent, a lack of shared values, and a profound disinclination to engage with those who are different from us, collective or community engagement across sectors is tough sledding. Look how hard it was to prevent a federal budget crisis and government shutdown in fall 2023, despite the highly publicized steep price that individuals and businesses would pay. Robert Putnam put it well when he recognized Americans' growing tendency to "bowl alone."[29]

Community-based schools have made some inroads. Individual communities also have made progress through projects like donated backpacks for students, containing food for the weekend and for holidays, and food pantries in schools and on campuses. There have been collaborations between companies and educational institutions to provide training, internships, and micro-credentials.[30]

Maybe we need a campaign that resembles the pods devised in communities when schools closed and people got together to have their children learn together. Maybe we can shift the orientation within the community to develop pods to improve the well-being of the many. And we shouldn't need a crisis to do that. We need the will to do it.

Owning What Was, What Is, and What Can Be

The idea of ownership as a component of establishing stickiness may appear self-evident at first blush. But it is hardly obvious. To make sticky change, we need to recognize what existed before the pandemic, with all its strengths and weaknesses. We need to own that the prepandemic world of education was far from perfect in many respects. While we often tried to ameliorate the deficiencies and build on the strengths, forward movement was slow. And the longer we waited, the harder change was, in part because the ground kept shifting under us. Student demographics changed; cultural gaps and divides mounted; and dissatisfaction grew, often without outlets for its expression.

Admitting and owning the status of what was and what is an inequitable mental health system is the beginning of the transformation. One of the coauthors brought supporters, allies, and resisters inside and outside the government to develop what the transformed system could be like. The transformation journey was challenging because of resistance and limited resources, recalling the analogy of the *stop* and *detour* road signs mentioned in Chapter 10. Passion alone did not make the job easier, but trust, community partnerships, authenticity, connectedness, and leadership do. Alleviating the poor mental health status of our students is equally daunting, and we need to apply similar strategies.[31]

During the pandemic, we needed to acknowledge what occurred, both the good and the bad. But in the middle of a crisis, it is difficult enough to evaluate what is happening in one's own piece of the world, let alone in the larger environment, even if one is aware of it. In a crisis, as we have observed and illustrated, time moves differently and the usual time to reflect and collaborate is truncated. As asserted earlier, education was building its plane as it was flying. That's risky business.

This book presents an opportunity, now and into the future, to view what occurred during the pandemic in classrooms across the country during a period when we did not have the time, inclination, or capacity to see and process it. If we can do that—not with eyes wide shut—we can begin to embrace change.

As we emerged from the pandemic, we had difficulty seeing forward and all we appeared to want in education (and other disciplines) was to move back to where we were, imperfect as that might have been. And our drive to return to "normalcy" overrode the desire to capture the positives and maintain them. The reversion was understandable too; moving into newness is uncomfortable and uncertain, and we feel uneasy and unprepared even if what went before remained far from ideal.

These behaviors account for why change based on the pandemic positives hasn't yet arrived. Addressing this conundrum, based on human behavior and the call to do things differently, when all we want to do is find peace and normalcy, visualized in Figure 11.1, is challenging. What it means is that we need to make the possibility of change easy, understandable, accessible, and nonstressful—and that's a high bar to reach.

To that end, we are reminded of Malcolm Gladwell's description of an experiment in which the aim was to get more undergraduate students at Yale to receive tetanus shots. The reasons were clear: Tetanus is serious, can lead to negative outcomes, and is easily preventable with a single injection. It was supposed that if students just knew these facts, they would rush to the infirmary for the injections.[32]

Those performing the experiment offered different groups of students different informational booklets. One showed the disastrous consequences of the disease; the other was easier to read and suggested the rationale for the injection. Bottom line, whichever booklet they received, students did not show up to get a tetanus shot. Of the small percentage who did, it did not matter which booklet they received. What mattered was that they were seniors in college; knew their way to the infirmary, having become familiar with the campus over 4 years as students; and had an idea of when the infirmary was open and could accommodate them.

The experiment team realized that the existing brochure was not the driver for the participating students. What the brochure needed were a map and the times when students could get the injection. The students then could mobilize. They could determine where to go and how to fit the injection into their schedule. They in essence would be empowered to find a way to do what was right for their health.

Transfer that idea into educational change. If we want educators to make changes, including integrating the pandemic positives at all levels, we need to offer easy access to the needed adjustments, provide a sense of the timing for making

Figure 11.1. Ed K. S. Wang, *Take Time*, 2018

change, and show how that time could be made to fit within the life of an educator. This is similar to the 20% rule that Google has used. The rule is named for the time allocated to employees when they are allowed to simply innovate; it is considered part of their job. The idea of time is critically important in education, where educators' role and workload are increasing, especially in the postpandemic era, with students' greater needs. If we have resources, the creation of an on-site education innovation lab to address specific school needs in the context of school and community will be an educational win-win for all. There is no reason why innovation, usually found in disciplines connected to technology and in start-up ventures, cannot be tried in our schools and colleges. The key is that the innovations are focused on education—not other fields in which such labs already exist.[33]

If we just expect change and implementation in addition to already assigned or undertaken tasks, they won't get done. To use a phrase from the business literature, you can't pour more water onto a piece of glass.[34]

Imagine, then, that we created a road map of the pandemic changes and the steps needed to implement them. Then we allowed educators a period of one school year to implement the changes they desired and gave them time slots for this work within their usual schedule (not added time or after-school time or lunchtime). If we did this, the changes would be more likely to be implemented.

Recalling the tetanus example, where students knew the value of the shot, educators (at least many of them) know the value of the pandemic positives. That being so, we need to find an easy way for them to implement that which they know has value for themselves and their students.

This could be accomplished in classrooms, throughout an institution, or as part of statewide or national change. Any adoption would be better than none and would yield the greatest promise of lasting, powerful, positive change. Adoption of this at different levels is addressed at length in Chapter 12.

Storytelling Power

For many, understanding change in the abstract is hard. That is why we have striven to ground our suggestions in the real-life, in-the-trenches work of educators. But even that may not be enough. We need personal stories that educators, leaders, and governing bodies can relate to, and if the stories are told by trusted educators they can rely on, that is all the more promising.

Gladwell points this out in the context of *Sesame Street*, an extraordinary program that changed how we viewed preschool engagement with television and with learning. Initially, based on the work of many child psychologists, the show divided real people from fantasy characters (such as Big Bird and Oscar the Grouch). The real people appeared on real streets (well, a set designed as a street) and the fantasy characters were in different, unreal spaces. What the studies showed is that, contrary to the perceptions of psychologists, children liked combining reality and fantasy. They wanted the human characters and the "fuzzy characters," the puppets, to appear together and engage.[35]

For us, this raises a critically important idea and not just vis-à-vis preschoolers. We need to combine logic, information, and hard facts (reality) with trial balloons, experimentation, wishes, and dreams. In other words, if we allow educators to focus only on the "real," they lose out on the "fuzzy." And what engages us and allows us to learn is not just the real but also the psychological power of the possible, the belief in things not yet proved with which we want to engage.

This means, in the context of the pandemic positives, that we need more than the hard facts about their benefits and the theoretical explanations for how they work, which we provided in Part II. We need something else—stickiness—if that is to happen. We need the educational equivalent of Big Bird and Oscar the Grouch. Perhaps that is captured by the words *hope* and *creativity*, but we see something else that is needed: permission to do the counterintuitive, permission to say that desks aren't optimal, classrooms are confining, and play has a place in education for all students regardless of age and stage. We need to do the opposite of coloring inside the lines.

In a real sense, *Sesame Street* was about storytelling in different ways that captivated preschoolers. The goal was to hone their attentiveness, which was accomplished through studying what did and did not work. If a show's segment got traction with only half the children, the producers discarded it and tried again. Once they found the right approach, the level of attentiveness was consistently about 85%.[36]

Stories and storytelling increase attentiveness in professionals too. Now, how we tell and share stories with adults is not as simple as combining real characters and fuzzy ones together on a street. But we think that if the pandemic story is told differently, as we discuss in Chapter 12, it is more likely that the pandemic positives will take hold. It isn't that there is no story; there is a story. We just haven't told it yet in ways that will capture educators, students, parents and caregivers, governing bodies, policymakers, and communities. And unlike what has happened with *Sesame Street*, we haven't yet given them a way to express how these pandemic positives make them feel.

We do have two inroads: our open-ended survey questions and the approach in this book. And in looking at the survey responses, consider the common themes that support the need for change with durability. In some ways, the responses, when read together, tell a story. Add to this that the present book, and the other two in the trilogy, are grounded in real stories and the voices of people. But there is also plentiful art in this volume, messaging the power of the imagination and the stories we can invent from what we see—fanciful stories, sad stories, hopeful stories.

Messaging

The brothers Chip and Dan Heath, mentioned earlier, maintain that messaging is key for change to have stickiness. As we reflect on this observation in the context of education in general and the pandemic positives in particular, we can't help but recognize that there are vastly different messages required in education when so many constituencies have a stake in educational outcomes. And we know too that messages for students differ from those for parents and caregivers, educators, administrators, and governing boards. We also know that the effectiveness of a message depends on gender, race, and ethnic and religious awareness and sensitivity. In messaging, one size does not fit all—all you have to do is see how advertisers market their products to segments of the economy, not to every single participant in the economy. Ads may target youth, seniors, men, women, a social or ethnic group, or a diverse audience. Different messages, and products, are directed toward different regions of the country. Messengers of all sorts tailor messaging and use different messaging strategies.[37]

Roger Martin thoughtfully observes (although we do not endorse all his ideas wholeheartedly) that we live in a heterogeneous world and a company's advertising needs to appeal to the biggest circle of people possible—or at least as big as the product can support. And we need to know where the fault lines lie, something important in our politicized world. He adds that we need to be cautious and ask when we message, "Are we turning a fault line into a fissure?"[38]

With the variety and diversity of the stakeholders in education, solitary messages aimed at the masses are unlikely to have stickiness. To use Martin's terminology, there are too many fault lines. We could hit one and have a fissure. That would move us backward. But finding opportunities for narrowly targeted messaging that is effective in education is a dubious proposition. Does that make messaging a poor approach for engendering stickiness for the pandemic positives?

In our view, messaging can work, but we need to be careful about it. We need to stage messaging if we want stickiness, and we should ask, Which are the most powerful constituencies we must convince that change in education is needed and that the pandemic positives are a pathway to that change? We suspect that students, parents and caregivers, and educators should not be our first stop on the convincing train, because many who work in or are affected by education already see its faults even if they do not agree on what they are or how to remedy them. We'd create fissures for sure. In short, education's direct stakeholders know that education is not benefiting all students optimally, even though they may disagree on what improvements are needed in their institutions.

Suppose that initially we focused our messaging largely on those who made educational policy: governing boards and the state and federal departments of education. These groups should be on the receiving end of messaging about the pandemic positives. Yes, this is top-down messaging, because the top is where the power to make change rests. While we believe in changes in classrooms and particular institutions, as evidenced throughout this book, big, sticky, large-scale change requires buy-in from those who wield power.

We acknowledge that concurrent messaging, as is used in advertising and marketing, might be another way forward. But it is time-consuming and expensive, and we'd need more bandwidth than we likely have. Moreover, as one of us with experience in educational messaging knows, it is hard to get messaging right for one constituency, say, prospective students, let alone the many constituencies of our schools and campuses. To add to the complexity, messaging must be sensitive to age, gender, and race and ethnicity. This is why admissions materials for colleges always look more or less the same. Not only are we not brave; we are not distinguishing ourselves from others, for fear our message will backfire.[39]

So instead of sending out traditional messages aimed at those who work in, attend, or have children who attend educational institutions, we must attract the immediate attention of school and governing boards, boards of trustees, and state and federal departments of education. They control funding and assessments and what we teach and spend money on, because they set the priorities—in dollars but also accreditation and ranking.

This suggests, for starters, that we should make a greater push on the legislative front. We need public hearings on the pandemic positives that draw the attention of state boards of education and the U.S. Department of Education. State and congressional education committees can be activated to hold hearings on these positives and then, if there is agreement, to push agencies in their purview to implement strategies involving regulations, letters of advice, accreditation alternations, and special funding.

We have used this approach in our own work. We have testified before committees and various boards. We have helped craft and comment on legislation. We have created and chaired committees. We have submitted reports to state legislatures and Congress. And we have identified advocates with access to the seats of power to help us bring the issues we care about—education and mental wellness among them—to the floor and the forefront.[40]

At some level, we wish that protests and in-the-trenches advocacy would produce widespread change, and in some cases, they can; this is work that should continue for sure. But we remain wary of the bottom-up approach to educational change because of the heterogeneity of the field. We need to approach change in ways that produce widespread consensus or at least as much as is needed to implement legislation and funding changes. As discussed in Chapter 10, we know that freestanding, top-down (macro) change is not enough. But it is where we think educational change can start (not stop).

We need school board members and trustees, the local locus of control for many institutions, to expand the realm of voices they listen to. Usually, their agendas are influenced by the voices of superintendents, presidents, chancellors, and sometimes students, alums, parents, and community leaders. We need board members to hear student and educator voices but also to learn about new developments in the education field outside their regions. And they need to be apprised of prospective trends and educators' predictions about the future of education in the context of demographics, resources, technology, social trends, and crises (whether current or on the horizon).

One way to accomplish this, and something tried by one of the authors, is to set aside time at each board meeting for opportunities to learn about future trends and suggestions from educational experts in or outside the institutions the board members oversee. Board members can get literature in advance; they can ask questions and work in small groups. In short, we can get boards to understand what education is and could be, hearing directly from those with experience working in the field. This would foster informed decision-making about priorities and actions to take. It also could lead to both informal more formal messaging.

One of us remembers going to Baby Presidents School (yes, that is its name) at Harvard Graduate School of Education and listening to a higher education specialist on educational governance talk about how boards were already well aware of the trends in education; our task was to help them strategize. His view was consistent with those of elite governing boards. Many of us at non-elite institutions had a sizable challenge in improving our board membership, and many of our board members were not familiar with current educational debates, issues, and data. They did not arrive on board (so to speak) as educational experts; they had been selected for reasons other than their expertise in the field.[41]

If these boards and, subsequently, governmental organizations appreciate the importance of the pandemic positives (among many other items), they can message their support widely and loudly.

The Jury System Approach

Writing in the *Boston Globe*, Hollie Russon Gilman and Amy Eisenstein addressed the power of the American jury system, where individuals from all walks of life (with some maneuvering at the margins, we would add) work together to reach a conclusion. For the most part, although there are hung juries, most juries are able to reach consensus when presented with the information from both sides of a case. In part they do this by finding where they agree and whether and which charges fit their areas of agreement. Rather than focusing on where they differ, juries get traction when they discover where they agree. Charges on which there is strong disagreement may be held for later or dismissed. Finding agreement—a shared decision—is the endgame. Jurors may differ in age, race, ethnicity, gender, social status, and educational levels. Yet even in the face of such diversity, resolution is reached. Of course, we know the system isn't perfect and juries are swayed in lots of ways, but overall it is the best system we know of to date for reaching the resolution of legal charges against individuals or entities.[42]

Gilman and Eisenstein suggest that this approach should be used in the context of citizens' assemblies, recalling a system adopted by the ancient Greeks. Such assemblies, in and outside the United States, have the power to make decisions that affect the population from which their members were chosen, just as juries are selected from the public to make decisions. Many organizations seek to operationalize citizens' assemblies, to narrow political divisiveness and make improvements with wide-ranging benefits. For people disappointed with political officials at every level, citizens' assemblies offer representation in a different manner. We may not trust our politicians, but surely, generally speaking, we can and do trust our neighbors and friends—the very groups from which citizens' assemblies are chosen.

To extrapolate, imagine educational assemblies composed of people engaged in one way or another in the educational process: students, alums, parents, teachers, leaders, researchers, and members of nonprofits and industry. Whether these groups were local, statewide, or national, if a group's members were put together in a room and charged with solving certain problems and given key information (including from all sides of debates), one would expect that they could come to some agreement that would satisfy most people.

In James Ryan's *Wait, What? and Life's Other Essential Questions*, among the five questions he suggests we ask of one another and ourselves (and he is talking in the context of education), is "Can we at least agree that . . . ?" Indeed, this is what citizens' assemblies would answer. They would find areas of agreement and not focus on disagreement. In a world as divided as ours, this approach has appeal.[43]

The name we give to the approach of juries, citizens' assemblies, and potential educational assemblies is *lumping*, which greatly contrasts with *splitting*. In science, there are those who do research and solve problems by looking for similarity, shared qualities; those are lumpers. And then there are those who do their work through splitting, homing in on differences and distinguishing features. Now, we can operate in ways that blend lumping and splitting, but we seem to accomplish more toward social change if we work as lumpers. We try to find areas in which we can reach agreement.[44]

Jury findings are taken seriously and not often overturned. We trust the system and accept the outcome. The same is true for citizens' assemblies; they engender trust and acceptance of their outcomes. If we want to change education, including in adopting the pandemic positives, we can look to the creation of educational assemblies, employing them in addition to school boards, boards of trustees, and state and national departments of education.[45]

Giving voice to stakeholders can increase stickiness.

Will and a Belief in Tree Planting

No change with stickiness can happen if people do not want it. Forced change simply does not have lasting power; a will to change is necessary. Usually a will to change arises in noncrisis contexts where the change has been planned, discussed, vetted, revised, and reconsidered by numerous individuals and groups. The pandemic positives are changes that arose through crisis and were not created in the way change most often occurs.

So we need a *will* to make change, and that desire for change is hard to bring about. After all, New Year's resolutions are well intentioned but rarely stick: We lack the will to make them happen. The same resistance applies to other aspirational changes: Stop eating sweets; stop drinking so much; stop smoking; exercise more. Sometimes our efforts bear fruit but frequently only for a short time. And sometimes they do not at all. Even short-term change is hard.[46]

There is, however, one belief that many individuals may hold, even without articulating or recognizing it. We call it the tree-planting theory. When we plant trees from seeds or saplings, we are not strictly planting them for ourselves, though we may feel pleasure from planting and nurturing them, especially with children. We really plant trees for following generations, because trees take many years to grow to maturity, bestowing shade, wood, clean air, and a healthier biosphere. The benefits will come in the next generation or two.[47]

That is the key. We plant today because we want following generations to have the benefit. We plant for the future; we plant for the long-term gain of the newly born or not yet born. And for some, the intention is to leave the world a better place for the future. One of us participated in a town's tree-planting initiative and was stunned by how moving it was to plant for the future; it was like creating a living legacy of sorts.[48]

We also can engage in activities as the trees we plant grow. What about pruning the trees as they grow, helping them become the shape of the trees we planned out, enabling them to become our "destination"?

The tree-planting theory is directly related to change and its stickiness. Unless we believe in creating a pathway for the next generation, we are not keen on changes that will occur over the longer haul. As observed earlier, we generally favor short-term thinking. We are dealing with the present and our own capacities to navigate it. We aren't focused on the future. But if we can encourage folks to think longer term, something that is immensely difficult, we can make forward progress that has stickiness.

Saving for retirement is an example. It's a good idea by almost any measure. Yet most people do not plan well enough and, often for good reasons, do not have enough today to save for tomorrow. In truth, people may need the money now, just to pay current expenses. And even those with enough funds underestimate future financial needs, a real worry with a generation that is outlasting earlier ones in longevity. We may be saving more but we are not saving enough. For a solution, in their *Nudge*, Richard Thaler and Cass Sunstein suggest that individuals be able to opt out of retirement contributions rather than having to opt in. At present, employers do not automatically provide retirement contributions to workers, who must opt in to receive them through payroll deductions, and many people will not take that step. Thaler and Sunstein advocate that employers be mandated to deduct a set, agreed-on amount (and perhaps even match some of it). If employees did not want the automatic deduction, they could opt out. Human behavior being what it is, we would be unlikely to opt out if such a system were created.[49]

The opt-in/opt-out approach was adopted for the first time (to the best of our knowledge) in consumer legislation during the Obama administration. In this legislation, which became law, individuals had to opt in if they wanted to overdraw on their credit card limit, even if it was expensive. (Banks like overdrafts, as they generate revenue.) The default provision in the law, then, is that no consumer can exceed the credit limit. This approach meant that most consumers accepted the status quo and did not opt in, thus saving them money. Had it been reversed and consumers had to opt out, most would not have done so and this expensive practice would have continued.[50]

What this suggests is that thinking about and protecting one's future is not easy or automatic for many. We're not, generally speaking, willing to go against the trend. But we have the capacity to nudge behavior, to encourage tree plant-ing, so to speak. We can get nudges to work and change choices. We can reflect on educational changes that work according to the tree-planting theory and use the nudge approach.

How can we make this happen, getting more people to plant trees and getting a nudge system in place in the educational arena? We acknowledge that our world is currently rife with inhumanity, and relying on goodness in human nature is not foolproof.

Consider this selection of possibilities:

- Although we are not doing so, we can learn from the COVID pandemic about how to handle a prospective pandemic or similar event. We can use what we learned to make plans. One way to convince people to plan now is to point out some of the chaos, confusion, and uncertainty that accompanied the pandemic. That lesson shows the need for longer-term thinking generally and in education in particular. We can appreciate the pandemic positives and their long-term stickiness as a response to what we lacked during the pandemic. In other words, our awareness of the problems in building the plane while flying should enable us to get greater stickiness. This is a fear-based approach: We don't like what happened to education during the pandemic so we take steps to make sure we don't repeat our mistakes.

- Another approach is grounded in self-interest, making it also not a choice based on generosity of spirit. We know from studies of how our brains function that in times of crisis, we receive benefit from helping others. Their appreciation and good experience reflects back to us because of our mirror neurons. So in addition to helping others survive a crisis, we help ourselves. And self-help is a good motivator.

- What our effort here in terms of stickiness calls for is the recognition that thinking of the future also will activate our mirror neurons, albeit somewhat differently; we are banking on the goodwill that comes from what will happen down the road, decades from now. We need to make our mirror neurons get the same profit from future good that they accrue from the delivery of current good. And we have no reason to suspect that our mirror neurons will be any less pleased (so to speak) with good feelings we give to others for the benefit of their future. Stated another way, our brains reward us for giving to the next generation. A bit of a stretch!

- Generally speaking, to some extent we do reflect on our lives—past, present, and future. But reflection is not acting. Stickiness is an act, not a thought, wish, fantasy, or intent. It is concrete action. This realization should give us an incentive to act because we do, or should, care about the future, as we are humans who live short lives and pass on the world to those who follow us. This isn't just philosophical optimism; it is the reality. Whether we do good things or not, the following generation is stuck with what we leave them.

- It is in this context that we reflect on a question that Jonas Salk considered deeply important: Are we being good ancestors? Now, that's odd phraseology. We think of those before us as our ancestors; we don't see ourselves as ancestors. But we are. Roman Krznaric, in his *The Good Ancestor*, asserts that the question needs to be framed with *we*, not *I*, because collective action works. To tie into our earlier references to the need for connection between individuals as a way of ameliorating trauma, he goes on to state, "We can nurture our need for connection and relationship by creating an empathic bond with future generations. . . . The quest to think long is full of existential sustenance."[51]

- In a world as difficult and complex as ours, with the likelihood of future crises looming, we would be wise to reflect on what we need to mend, manage, and sustain ourselves.

The Significance of Smallness

As mentioned in Chapter 9, we both have personal experiences in fostering transformative change at the local, regional, national, and international levels. Public policy change is neither easy nor guaranteed. Politics and priorities, including in funding, interfere.

Nonetheless, we know that the absence of effort and conceding impossibility disable change. We are reminded that even small changes can have an impact. While both authors would prefer a huge uptake of the pandemic positives, we appreciate the presence of incremental change and change that requires reminders of what it can offer. We are neither discouraged nor lacking in hope. We would have retired long ago if we did not retain hope that change can and does happen, even if not at the pace or breadth we seek.[52]

The stickiness point is this. We need people to advocate for change. It does not just happen. In the field of education, we need to speak truth to power, as the saying goes. Yes, we can continue our work at the local level and improve schools in which we work, teach, and consult. But we need to do more. We need to stick our necks out and speak up, even on controversial topics.

One of us remembers that when an early book was published, someone close to the author remarked, "You're putting your head on a chopping block with this book. Do you realize that?" Call it a warning and something of a lack of confidence in the author herself.[53]

It is true that the book did generate controversy. It also generated some horrible reviews. But over 25 years the tide shifted, and ideas that were radical when the book was written ceased to be so radical. At a planned anniversary of the book's publication at a university abroad (sadly canceled by the pandemic), the goal was to show how the book's central premises had taken root in policy and practice over time. And years later at a U.S. Senate hearing on protecting individual creditor interest in the corporate reorganization of companies that committed torts, a scholar from the following generation carried the book's themes forward. The lesson: The chopping block is not always permanent.[54]

Getting the pandemic positives to stick so they can become game changers is not a simple task. We know that. But the 10 streets leading to stickiness detailed earlier help us sustain hope. The street map we created isn't simple, but it does give guidance. It does allow us to say with confidence that we think the pandemic positives, at least some of them, can change the trajectory of education in a good way over the near and longer terms. We can mend education—if we see the benefits of doing so. It is to that topic that we now turn and with which we conclude.

CHAPTER 12

The Art of Mending

MENDING MATTERS

Mending starts with recognizing the beauty of cracks that appear, as they did in education during the pandemic. We have to adjust our attitude toward cracks and how they can benefit us. Instead of viewing them as negative (which is how many view what happened in education), we see cracks as positives. This viewpoint is deeply informed by two art forms, Kintsugi and Ju Ci, referred to earlier. We now turn to these as our guide, our source of the positive, and our representation for how to mend education.

Historically, Japanese and Chinese cultures were reluctant to discard broken objects, while Americans have tended to simply toss away damaged items and buy new ones to replace them. With all that has gone wrong in education, we could just leave education's pandemic shards where they are—consistent with America's throwaway culture. But we have chosen to pick up the pieces of education and allow them to lead us forward. Kintsugi and Ju Ci are art forms that make use of broken objects, and they give us hope that we actually can use some of education's shards. Crises can and do create opportunities.[1]

Kintsugi in Japan and Ju Ci in China are art forms in which broken porcelain dishware is mended. Their adherents put broken objects back together, and specifically in Kintsugi, they replace missing pieces with new ones. And while these traditional art forms are rarer in today's world, their long and storied history remains valuable.[2]

With Kintsugi, the lines of a break in dishware are connected and the "scars" are painted in gold. With these new creations, this phrase is uttered: "More beautiful for being broken." And the objects pieced together are truly beautiful—when viewed from both the top and the underside. One of the authors has always kept several Kintsugi pieces in her home and office, reminders that trauma can enable some positive outcomes. She has created artworks from shards. As she puts it, you can create peace from pieces. She has even re-created Kintsugi art with audiences, breaking plates, cups, and bowls and putting them back together with glue and gold paint (or sometimes gold nail polish) to demonstrate our capacity for repair and beauty that comes from restoration.[3]

In Ju Ci, small holes are bored into the broken pieces of dishware; then handmade hinges and staples are inserted to enable reconnection and usability. It is delicate work. The goal is not necessarily to create perfection; it is to find beauty in imperfection. When one of the authors looks at the mended pieces, it raises questions in his mind about the context of the repair. Who was the owner? How long did the owner have the porcelain? How did the porcelain break? Why did the owner even want to repair the porcelain? How long did it take to repair the piece? And what happens to the porcelain after it is mended? In any event, the mended porcelain is not viewed as flawed. It brings beauty and a new understanding of and appreciation for the dishware.

In both these arts of mending, the messaging is about creating a new whole with new meaning, a repair that enables transformation and forward movement. Both art forms also maintain a sense of history, since the original piece is not discarded. For one of the authors, the repurposing of discarded things into decorative pieces is a hobby and a reminder of the power of transformation of both people and things. Both authors' collections of repaired art in their homes grew during the pandemic as the need for creative healing kept rising.

Kintsugi and Ju Ci are symbols for rethinking and mending education. Call them the golden glue and hinges. Imagine that education is a bowl. Suppose the bowl breaks and some of the pieces have gone missing. To put the bowl back together after the pandemic, we need to mend the existing pieces and add new ones. While the precise shape of the bowl may change, it remains *education*. If we mend it through Kintsugi and Ju Ci, if we apply golden glue and hinges, we are suggesting that the repaired bowl is transformed into something new but not without a recognition of history and context. Importantly, the mending in education is not limited to the outward changes; we recognize when our mental health is "broken," so mending the pieces of our minds and creating mental wellness are integral too.

In a very real way, this book, as reflected also in its cover, is the golden glue and hinges that enable us to improve education. It proffers an approach for repairing, reconfiguring, and reinvigorating education by contextualizing positive strategies garnered during the pandemic. We are offering up a more beautiful education bowl, so to speak—a bowl many have not seen. We employ a host of concrete examples that mend (represented in part by a three-legged stool to message the needed changes), but we also see education as being like the art forms just described. Education must evolve, and postpandemic, it reemerges and its importance is augmented by the repairs. And with the improvements to education, we can find both healing and hope, something also fostered and messaged through Kintsugi and Ju Ci.

It would be easier, we acknowledge, to leave the detritus of education caused by the pandemic sitting on the ground of the educational landscape, unpieced together and unused. We could just lament over and discard the experience of the pandemic like old porcelain dishware. We could cease using glue and hinges. We could cease seeing things through a pandemic lens. But for us, there is power and hope in repair.

Throughout the pandemic, we transmuted these art forms (see Figure 12.1) into ways of navigating forward in difficult times, where much is broken and we need to find ways quickly to repair our lives, our schools, our businesses, our health

Figure 12.1. Karen Gross, *Well-Broken*, 2023

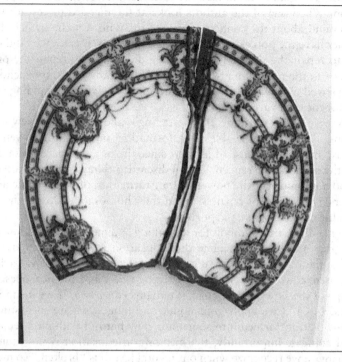

care system, our economy, our spirit, our health. We have found these pathways in the positives that many educators created for their students. Commonly grounded in in-the-trenches experience and wisdom, partnered with hope and creativity, many of our educators across ages, genders, races, ethnicities, religions, and locations found ways to improve education.

WALKING FORWARD

We are better and more beautiful for being broken by the pandemic crisis. We just have to absorb that realization and appreciate the value of the golden glue and hinges that enable us to see and not forget the pandemic changes. To return to the parable that opened this book, education needs to molt.

With this book, we think that molting not only has begun but also can continue. Time will be the truth teller about whether the pandemic positives have had a role in mending education by becoming game changers. And you, our readers, can be catalysts for the mending process; you can continue to use the golden glue and hinges.

Many of you are already doing just that: taking education's many shards and piecing them together with golden glue and hinges. This is work that can continue, and we are here supporting you every step of the way. This book, taken as a whole, is showing how mending with golden glue and hinges—pandemic positives—can occur. We keep the pandemic's influences and changes close to us; they are our lens. And we are here to walk with you as we make repairs. So, reach out, connect with us, share your successes. We'd welcome that.

Epilogue

A Conversation (Excerpts)

We intended to end this book with a conversation between the coauthors, to informally share our voices—reflecting the importance we place on voices throughout the book. Our dialogue became extensive; the full conversation is available through the QR code at the end of this book. What follows are condensed, lightly edited excerpts. Enjoy this "epologic appetizer."

Ed: Share why you decided to write a book with a coauthor (me in particular).
Karen: COVID was isolating and writing is solipsistic, so I welcomed a writing partner. Because we had worked together earlier, I had an intuition that we shared a vision for helping struggling youth. I knew we had to find a way to expand that vision. This book reflects our shared vision. And you?
Ed: Your encouragement and support made me realize that it was a no-brainer to write a book together. When we discussed this book's theme (pandemic positives), it motivated me because of my brother's death by suicide while he was in college. With you, I could ensure that we spoke loudly about student mental wellness.
Karen: What do you hope this book will accomplish outside education—in the worlds where you engage regularly? This will be the answer to why we wrote this book together, right?
Ed: The pandemic positives we identified and the principles of public stewardship we addressed work across all governmental agencies and nonprofits in different disciplines and across many nations. I hope this book is a catalyst for others interested in transformations to act in their own settings and disciplines. The book reveals the value of cross-disciplinary work too. And you?
Karen: I hope those outside education will value the pandemic positives and ignite change for the better. I hope readers recognize, as you observe, the intersectionality of disciplines. The book begs for action. My message is: Have hope; believe in change. And yours?
Ed: Seize this moment in history; be a game changer; work across silos.
Karen: You asked me many times about future books you were contemplating and whether we would be writing an additional book together. Here's my answer: I think so.
Ed: Thus, this book ends and we begin a new journey. Onward.

Supplementary Material

As referenced throughout the book, additional sections are available through a QR code, which appears below. Scan the code to access the following:

Epilogue: A Conversation
Survey for Educators
Tables
Related Sources

Endnotes

Prologue

1. Anya Kamenetz, *The Stolen Year: How COVID Changed Children's Lives, and Where We Go Now* (Public Affairs, 2022); Fernando M. Reimers, ed., *Primary and Secondary Education During Covid-19: Disruptions to Educational Opportunity During a Pandemic* (Springer, 2022), https://link.springer.com/book/10.1007/978-3-030-81500-4; Emily Schwickerath, *Unprecedented: Teaching in a Pandemic* (Dorrance, 2022); "COVID-19 Pandemic Massively Set Back Learning, Especially for High-Poverty Areas," *PBS NewsHour*, October 28, 2022, https://www.pbs.org/newshour/education/covid-19-pandemic-massively-set-back-learning-especially-for-high-poverty-areas; Gema Zamarro et al., "How the Pandemic Has Changed Teachers' Commitment to Remaining in the Classroom," Brookings, September 8, 2021, https://www.brookings.edu/blog/brown-center-chalkboard/2021/09/08/how-the-pandemic-has-changed-teachers-commitment-to-remaining-in-the-classroom; Natasha Singer, "Teaching in the Pandemic: 'This Is Not Sustainable,'" *New York Times*, November 30, 2020, updated December 3, 2020, https://www.nytimes.com/2020/11/30/us/teachers-remote-learning-burnout.html; Emma Dorn et al., "COVID-19 and Education: The Lingering Effects of Unfinished Learning," McKinsey, July 27, 2021, https://www.mckinsey.com/industries/education/our-insights/covid-19-and-education-the-lingering-effects-of-unfinished-learning; Anna D. Johnson et al., "Predictors of First-Grade Teachers' Teaching-Related Time During COVID-19," *Aera Open*, January 20, 2022, https://journals.sagepub.com/doi/full/10.1177/23328584211067798; Brea L. Perry, Brian Aronson, and Bernice A. Pescosolido, "Pandemic Precarity: COVID-19 Is Exposing and Exacerbating Inequalities in the American Heartland," *PNAS* 118, no. 8 (2021), https://www.pnas.org/doi/full/10.1073/pnas.2020685118.

2. Iago Sávyo Duarte Santiago et al., "The Impact of the COVID-19 Pandemic on the Mental Health of Teachers and Its Possible Risk Factors: A Systematic Review," *International Journal of Environmental Research and Public Health* 20, no. 3 (2023), https://www.ncbi.nlm.nih.gov/pmc/articles/PMC9914333; Joseph M. Kush et al., "Teachers' Mental Health During the COVID-19 Pandemic," *Educational Researcher* 51, no. 9 (2022), https://journals.sagepub.com/stoken/default+domain/G4BZPSGF2I3SPUAUBHSK/full; "School During the Pandemic: Mental Health Impacts on Students," NAMI California, n.d., https://namica.org/blog/impact-on-the-mental-health-of-students-during-covid-19; Devin Dwyer and Patty See, "Schools Stock Naloxone as Student Drug Overdoses Surge," *ABC News*, May 15, 2023, https://abcnews.go.com/Politics/schools-stock-naloxone-student-drug-overdoses-surge/story?id=98662979; Elissa Nadworny and Lee V. Gaines, "As More Teens Overdose on Fentanyl, Schools Face a Drug Crisis Unlike Any Other," *All Things Considered*, August 30, 2023, https://www.npr.org/2023/08/30/1196343448/fentanyl-deaths-teens-schools-overdose; Evie Blad, "'Swatting' Hoaxes

Disrupt Schools Across the Country. What Educators Need to Know," *Education Week*, September 21, 2022, https://www.edweek.org/leadership/swatting-hoaxes-disrupt-schools -nationwide-what-educators-need-to-know/2022/09; Amy Rock, "School Swatting: Why It's So Dangerous and How to Combat It," *Campus Safety*, April 11, 2023, https://www .campussafetymagazine.com/podcast/school-swatting-dangers; "Mental Health Found to Be Worsening Among U.S. High School Students," *Psychiatric News*, February 14, 2023, https://alert.psychnews.org/2023/02/mental-health-found-to-be-worsening.html?m=1; Centers for Disease Control and Prevention (CDC) Division of Adolescent and School Health (DASH), *Youth Risk Behavior Survey Data Summary & Trends Report: 2011–2021*, CDC DASH, [2023], https://www.cdc.gov/healthyyouth/data/yrbs/pdf/YRBS_Data -Summary-Trends_Report2023_508.pdf.

3. Mike Morrison and Clint Kofford, *Creating Meaningful Change: A Timeless Leadership Path to Transforming the Modern Work Culture* (Archangel Ink, 2022); Faisal Hoque, *Lift: Fostering the Leader in You Amid Revolutionary Global Change* (Fast Company Press, 2022); Dorie Clark, *The Loooooong Game* (Harvard Business Review Press, 2021); Chip Heath and Dan Heath, *Switch: How to Change Things When Change Is Hard* (Broadway Books, 2010); Cass R. Sunstein, *How Change Happens* (MIT Press, 2019); Erika Andersen, "Change Is Hard; Here's How to Make It Less Painful," *Harvard Business Review*, April 7, 2022, https://hbr.org/2022/04/change-is-hard-heres-how-to-make-it -less-painful.

No discussion about change would be possible without referencing the late Clayton Christianson and his theory of disruptive innovation, whether one agrees with it or not. See Clayton M. Christensen, Michael E. Raynor, and Rory McDonald, "What Is Disruptive Innovation?" *Harvard Business Review*, December 2015, https://hbr.org/2015/12 /what-is-disruptive-innovation.

4. Many have written about the lobster parable and its meaning. In addition to religious interpretations, there are repeated references to the parable in the lessons it teaches business leaders about change. See, e.g., Sylvia Lafair, "Here's Good Advice You Can Learn From a Lobster," *Inc.*, n.d., https://www.inc.com/sylvia-lafair/heres-good-advice-you-can -learn-from-a-lobster.html.

5. Paul H. Wise and Lisa J. Chamberlain, "Adversity and Opportunity—the Pandemic's Paradoxical Effect on Child Health and Well-Being," *JAMA Pediatrics* 176, no. 7 (2022): e220063, https://jamanetwork.com/journals/jamapediatrics/fullarticle/2789950; Emily E. Smith, "Pandemic Brought Out Something Positive for Some People—Resilience," *Washington Post*, June 20, 2021, https://www.washingtonpost.com/health/pandemic-resilience /2021/06/18/a82d69fc-a9f0-11eb-8d25-7b30e74923ea_story.html.

6. Emiliana Vegas and Rebecca Winthrop, "Beyond Reopening Schools: How Education Can Emerge Stronger Than Before COVID-19," Brookings, September 8, 2020, https://www.brookings.edu/articles/beyond-reopening-schools-how-education-can-emerge -stronger-than-before-covid-19; "How the COVID-19 Pandemic Changed Society," *UAB News*, March 14, 2022, https://www.uab.edu/news/youcanuse/item/12697-how-the-covid -19-pandemic-changed-society; "Pandemic Data Tracking," *CRPE*, Arizona State University, n.d., https://crpe.org/pandemic-learning/tracking-district-actions; Stephen Schramm, Jack Frederick, and Leanora Minai, "Three Years Later: How the Pandemic Changed Us," *Duke Today*, March 8, 2023, https://today.duke.edu/2023/03/three-years-later-how -pandemic-changed-us. For a discussion of the terms *game changers* and *game-changing moments*, see Will Kenton, "Game-Changer: Definition and Examples in Business," *Investopedia*, updated May 2, 2023, https://www.investopedia.com/terms/g/game-changer

.asp; Ron Dawson, "What Makes a True Game-Changer? Twelve Film Industry Leaders Weigh In," Frame.io Insider, n.d., https://blog.frame.io/2018/04/16/game-changers.

Chapter 1

1. Karen Gross, *Breakaway Learners: Strategies for Post-Secondary Success With At-Risk Students* (Teachers College Press, 2016); Karen Gross, *Trauma Doesn't Stop at the School Door: Strategies and Solutions for Educators, PreK–College* (Teachers College Press, 2020).

2. See Emiliana Vegas and Rebecca Winthrop, "Beyond Reopening Schools: How Education Can Emerge Stronger Than Before COVID-19," Brookings, September 8, 2020, https://www.brookings.edu/articles/beyond-reopening-schools-how-education-can-emerge-stronger-than-before-covid-19. For positives in education that arose during the pandemic and have been written about, see, e.g., Gregory C. Hutchings and Douglas S. Reed, *Getting Into Good Trouble at School: A Guide to Building an Antiracist School System* (Corwin, 2022); Wayne Journell, ed., *Post-Pandemic Social Studies: How COVID-19 Has Changed the World and How We Teach* (Teachers College Press, 2021); Stéphan Vincent-Lancrin, "Educational Innovation and Digitalisation During the COVID-19 Crisis: Lessons for the Future," in *How Learning Continued During the COVID-19 Pandemic: Global Lessons From Initiatives to Support Learners and Teachers*, ed. Stéphan Vincent-Lancrin, Cristóbal Cobo Romaní, and Fernando Reimers (OECD, 2022); Karen Gross, *Finding Hope Amidst Traumatic Events: Can Trauma Improve Education?* Samuel Dewitt Proctor Institute for Leadership, Equity, and Justice, n.d., https://proctor.gse.rutgers.edu/sites/default/files/Can%20Trauma%20Improve%20Education%3F.pdf; Eleonora Farina and Carmen Belacchi, "Social Status and Emotional Competence in Bullying: A Longitudinal Study of the Transition From Kindergarten to Primary School," *Frontiers in Psychology* 13 (April 29, 2022), https://www.ncbi.nlm.nih.gov/pmc/articles/PMC9106559; "How Did COVID-19 Change Your Teaching, for Better or Worse? See Teachers' Responses," *Education Week*, June 2, 2020, https://www.edweek.org/technology/how-did-covid-19-change-your-teaching-for-better-or-worse-see-teachers-responses/2020/06; Nate Herpich, "Taking Best of Innovations, Lessons of Pandemic Education," *Harvard Gazette*, March 9, 2022, https://news.harvard.edu/gazette/story/2022/03/taking-best-of-innovations-lessons-of-pandemic-education; Alex Ntsiful et al., "Transitioning to Online Teaching During the Pandemic Period: The Role of Innovation and Psychological Characteristics," *Innovative Higher Education* 48 (2023): 197–218, https://link.springer.com/article/10.1007/s10755-022-09613-w; Susan D'Agostino, "How COVID Spurred Digital Innovation and Empathy," *Inside Higher Ed*, October 19, 2022, https://www.insidehighered.com/news/2022/10/20/how-covid-spurred-online-education-innovation-and-empathy; Jenny Brundin, "The Pandemic Taught Teachers a Bunch of Lessons; Now, They Want Their Schools to Listen," *CPR News*, July 19, 2021, https://www.cpr.org/2021/07/19/covid-pandemic-colorado-what-teachers-learned; Nadia Tamez-Robledo, "There's Still Time to Do School Discipline Differently, Researcher Says," EdSurge, August 11, 2022, https://www.edsurge.com/news/2022-08-11-there-s-still-time-to-do-school-discipline-differently-researcher-says; National School Climate Center, "School Community Engagement in the Time of COVID-19," Creating Communities of Courage in the Time of COVID-19, n.d., https://myemail.constantcontact.com/What—School-Community-Engagement—Means-in-the-Time-of-COVID-19.html?soid=1102681734147&aid=IOigHm4sZZA; Saima Firdaus Mohammed Yaseen and Smt. Shubhada Ramesh Joshi, "Positive Impact of Covid-19 on Education," *International Research Journal on Advanced Science Hub* 3, no. 6S (June 2021),

https://rspsciencehub.com/article_15323_8369972babe711668fcc3879729cec30.pdf; "Research Reveals Positive Impact of COVID Remote Learning on Educators' Cultural Awareness," News, University of Arkansas, February 19, 2021, https://news.uark.edu /articles/55996/research-reveals-positive-impact-of-covid-remote-learning-on-educators -cultural-awareness.

3. Hong Wang Fung et al., "The Relationship Between Perceived Family Support and Depressive Symptoms: Longitudinal Findings From Two Culturally Different Samples" (under review; copy available upon request), 2023; Hong Wang Fung et al., "Interpersonal Stress Mediates the Relationship Between Childhood Trauma and Depressive Symptoms: Findings From Two Culturally Different Samples," *Australian & New Zealand Journal of Psychiatry* 57, no. 7 (2022), https://doi.org/10.1177/00048674221138501; K. Lee et al., "Recognizing Trauma Among Mothers in Taiwan: Relationship With Parenting Over-Reactivity and Children's Emotional and Behavioral Problems" (under review; copy available upon request), 2023.

4. For a thoughtful discussion of how different emotions are interpreted in different cultures and the need for an understanding of cross-cultural behavior, see Andy Molinsky, "Emotional Intelligence Doesn't Translate Across Borders," *Harvard Business Review*, April 20, 2015, https://hbr.org/2015/04/emotional-intelligence-doesnt-translate-across -borders.

Added insights into cultural competencies appear in "Section 1: The Project One Billion Health Survey," in *Global Mental Health: Trauma and Recovery* (Harvard Program in Refugee Trauma, 2011).

5. For a definition of *whole-brain child*, see "Summary of the Whole-Brain Child," Montessori Notebook, n.d., https://themontessorinotebook.com/summary-of-the-whole -brain-child; Daniel J. Siegel and Tina Payne Bryson, *The Whole-Brain Child: 12 Revolutionary Strategies to Nurture Your Child's Developing Mind, Survive Everyday Parenting Struggles, and Help Your Family Thrive* (Delacorte Press, 2011), https://drdansiegel .com/book/the-whole-brain-child. See also Libby Stanford, "Students Are Missing School Because They're Too Anxious to Show Up," *Education Week*, October 6, 2023, https:// www.edweek.org/leadership/students-are-missing-school-because-theyre-too-anxious-to -show-up/2023/10.

6. Edward K. Wang, A Journey of Public Stewardship on Asian American and Pacific Islander Mental Health: Massachusetts's Approach to Addressing Disparities," *Asian American Policy Review* 29 (Spring 2019), https://www.proquest.com/docview /2317571852?pq-origsite=summon&sourcetype=Scholarly%20Journals.

7. Centers for Disease Control and Prevention, *Youth Risk Behavior Survey Data Summary & Trends Report: 2011–2021* (CDC, [2023]), https://www.cdc.gov/healthyyouth /data/yrbs/pdf/YRBS_Data-Summary-Trends_Report2023_508.pdf.

8. To learn more about the Virtual Teachers' Lounge, see "Virtual Teachers' Lounge Resources for Educators," Virtual Teachers' Lounge, n.d., https://vtl4today.com. On the importance of voice and storytelling in research in general and education in particular, see, e.g., Becky McCall et al., "Storytelling as a Research Tool Used to Explore Insights and as an Intervention in Public Health: A Systematic Narrative Review," *International Journal of Public Health* 66 (November 2, 2021), https://www.ncbi.nlm.nih.gov/pmc/articles/ PMC8592844; Beth Stackpole, "The Next Chapter in Analytics: Data Storytelling," MIT Management, Sloan School, May 20, 2020, https://mitsloan.mit.edu/ideas-made-to-matter /next-chapter-analytics-data-storytelling; Judith E. Krauss et al., "Bringing Research Alive Through Stories: Reflecting on Research Storytelling as a Public Engagement Method,"

Research for All, September 20, 2022, https://uclpress.scienceopen.com/hosted-document
?doi=10.14324/RFA.06.1.20; Jennifer Friend and Loyce Caruthers, "Transforming the
School Reform Agenda: A Framework for Including Student Voice in Urban School Re-
newal," *Journal of Urban Learning Teaching and Research* 11 (2015): 14–25, https://files
.eric.ed.gov/fulltext/EJ1071419.pdf; Marc Brasof and Joseph Levitan, "Student Voice Research: Theory, Methods, and Innovations From the Field," *ResearchGate*, October 2022,
https://www.researchgate.net/publication/360196115_Student_Voice_Research_Theory
_Methods_and_Innovations_From_the_Field; "Why Storytelling Is Important in Education," *Labster Blog*, Fierce Education, August 8, 2022.

9. Mind Tools Content Team, "Managing in a VUCA World," *Mind Tools*, n.d.,
https://www.mindtools.com/asnydwg/managing-in-a-vuca-world; "Examples of VUCA,"
Harappa, November 19, 2021, https://harappa.education/harappa-diaries/vuca-examples;
Jeroen Kraaijenbrink, "What Does VUCA Really Mean?" *Forbes*, December 19, 2018,
https://www.forbes.com/sites/jeroenkraaijenbrink/2018/12/19/what-does-vuca-really
-mean/?sh=1bcd11ab17d6.

For a discussion of permacrises, see "Permacrisis: What It Means and Why It's Word
of the Year for 2022," *The Conversation*, November 11, 2022, https://theconversation
.com/permacrisis-what-it-means-and-why-its-word-of-the-year-for-2022-194306. For understanding the role of context in educational research, see generally Lynn McBrien, "The
Importance of Context: Vietnamese, Somali, and Iranian Refugee Mothers Discuss Their
Resettled Lives and Involvement in Their Children's Schools," *Compare: A Journal of
Comparative and International Education* 41, no. 1 (2011): 75–90, https://doi.org/10
.1080/03057925.2010.523168.

10. See "Summary of the Whole-Brain Child"; Siegel and Payne Bryson, *The Whole-
Brain Child*.

For a description of how the left and right brain hemispheres function, see "Left Brain
vs. Right Brain: Fact and Fiction," *Medical News Today*, December 22, 2022, https://www
.medicalnewstoday.com/articles/321037#differences-between-people; Eagle Gamma, "Left
Brain vs. Right Brain: Hemisphere Function," *Simply Psychology*, updated October 20,
2023, https://www.simplypsychology.org/left-brain-vs-right-brain.html.

For a summary of the long-standing and growing equity divide in education, see Sandy Baum and Michael McPherson, *Can College Level the Playing Field? Higher Education in an Unequal Society* (Princeton University Press, 2022); Emma García and Elaine
Weiss, *Education Inequalities at the School Starting Gate: Gaps, Trends, and Strategies to Address Them* (Economic Policy Institute, September 27, 2017), https://www.epi
.org/publication/education-inequalities-at-the-school-starting-gate; Clea Simon, "How
COVID Taught America About Inequity in Education," *Harvard Gazette*, July 9, 2021,
https://news.harvard.edu/gazette/story/2021/07/how-covid-taught-america-about-inequity
-in-education; Linda Darling-Hammond, "Unequal Opportunity: Race and Education,"
Brookings, March 1, 1998, https://www.brookings.edu/articles/unequal-opportunity-race
-and-education; Brian D. Smedley et al., *The Right Thing to Do, the Smart Thing to Do:
Enhancing Diversity in the Health Professions: Summary of the Symposium on Diversity
in Health Professions in Honor of Herbert W. Nickens, M.D.* (National Academies Press,
2001), https://www.ncbi.nlm.nih.gov/books/NBK223640.

11. For a comparison of the pandemic crisis and the Spanish flu, see Omar Sim-
onetti, Mariano Martini, and Emanuele Armocid, "COVID-19 and Spanish Flu-18: Review of Medical and Social Parallelisms Between Two Global Pandemics," *Journal of
Preventive Medicine and Hygiene* 62 (2021): E613–E620, doi: 10.15167/2421-4248/

jpmh2021.62.3.2124; Lakshmi Krishnan, S. Michelle Ogunwole, and Lisa A. Cooper, "Historical Insights on Coronavirus Disease 2019 (COVID-19), the 1918 Influenza Pandemic, and Racial Disparities: Illuminating a Path Forward," *Annals of Internal Medicine* 173, no. 6 (2020): 474–81, doi: 10.7326/M20-2223.

12. Many lessons have been learned from the pandemic and there is a fear that these will be lost, within and outside the education field. See Kathy Katella, "8 Lessons We Can Learn From the COVID-19 Pandemic," *Yale Medicine*, May 14, 2021, https://www .yalemedicine.org/news/8-lessons-covid-19-pandemic; Mohammed Saqr and Barbara Wasson, "COVID-19: Lost Opportunities and Lessons for the Future," *International Journal of Health Sciences* (Qassim) 14, no. 3 (2020): 4–6; Stephen Handel and Eileen Strempel, "Lessons the Pandemic Taught Us: We Missed the Signals; Let's Not Miss the Lessons," *Beyond Transfer* (blog), *Inside Higher Ed*, October 30, 2022, https://www.insidehighered .com/blogs/beyond-transfer/lessons-pandemic-taught-us; Sheryl Gay Stolberg and Noah Weiland, "Experts See Lessons for Next Pandemic as Covid Emergency Comes to an End," *New York Times*, May 11, 2023, https://www.nytimes.com/2023/05/11/us/politics/covid -response-lessons.html.

Chapter 2

1. In thinking about both hope and creativity, we relied on the following: Karen Gross, *Trauma Doesn't Stop at the School Door: Strategies and Solutions for Educators, PreK– College* (Teachers College Press, 2020), chap. 12; Jane Goodall with Douglas Abrams, *The Book of Hope: A Survival Guide for Trying Times*, 1st ed. (Celadon Books, 2021); Scott Barry Kaufman and Carolyn Gregory, *Wired to Create: Unraveling the Mysteries of the Creative Mind* (Perigee, 2015); Harvard Business Review et al., *HBR's 10 Must Reads on Creativity* (Harvard Business Review Press, 2021); Mihaly Csikszentmihalyi, *Creativity: Flow and the Psychology of Discovery and Invention* (HarperCollins, 2007); Sophia Richman, *Mended by the Muse: Creative Transformations of Trauma* (Routledge, 2014); Tobi Zausner, *When Walls Become Doorways: Creativity and the Transforming Illness* (Harmony Books, 2006); Scott Barry Kaufman, "The Will and Ways of Hope," *Creativity Post*, December 25, 2011, https://www.creativitypost.com/article/the_will_and_ways _of_hope; "Hope," *Stanford Encyclopedia of Philosophy Archive*, Winter 2021, https:// plato.stanford.edu/Archives/win2021/entries/hope; "The Psychological Basis of Hope and How It Gets Us Through Hard Times," *Forbes*, November 2, 2021, https://www.forbes .com/sites/womensmedia/2021/11/02/the-psychological-basis-of-hope-and-how-it-gets-us -through-hard-times/?sh=33f5fc3b67fe; Drew Boyd, "Where There Is Hope, There Is Creativity: Your Sense of Hope Affects Your Creative Output," *Psychology Today*, June 24, 2013, https://www.psychologytoday.com/us/blog/inside-the-box/201306/where-there-is -hope-there-is-creativity; Joanne Foster, "Hope," *Creativity Post*, August 31, 2022, https:// www.creativitypost.com/article/hope; Kelly Morr, "What Is Creativity? The Ultimate Guide to Understanding Today's Most Important Ability," 99 Designs, https://99designs .com/blog/creative-thinking/what-is-creativity; Dean Keith Simonton, "What Is a Creative Idea? Little-C Versus Big-C Creativity," in *Handbook of Research on Creativity*, ed. Kerry Thomas and Janet Chan (Edward Elgar, 2013), 69–83; Marie J. C. Forgeard et al., "Bringing the Whole Universe to Order: Creativity, Healing, and Posttraumatic Growth," in *Creativity and Mental Illness*, ed. James C. Kaufman (Cambridge University Press, 2014), 321–42, doi: 10.1017/CBO9781139128902.021.

2. Boyd, "Where There Is Hope"; Yinyinzi Yang et al., "Hope and Creative Self-Efficacy as Sequential Mediators in the Relationship Between Family Socioeconomic Status

and Creativity," *Frontiers in Psychology* 11, article 438 (March 17, 2020), doi: 10.3389/fpsyg.2020.00438; "Marcel on Creativity and Hope," *Reason and Meaning*, August 31, 2020, https://reasonandmeaning.com/2020/08/31/marcel-on-creativity-and-hope.

3. Boyd, "Where There Is Hope."

4. Darren Webb, "Pedagogies of Hope," *Studies in Philosophy and Education* 32, no. 4 (2012): 397–414; Darren Webb, "Modes of Hoping," *History of the Human Sciences*, 20 (2007): 65–83, cited in Boyd, "Where There Is Hope."

5. The complexity of hope should not be ignored. For example, some use the term *hope* even when the future is not involved. One can hope that a loved one did not suffer. Some see hope as episodic. Others see it as a personality stance that does not waiver, which explains why Desmond Tutu described himself as a "prisoner of hope," despite being in perilous situations that were anything but hopeful. "Prisoners of Hope," interview with Desmond Tutu, *Sojourners*, February 1985, https://sojo.net/magazine/february-1985/prisoner-hope.

Some see hope as a door opening to personal change. See Radha Ruparell, "How Getting COVID-19 Forced Me to Re-Examine My Life," *Greater Good Magazine*, October 12, 2020, https://greatergood.berkeley.edu/article/item/how_getting_covid_19_forced_me_to_reexamine_my_life. For more on the profit gained by hope, see Andrea Bonior, "The Health Benefits of Hope," *Psychology Today*, March 30, 2021, https://www.psychologytoday.com/us/blog/friendship-20/202103/the-health-benefits-hope; "Why Is Hope So Important?" PsychCentral, last medically reviewed on September 26, 2022, https://psychcentral.com/blog/the-psychology-of-hope#the-importance-of-hope; Michael Smithson et al., "The Psychological Benefits of an Uncertain World: Hope and Optimism in the Face of Existential Threat," *Frontiers in Psychology* 13 (March 22, 2022), https://www.frontiersin.org/articles/10.3389/fpsyg.2022.749093/full; Carlos Laranjeira and Ana Querido, "Hope and Optimism as an Opportunity to Improve the 'Positive Mental Health' Demand," *Frontiers in Psychology* 13 (February 24, 2022), https://www.ncbi.nlm.nih.gov/pmc/articles/PMC8907849.

6. The full epilogue is available through the QR code at the end of this book. While Goodall's focus is on the natural world, her approach has broader applicability: Nature is but one topic from which we can learn and to which we should pay attention, to improve wellness. Goodall's work crossed over into education, with an emphasis on the power and voices of youth, a belief in which we share; applying her theory of hope ties in well with our focus on education. Sam Linnerooth, "Jane Goodall to Teach Newest MOOC on Developing Compassionate Leaders," *CU Boulder Today*, February 12, 2018, https://www.colorado.edu/today/2018/02/12/jane-goodall-teach-newest-mooc-developing-compassionate-leaders.

7. Quotations from Goodall and Abrams, *The Book of Hope*, are taken from the Kindle version, xiii, 11, and 27.

8. Boyd, "Where There Is Hope." In *The Book of Hope*, Goodall sets out four elements needed for and supportive of hope: (1) The Amazing Human Intellect (as distinguished from intelligence) includes the capacity to communicate through words and collectively problem-solve. (2) The Resilience of Nature is a concept she grounds in our realization that nature rebounds in the face of calamity. She cites the Survivor Tree from 9/11 that was saved by Rebecca Clough and continues to thrive today. Nature teaches us about playing the long game, a topic we address in the present book. (3) The Power of Young People involves our freeing them from constraints and allowing them to share their voices and be nurtured and recognize the impact they can have, including in small changes,

which accumulate. (4) The Indominable Human Spirit allows us to not give up or give in and to address what seems impossible. We'd call it the Power of the Possible, as evidenced by the pandemic positives. This idea embodies a forward-looking notion exemplified by the terms *resilience* and *lasticity* described in Part II.

9. Simonton, "What Is a Creative Idea?"

10. Forgeard et al., "Bringing the Whole Universe to Order"; Scott Barry Kaufman, "Post-Traumatic Growth: Finding Meaning and Creativity in Adversity, *Beautiful Minds* (blog), *Scientific American*, April 20, 2020, https://blogs.scientificamerican.com/beautiful -minds/post-traumatic-growth-finding-meaning-and-creativity-in-adversity.

11. For an example of crisis creativity in a noneducational setting, see Jeremy Klemin, "My Parents Are Hackers out of Necessity," *New York Times*, September 25, 2022, https://www.nytimes.com/2022/09/25/opinion/skateboarding-disability-hacks.html.

12. "Creativity & COVID: A Lesson From Art Educators on the Importance of Creativity in a Crisis," *National Geographic Education Blog*, May 29, 2020, https:// blog.education.nationalgeographic.org/2020/05/29/creativity-covid-a-lesson-from-art -educators-on-the-importance-of-creativity-in-a-crisis/amp.

Chapter 3

1. "The Feeling Alphabet Practice Set," Karen Gross Education, n.d., https:// karengrosseducation.com/thefeelingalphabet; Karen Gross and Ed Wang, *The Feeling Alphabet Activity Set* (Amazon Press, 2022).

2. Substance Abuse and Mental Health Services Administration, *Trauma-Informed Care in Behavioral Health Services*, Treatment Improvement Protocol (TIP) Series 57 (U.S. Department of Health and Human Services, n.d.), part 3, A Review of the Literature, https:// store.samhsa.gov/sites/default/files/d7/priv/sma14-4816_litreview.pdf. For an overview of trauma theory, see Karen Gross, *Trauma Doesn't Stop at the School Door: Strategies and Solutions for Educators, PreK–College* (Teachers College Press, 2020), chaps. 1–4. See also Gross and Wang, *Feeling Alphabet*; John O. Harney and Karen Gross, "Trauma in the Time of Coronavirus and Beyond: A *NEJHE* Q&A With Karen Gross," New England Board of Higher Education, April 2020, https://nebhe.org/journal/trauma-in-the-time-of-coronavirus -and-beyond-a-nejhe-qa-with-karen-gross; Karen Gross and Cynthia Prather, "Well-Being in Classrooms After COVID-19: A '3-D' Approach for Addressing Student Trauma," *Delta Kappa Gamma Bulletin* 88, no. 1 (2021): 6–13.

3. "COVID-19 Q&A: Dr. Debra Kaysen on Individual and Collective Stress and Grief," Stanford Medicine, Department of Psychiatry and Behavioral Sciences, n.d., https://med.stanford.edu/psychiatry/about/covid19/stress.html.

4. See Gross, *Trauma*, 17.

5. Bessel van der Kolk, *The Body Keeps the Score: Brain, Mind, and Body in the Healing of Trauma* (Viking, 2014). See also Gross, *Trauma*, chaps. 1–4. On the concept of brain plasticity, see Karen Gross, *Breakaway Learners: Strategies for Post-Secondary Success With At-Risk Students* (Teachers College Press, 2016), chap. 7.

We are mindful of the recent criticism of van der Kolk and the neuroscience of trauma. While we recognize these criticisms, we think they miss the point. We may not have everything right, as the field of neuroscience is evolving, but we have plentiful studies and experiential evidence about trauma, its retriggering, and our responses to it. Eleanor Cummins, "The Self-Help That No One Needs Right Now," *Atlantic*, October 18, 2021, https://www .theatlantic.com/health/archive/2021/10/trauma-books-wont-save-you/620421; Danielle Carr, "Tell Me Why It Hurts: How Bessel van der Kolk's Once Controversial Theory of

Trauma Became the Dominant Way We Make Sense of Our Lives," Intelligencer, *New York Magazine*, July 31, 2023, https://nymag.com/intelligencer/article/trauma-bessel-van -der-kolk-the-body-keeps-the-score-profile.html; Kristen Martin, "'The Body Keeps the Score' Offers Uncertain Science in the Name of Self-Help. It's Not Alone," *Washington Post*, August 2, 2023, https://www.washingtonpost.com/books/2023/08/02/body-keeps -score-grieving-brain-bessel-van-der-kolk-neuroscience-self-help; Jill Filipovic, "I Was Wrong About Trigger Warnings: Has the National Obsession With Trauma Done Real Damage to Teen Girls?" *Atlantic*, August 9, 2023, https://www.theatlantic.com/magazine /archive/2023/09/trigger-warnings-feminism-teen-girls-mental-health/674759.

6. Gross, *Trauma*, chaps. 3–4; "Afterwar: Healing the Moral Wounds of Our Soldiers," Nancy Sherman, https://www.nancysherman.com/afterwar; Patrick Spencer, "Dr. Nancy Sherman, 'Afterwar,'" *Georgetown Public Policy Review*, November 11, 2015, https:// gppreview.com/2015/11/11/dr-nancy-sherman-afterwar; Meira Levinson, "Moral Injury and the Ethics of Educational Injustice," *Harvard Educational Review* 85, no. 2 (2015): 203–28, https://www.researchgate.net/publication/279277845_Moral_Injury_and_the_Ethics_of _Educational_Injustice.

7. H. Stefan Bracha, "Freeze, Flight, Fight, Fright, Faint: Adaptationist Perspectives on the Acute Stress Response Spectrum," *CNS Spectrums* 9, no. 9 (2004): 679–85, https:// pubmed.ncbi.nlm.nih.gov/15337864; Martin Taylor, "What Does Fight, Flight, Freeze, Fawn Mean?" WebMD, n.d., https://www.webmd.com/mental-health/what-does-fight -flight-freeze-fawn-mean; Crystal Raypole, "The Beginner's Guide to Trauma Responses," *Healthline*, August 26, 2021, https://www.healthline.com/health/mental-health/fight-flight -freeze-fawn; Karen Gross, "The Fawning Response to Trauma: An Incident That Haunts Me Still," Medium, August 3, 2021, https://karengrossedu.medium.com/the-fawning -response-to-trauma-an-incident-that-haunts-me-still-bfa7a6181ad7.

8. Judith Lewis Herman, "Complex PTSD: A Syndrome in Survivors of Prolonged and Repeated Trauma," *Journal of Traumatic Stress* 5 (July 1992): 377–91, https://link .springer.com/article/10.1007/BF00977235; Kristen L. Zaleski, Daniel K. Johnson, and Jessica T. Klein, "Grounding Judith Herman's Trauma Theory Within Interpersonal Neu-roscience and Evidence-Based Practice Modalities for Trauma Treatment," *Smith College Studies in Social Work* 86, no. 4 (2016): 377–93, http://dx.doi.org/10.1080/00377317 .2016.1222110.

9. For a discussion of ACEs, see Gross, *Trauma*, 18–21; Centers for Disease Control and Prevention, "Adverse Childhood Experiences (ACEs)," National Center for Injury Prevention and Control, Division of Violence Prevention, last reviewed June 29, 2023, www.cdc.gov/violenceprevention/aces/index.html.

10. Sarah Gonser, "What to Do About Increasing Dysregulation in the Early Grades," Edutopia, August 25, 2023, https://www.edutopia.org/article/tackling-misbehavior-in -the-early-grades; Chris Leonard, "Emotional Dysregulation: Support for Teachers and Students," The Learning Counsel, May 30, 2023, https://thelearningcounsel.com/articles /emotional-dysregulation-support-for-teachers-and-students; Hannah Lawrence, "Melt-downs, Shutdowns, and Dysregulation: Supporting Children and Young People With Emo-tional or Sensory Overwhelm," Twinkl, August 24, 2022, https://www.twinkl.com/blog /meltdowns-shutdowns-and-dysregulation-supporting-children-and-young-people-with -emotional-or-sensory-overwhelm; Karen Gross, "Behavior Is the Language of Trauma," Medium, July 24, 2022, https://karengrossedu.medium.com/behavior-is-the-language-of -trauma-ab9ba15b7071; Karen Gross, "Trauma and Adult Learners," Karen Gross Edu-cation, [December 18, 2019], https://karengrosseducation.com/trauma-and-adult-learners.

Gross, *Breakaway Learners*, chap. 4, may be helpful too; Gross and Wang, *Feeling Alphabet*; Karen Gross, "Mourning and Missing: A Price of Love," Medium, July 15, 2022, https://medium.com/age-of-awareness/mourning-and-missing-a-price-of-love-8728cfc-ca5a.

11. Karen Gross, "Learning to Play Again in a World Filled With Trauma," Medium, October 7, 2021, https://medium.com/age-of-awareness/learning-to-play-again-in-a-world-filled-with-trauma-689d09824406; Karen Gross, "I Beg to Differ on How to Deal With Trauma 'Anniversaries,'" Medium, January 24, 2020, https://medium.com/age-of-awareness/i-beg-to-differ-on-how-to-deal-with-trauma-anniversaries-c10d5304075; "Supporting Survivors of Trauma: How to Avoid Re-Traumatization," Online MSW Programs, n.d., https://www.onlinemswprograms.com/resources/how-to-be-mindful-re-traumatization; Stephanie A. Wright, "How to Identify and Overcome Trauma Triggers," PsychCentral, November 8, 2021, https://psychcentral.com/health/trauma-triggers; Angela Sweeney et al., "A Paradigm Shift: Relationships in Trauma-Informed Mental Health Services," *British Journal of Psychiatry Advances* 24, no. 5 (2018): 319–33, https://www.ncbi.nlm.nih.gov/pmc/articles/PMC6088388.

12. Gross and Prather, "Well-Being in Classrooms After COVID-19"; Gross and Wang, *Feeling Alphabet*.

There is some confusion and overlap in the use of the terms *trauma-sensitive schools*, *trauma-responsive schools*, and *trauma-informed schools*. (The U.S. Department of Education uses *trauma sensitive*.) For a discussion of these terms, see Gross, *Trauma*, 85–87. See also "Frequently Asked Questions About Trauma-Sensitive Schools," Trauma and Learning Policy Initiative, n.d., https://traumasensitiveschools.org/frequently-asked-questions; David Osher et al., "Trauma-Sensitive Schools and Social and Emotional Learning: An Integration," Edna Bennett Pierce Prevention Research Center, Penn State College of Health and Human Development, May 2021, https://prevention.psu.edu/wp-content/uploads/2022/09/TSS-SEL-Brief-Final-June2021R.pdf; "Becoming a Trauma Responsive School," TREP Project, n.d., https://www.trepeducator.org/trauma-responsive-school.

In this book, we use *trauma-responsive schools*, recognizing that different organizations, governments, and schools use various terminology. For us, the key is that *trauma responsiveness* puts an emphasis on action and doing: It is proactive, rather than reactive.

13. For the importance of play, see Gross, *Trauma*, 126–127; "The Power of Play for Addressing Trauma in the Early Years," Childhood Education International, n.d., https://ceinternational1892.org/wp-content/uploads/2020/05/TraumaPowerPlayBrief.pdf.

See Gross, *Breakaway Learners*, chap. 9, on reciprocity; Gross and Wang, *Feeling Alphabet*; Karen Gross, "Stress Abounds: What Can We Do to Help Youth?" Medium, October 3, 2022, https://medium.com/age-of-awareness/stress-abounds-what-can-we-do-to-help-youth-e8b6adc06b5d; Jeremy Sutton, "Mirror Neurons and the Neuroscience of Empathy," *PositivePsychology.com*, September 7, 2023, https://positivepsychology.com/mirror-neurons; Richard Praszkier, "Empathy, Mirror Neurons and SYNC," *Mind and Society* 15 (2016): 1–25, https://doi.org/10.1007/s11299-014-0160-x; Daniela D'Elia, Luna Carpinelli, and Giulia Savarese, "Post-Traumatic Play in Child Victims of Adverse Childhood Experiences: A Pilot Study With the MCAST—Manchester Child Attachment Story Task and the Coding of PTCP Markers," *Children* (Basel) 9, no. 12 (1991), https://www.ncbi.nlm.nih.gov/pmc/articles/PMC9776711. Because trauma truncates neural connections, restoring connections is critical in being trauma responsive. See, e.g., Laura Waters, "Human Connections and Healing From Trauma," January 8, 2019, https://www.unitedfamilies.org/family/human-connections-and-healing-from-trauma; Lori Desautels,

"Connections Go a Long Way for Students With Trauma," Edutopia, July 18, 2018, https://www.edutopia.org/article/connections-go-long-way-students-trauma.

14. World Health Organization, *Health Promotion Glossary of Terms* (World Health Organization, 2021), https://iris.who.int/bitstream/handle/10665/350161/9789240038349 -eng.pdf?sequence=1.

15. "8 Dimensions of Wellness," *Your Guide to Living Well* (blog), University of Maryland, n.d., https://umwellness.wordpress.com/8-dimensions-of-wellness; Leanne Lester and Donna Cross, "The Relationship Between School Climate and Mental and Emotional Wellbeing Over the Transition From Primary to Secondary School," *Psychological Well Being* 5, no. 1 (2015): 9, https://www.ncbi.nlm.nih.gov/pmc/articles/PMC4615665.

16. See Debbie L. Stoewen, "Dimensions of Wellness: Change Your Habits, Change Your Life," *Canadian Veterinary Journal* 58, no. 8 (2017): 861–62, https://www.ncbi .nlm.nih.gov/pmc/articles/PMC5508938; "8 Dimensions of Wellness"; "Seven Facets of Wellbeing," UChicago Student Wellness, n.d., https://wellness.uchicago.edu/healthy-living /outreach. See also Hong Wang Fung et al., "Clinical Features of a Chinese Sample With Self-Reported Symptoms of Pathological Dissociation," *Journal of Trauma and Dissociation* 22, no. 3 (2021): 378–393.

17. Gabriel A. Orenstein and Lindsay Lewis, "Eriksons [*sic*] Stages of Psychosocial Development," StatPearls, November 7, 2022, https://www.ncbi.nlm.nih.gov/books/NBK556096; Jeremy Sutton, "Erik Erikson's Stages of Psychosocial Development Explained," Positive-Psychology.com, August 5, 2020, https://positivepsychology.com/erikson-stages; Paul Main, "Erikson's Psychosocial Development Stages Explained," Structural Learning, March 23, 2023, https://www.structural-learning.com/post/eriksons-psychosocial-development-stages.

18. Doris Buckley and Deirdre Budzyna, "Psychosocial Theory," in *The Whole Child: Development in the Early Years*, Rotel Project, n.d., https://rotel.pressbooks.pub/whole -child/chapter/psychosocial-theory; Erin Martise, "How to Apply Erikson's Theory in Instruction," *The Classroom*, updated April 22, 2023, https://www.theclassroom.com/apply -eriksons-theory-instruction-8400675.html; Hong Wang Fung et al., "Psychosocial and Mental Health Correlates of Perceived Teacher Support Among Young Adults Across Cultures (China, US, and Canada): Above and Beyond the Effects of Childhood Trauma" (under review).

19. "Fundamentals of SEL," CASEL, n.d., https://casel.org/fundamentals-of-sel; Mark T. Greenberg, *Evidence for Social and Emotional Learning in Schools*, Learning Policy Institute, March 6, 2023, https://learningpolicyinstitute.org/product/evidence-social -emotional-learning-schools-report; Nancy Frey, Douglas Fisher, and Dominique Smith, *Social and Emotional Learning Playbook: A Guide to Student and Teacher Well-Being* (Corwin, 2022); Geoffrey L. Cohen, *Belonging: The Science of Creating Connection and Bridging Divides* (W. W. Norton, 2023).

20. Paulo Freire, *Pedagogy of the Oppressed* (Penguin, 2017); Gross, *Breakaway Learners*, 65–66, 72–73; Gross, *Trauma*, 25–27.

21. "Fundamentals of SEL"; Greenberg, *Evidence for Social and Emotional Learning in Schools*; Frey, Fisher, and Smith, *Social and Emotional Learning Playbook*; Cohen, *Belonging*; Nick Morrison, "It's Not Their Mindset That's Holding Children Back at School, Study Finds," *Forbes*, December 18, 2023, https://www.forbes.com/sites/nickmorrison /2023/12/18/its-not-their-mindset-thats-holding-children-back-at-school-study-finds/?sh =2572848128a6.

22. See Part II of the present book; Emily Tate Sullivan, "Demystifying Social–Emotional Learning and the Controversy Surrounding It," EdSurge, September 30, 2022,

https://www.edsurge.com/news/2022-09-30-demystifying-social-emotional-learning-and
-the-controversy-surrounding-it.

23. Gross, *Trauma*, 79–82; Osher et al., "Trauma-Sensitive Schools and Social and
Emotional Learning."
See the following working papers by coauthor Edward K. S. Wang, all available on request: "Trauma-Informed Care: Hope, Strengths, Resilience, Growth, and Healing," 2019;
"Wellness and Resilience in Children and Their Communities," 2020; "Asian Perspectives: A Train-the-Trainer Manuscript on Multicultural Competency," Massachusetts Department of Mental Health, 1994; "Integrating Culture Into Practice: Training Curricula
for Clinicians, Supervisors, and Administrators," Massachusetts Department of Mental
Health, 2004.

24. Gregory C. Hutchings and Douglas S. Reed, *Getting Into Good Trouble at
School: A Guide to Building an Antiracist School System* (Corwin, 2022); Wayne Journell,
ed., *Post-Pandemic Social Studies: How COVID-19 Has Changed the World and How
We Teach* (Teachers College Press, 2021); Stéphan Vincent-Lancrin, "Educational Innovation and Digitalisation During the COVID-19 Crisis: Lessons for the Future," in *How
Learning Continued During the COVID-19 Pandemic: Global Lessons From Initiatives
to Support Learners and Teachers*, ed. Stéphan Vincent-Lancrin, Cristóbal Cobo Romaní,
and Fernando Reimers (OECD, 2022), https://doi.org/10.1787/93c3dc5e-en; Osher et al.,
"Trauma-Sensitive Schools and Social and Emotional Learning." See also Related Sources
through the QR code that appears at the end of this book.

25. Emiliana Vegas and Rebecca Winthrop, "Beyond Reopening Schools: How Education Can Emerge Stronger Than Before COVID-19," Brookings, September 8, 2020,
https://www.brookings.edu/articles/beyond-reopening-schools-how-education-can-emerge
-stronger-than-before-covid-19.

26. "Accelerating Structural and Systemic Change in K–12 Education: Insights
From Colorado Educators," Teach + Plus, July 8, 2021, https://teachplus.org/resource
/accelerating-structural-and-systemic-change-in-k-12-education-insights-from-colorado
-educators.

27. "Accelerating Structural and Systemic Change in K–12 Education." See Jenny
Brundin, "The Pandemic Taught Teachers a Bunch of Lessons; Now, They Want Their
Schools to Listen," *CPR News*, July 19, 2021, https://www.cpr.org/2021/07/19/covid
-pandemic-colorado-what-teachers-learned.

28. Edward K. Wang, "A Journey of Public Stewardship on Asian American and
Pacific Islander Mental Health: Massachusetts's Approach to Addressing Disparities,"
Asian American Policy Review 29 (Spring 2019), https://www.proquest.com/docview
/2317571852?pq-origsite=summon&sourcetype=Scholarly%20Journals.

29. See, e.g., L. Rosi and E. K. Wang, "The Project One Billion Global Mental Health
Survey," in *Textbook of Global Mental Health: Trauma and Recovery; A Companion
Guide for Field and Clinical Care of Traumatized People Worldwide*, ed. Richard F. Molli-
ca (Harvard Program in Refugee Trauma, 2011), 61–88. For a survey conducted by Karen
Gross in 1986 and released by the American Bankruptcy Institute and for her testimony
before Congress, see "Hearing Before the Subcommittee on Courts and Administrative
Practice of the Committee on the Judiciary; United States Senate One Hundredth Congress,
Second Session, on S. 1626, S. 1358, S. 1863, and S. 2279," U.S. Government Printing
Office, June 10, 1988, https://ipmall.law.unh.edu/sites/default/files/hosted_resources/lipa
/trademarks/S.Hrg.100-1067%20Am.%20Bankruptcy%20Inst.%20Survey%20%2806
_%2010,%201988%29%20A.pdf.

30. Julie Ponto, "Understanding and Evaluating Survey Research," *Journal of the Advanced Practitioner in Oncology* 6, no. 2 (2015): 168–71, https://www.ncbi.nlm.nih.gov /pmc/articles/PMC4601897; Jason Mander, "Why Survey Data Is More Valuable Than Ever for Consumer Research," GWI, February 10, 2020, https://blog.gwi.com/marketing /survey-data-for-consumer-research; "Survey Research," chap. 8, n.d., https://www.sagepub .com/sites/default/files/upm-binaries/43589_8.pdf.

31. "Combine Qualitative and Quantitative Data," Better Evaluation, n.d., https:// www.betterevaluation.org/frameworks-guides/rainbow-framework/describe/combine -qualitative-quantitative-data; Marja J. Verhoef and Ann L. Casebeer, "Broadening Horizons: Integrating Quantitative and Qualitative Research," *Canadian Journal of Infectious Diseases and Medical Microbiology* 8, no. 2 (1997): 65–66, https://www.ncbi.nlm.nih.gov /pmc/articles/PMC3327344; Eric "ERock" Christopher, "Why Both Quantitative and Qualitative Data Are Vital for Results-Driven Businesses," *Entrepreneur*, December 24, 2020, https://www.entrepreneur.com/science-technology/why-both-quantitative-and-qualitative -data-are-vital-for/361314.

Chapter 4

1. On the school closure and reopening timeline, see "The Coronavirus Spring: The Historic Closing of U.S. Schools (a Timeline)," *Education Week*, July 1, 2020, https://www .edweek.org/leadership/the-coronavirus-spring-the-historic-closing-of-u-s-schools-a-timeline /2020/07; "A Year of COVID-19: What It Looked Like for Schools; A Timeline," *Education Week*, March 4, 2021, https://www.edweek.org/leadership/a-year-of-covid-19-what-it -looked-like-for-schools/2021/03; Andrew Smalley, "Higher Education Responses to Coronavirus (COVID-19)," NCSL, updated March 22, 2021, https://www.ncsl.org/education /higher-education-responses-to-coronavirus-covid-19; Amelia Nierenberg and Adam Pasick, "Schools Briefing: The Outlook for In-Person Classes," *New York Times*, updated August 26, 2020, https://www.nytimes.com/2020/08/24/us/college-university-reopening -coronavirus.html.

2. For the international perspective on school closures, see Deni Mazrekaj and Kristof De Witte, "The Impact of School Closures on Learning and Mental Health of Children: Lessons From the COVID-19 Pandemic," *Perspectives on Psychological Science*, July 10, 2023, https://journals.sagepub.com/doi/full/10.1177/17456916231181108.

3. COVID-related shutdowns, quarantines, and absence of travel contributed to a change in how we viewed time during the pandemic. In fact, some would say we lost our sense of time. See "How (and Why) Coronavirus Is Changing Our Sense of Time," University of California, May 7, 2020, https://www.universityofcalifornia.edu/news/how-and -why-coronavirus-changing-our-sense-time; Yuki Noguchi, "How Did COVID Warp Our Sense of Time? It's a Matter of Perception," NPR, December 14, 2022, https://www.npr .org/sections/health-shots/2022/12/14/1127361435/how-covid-warped-time-perception.

Andrea Frazzetta's photograph of a sculpture by Stefano Bombardieri in a series titled Suspended in Time appears in *National Geographic*'s From Our Photographers column, September 2023, 136.

4. "Private Schools Stayed Open While Public Schools Closed," *Covid Chronicles*, updated August 25, 2023, https://www.covidchronicles.cc/private-schools-stayed -open-while-public-schools-closed.html; Aaron Garth Smith and Jordan Campbell, "Homeschooling Is on the Rise, Even as the Pandemic Recedes," Reason Foundation, May 31, 2023, https://reason.org/commentary/homeschooling-is-on-the-rise-even-as-the -pandemic-recedes.

5. "Fact Sheet: Anti-Asian Prejudice, March 2021," Center for the Study of Hate and Extremism, n.d., https://www.csusb.edu/sites/default/files/FACT%20SHEET-%20 Anti-Asian%20Hate%202020%20rev%203.21.21.pdf; Kimmy Yam, "Anti-Asian Hate Crimes Increased by Nearly 150% in 2020, Mostly in N.Y. and L.A., New Report Says," *NBC News*, March 9, 2021, https://www.nbcnews.com/news/asian-america/anti-asian-hate -crimes-increased-nearly-150-2020-mostly-n-n1260264; "Anti-Asian Hate Crime Events During the COVID-19 Pandemic," Research Center, California Justice Information Services Division, California Department of Justice, n.d., https://oag.ca.gov/system/files/media/anti -asian-hc-report.pdf.

6. Janice Gassam Asare, "Why More Black Families Are Choosing to Homeschool Their Children," *Forbes*, February 16, 2023, https://www.forbes.com/sites/janicegassam /2023/02/16/why-more-black-families-are-choosing-to-homeschool-their-children/?sh =1d4bfc52641c; Moriah Balingit and Kate Rabinowitz, "Home Schooling Exploded Among Black, Asian, and Latino Students. But It Wasn't Just the Pandemic," *Washington Post*, July 27, 2021, https://www.washingtonpost.com/education/2021/07/27/pandemic -homeschool-black-asian-hispanic-families; Anya Kamenetz, "Why So Many Asian Americans Are Learning Remotely," NPR, April 9, 2021, https://www.npr.org/2021/04/09/984789341 /why-so-many-asian-americans-are-learning-remotely#:~:text=Asian%20American%20 students%20are%20far,Education%20Department%27s%20latest%20school%20 survey; "AANHPI Service Providers in All Fifty States," NAAPIMHA (National Asian American Pacific Islander Mental Health Association), n.d., https://www.naapimha.org /aanhpi-service-providers.

7. The following are selected from the many articles on how parents struggled when schools closed—a worldwide phenomenon: Mazrekaj and De Witte, "The Impact of School Closures on Learning and Mental Health of Children"; Madeline Holcombe, "'Kids Very Rarely Do Better Than Their Parents Are Doing.' Here's What to Do," CNN, January 18, 2022, https://amp.cnn.com/cnn/2022/01/18/health/children-impact-school -closing-coronavirus-wellness/index.html; Raya Maggay, "Effects of Coronavirus School Closures on Parents and Children," Study.com, n.d., https://study.com/academy/popular /effects-of-coronavirus-school-closures-on-parents-and-children.html.

The problem of school closure was particularly acute for children with disabilities. Molly Lipkin and Franci Crepeau-Hobson, "The Impact of the COVID-19 School Closures on Families With Children With Disabilities: A Qualitative Analysis," *Psychology in the Schools* 10 (April 12, 2022), https://www.ncbi.nlm.nih.gov/pmc/articles/PMC9088372 /#:~:text=Parents%20had%20difficulties%20related%20to,a%20learner%20during%20 online%20learning.

8. Office of Civil Rights, U.S. Department of Education, *Education in a Pandemic: The Disparate Impacts of COVID-19 on America's Students*, Office of Civil Rights, U.S. Department of Education, n.d., https://www2.ed.gov/about/offices/list/ocr/docs/20210608 -impacts-of-covid19.pdf; Mazrekaj and De Witte, "The Impact of School Closures on Learning and Mental Health of Children"; Heather J. Hough, "COVID-19, the Educational Equity Crisis, and the Opportunity Ahead," Brookings, April 29, 2021, https://www .brookings.edu/articles/covid-19-the-educational-equity-crisis-and-the-opportunity-ahead; Emma Dorn et al., "COVID-19 and Learning Loss—Disparities Grow and Students Need Help," McKinsey, December 8, 2020, https://www.mckinsey.com/industries/public-sector /our-insights/covid-19-and-learning-loss-disparities-grow-and-students-need-help.

The gap was not just for children; it existed in colleges and universities too. Paul Fain, "Higher Education and Work Amid Crisis," *Inside Higher Ed*, June 16, 2020, https://

www.insidehighered.com/news/2020/06/17/pandemic-has-worsened-equity-gaps-higher
-education-and-work.

9. Jasmine Aguilera, Madeleine Carlisle, and Katie Reilly, "From Teachers to Cus-
todians, Meet the Educators Who Saved a Pandemic School Year," *Time*, September 2,
2021, https://time.com/6094017/educators-covid-19-school-year; "Teachers Make Home
Visits During Closure," Positive Tomorrows, n.d., https://www.positivetomorrows.org
/teachers-make-home-visits-during-school-closure; Neal Morton, "Teachers Visit Families at Home in 700 Communities Nationwide. The Idea Is Earning Attention in Seattle," *Seattle Times*, April 19, 2019, updated April 20, 2019, https://www.seattletimes
.com/education-lab/when-teachers-visit-homes-students-do-better-and-parents-learn-too;
Thaddeus Mast, "Teacher's Touching Message Spelled Out in Chalk Brings Comfort to
Students," *Naples (Florida) Daily News*, March 22, 2020, https://www.naplesnews.com
/story/news/local/2020/03/22/coronavirus-florida-teachers-touching-message-comforts
-students/2895342001.

10. Katie Morosky, "During Coronavirus School Closures, Riverhead Teachers Find
Creative Ways to Cheer Up Students Stuck at Home," *Riverhead Local*, March 30, 2020,
https://riverheadlocal.com/2020/03/30/during-coronavirus-school-closures-riverhead
-teachers-find-creative-ways-to-cheer-up-students-stuck-at-home.

11. Joyce Kasman Valenza et al., "We Were the Glue: Contributions, Compromises, and
Continuing Concerns of School Librarians During the COVID-19 Pandemic," February 19,
2023, https://files.eric.ed.gov/fulltext/ED626437.pdf; American Association of School Librarians (AASL), "School Librarian Role in Pandemic Learning Conditions," AASL, https://
www.ala.org/aasl/sites/ala.org.aasl/files/content/advocacy/SchoolLibrarianRolePandemic
_Resources_Chart_200713.pdf; Deborah Rinio, "Schools May Be Closed, but Your School
Librarian Is Only a Few Clicks Away," *Anchorage Daily News*, April 9, 2020, https://www
.adn.com/opinions/2020/04/09/schools-may-be-closed-but-your-school-librarian-is-only-a
-few-clicks-away; American Association of School Librarians, "Snapshot of School Librarian
Roles During School Closures," *Knowledge Quest*, April 10, 2020, https://knowledgequest
.aasl.org/snapshot-of-school-librarian-roles-during-school-closures; Caitlin O'Kane, "Librarian Uses Drones to Deliver Books to Kids Stuck at Home due to Coronavirus," *CBS
News*, June 16, 2020, https://www.cbsnews.com/amp/news/librarian-uses-drone-to-deliver
-books-to-kids-stuck-at-home-due-to-coronavirus.

12. For the videos and related materials, see Related Sources, available through the
QR code at the end of the book.

13. Karen Gross and Ed Wang, *The Feeling Alphabet Activity Set* (Amazon Press,
2022).

14. Emma García, "The Pandemic Sparked More Appreciation for Teachers, but Will
It Give Them a Voice in Education and Their Working Conditions?" *Working Economics Blog*, Economic Policy Institute, May 7, 2020, https://www.epi.org/blog/the-pandemic
-sparked-more-appreciation-for-teachers-but-will-it-give-them-a-voice-in-education
-and-their-working-conditions; Erin Richards, Arika Herron, and MJ Slaby, "Teacher
Appreciation Week: They Wanted Respect. It Only Took a Coronavirus Pandemic and
Worldwide Economic Collapse," *USA Today*, May 4, 2020, https://www.usatoday.com
/story/news/education/2020/05/04/teacher-appreciation-week-2020-coronavirus-virtual
/3066238001; "Harris Poll Finds 82% of Parents Have a Greater Appreciation for Teachers Since the Start of the COVID-19 Pandemic," Business Wire, May 3, 2021, https://www
.businesswire.com/news/home/20210503005350/en/Harris-Poll-finds-82-of-parents-have
-a-greater-appreciation-for-teachers-since-the-start-of-the-COVID-19-pandemic.

For the role and importance of educators, see Alexander Robbins, *The Teachers: A Year Inside America's Most Vulnerable, Important Profession* (Dutton, 2023).

15. Annamaria Colao et al., "Rethinking the Role of the School After COVID-19," *Lancet*, May 25, 2020, https://www.thelancet.com/journals/lanpub/article/PIIS2468 -2667(20)30124-9/fulltext; Jacob Fay et al., *Schools During the COVID-19 Pandemic: Sites and Sources of Community Resilience*, COVID-19 Rapid Response Impact Initiative, White Paper 20, June 11, 2020, https://ethics.harvard.edu/files/center-for-ethics/files /20schoolsduringpandemic2.pdf; Stephen Sawchuk, "When Schools Shut Down, We All Lose," *Education Week*, March 20, 2020, https://www.edweek.org/leadership/when -schools-shut-down-we-all-lose/2020/03; Emiliana Vegas and Rebecca Winthrop, "Beyond Reopening Schools: How Education Can Emerge Stronger Than Before COVID-19," Brookings, September 8, 2020, https://www.brookings.edu/articles/beyond-reopening -schools-how-education-can-emerge-stronger-than-before-covid-19.

16. Emily Graham, "Teacher Appreciation Goes Mainstream During School Closures," *PTO Today*, July 20, 2021, https://www.ptotoday.com/pto-today-articles/article /9040-teacher-appreciation-goes-mainstream-during-school-closures.

17. Teacher respect grew during the pandemic. García, "The Pandemic Sparked More Appreciation for Teachers." See also "In COVID's Wake, Educators Cite Increased Respect for Teachers as Positive Outcome of Pandemic, Are Prepared for Significant Change Heading Into the New School Year, With Social–Emotional Learning, Safety Concerns Ranking Most Important to Educators," *PR Newswire*, July 28, 2020, https://www.prnewswire.com /news-releases/in-covids-wake-educators-cite-increased-respect-for-teachers-as-positive -outcome-of-pandemic-are-prepared-for-significant-change-heading-into-the-new-school -year-with-social-emotional-learning-safety-concerns-ranking-most-imp-301101262.html.

Trends show that respect is waning and more educators are leaving the profession. Matt Zalaznick, "The 3 States Where Teachers Say Respect for Educators Has Fallen the Most," District Administration, September 15, 2022, https://districtadministration.com /respect-for-teachers-falling-shortages-vacancies-aasa; Ned Hoskin, "Two Years Into Pandemic, Educators Need Respect, Cooperation, and Patience,"NYSUT, February 4, 2022, https://www.nysut.org/news/2022/february/respect.

18. Sarah D. Sparks, "Lessons Learned From Pandemic Learning Pods," *Education Week*, February 23, 2022, https://www.edweek.org/leadership/lessons-learned-from -pandemic-learning-pods/2022/02.

19. Karen D'Souza, "Outdoor Classes and 'Forest Schools' Gain New Prominence Amid Distance Learning Struggles," EdSource, October 1, 2020, https://edsource.org/2020 /outdoor-classes-and-forest-schools-gain-new-prominence-amid-distance-learning-struggles /640853; Bryan C. Hassel and Sharon Kebschull Barrett, "Will Learning Pods Be Only for the Rich?" *Education Week*, August 25, 2020, https://www.edweek.org/leadership/opinion -will-learning-pods-be-only-for-the-rich/2020/08.

20. Maurice J. Elias, "What Kind of Ecosystem Is Your School?" Edutopia, March 21, 2016, https://www.edutopia.org/blog/what-kind-ecosystem-your-school-maurice-elias; Vegas and Winthrop, "Beyond Reopening Schools."

21. Andrew Bauld, "Make Outdoor Learning Your Plan A," Harvard Graduate School of Education, August 18, 2021, https://www.gse.harvard.edu/ideas/usable-knowledge/21 /08/make-outdoor-learning-your-plan.

22. Trust for Public Land, "During COVID-19, Schools Turn to Outdoor Learning," Trust for Public Land, n.d., https://www.tpl.org/blog/thinking-outside-classroom -during-covid-19-schools-turn-outdoor-learning; Trust for Public Land, *School's Out: In*

a Time of Compounding Crises, America's Schoolyards Are Packed With Potential, Trust for Public Land, n.d., https://www.tpl.org/wp-content/uploads/2020/08/Schools-Out_A -Trust-for-Public-Land-Special-Report.pdf; "Playground Power: Initiative Brings Green Spaces to Urban Schoolyards," National School Boards Association, August 1, 2022, https://www.nsba.org/ASBJ/2022/august/playground-power; Jan Cohen and Tiffany Briery, "Math on the Playground," Green Schools National Network, March 12, 2020, https:// greenschoolsnationalnetwork.org/math-on-the-playground.

Before the pandemic, there were schools that largely functioned out of doors (weather permitting); these employed largely project-based learning programs where learning happened by doing. For some students this was an optimal learning modality. With the pandemic, students who had not been involved in "thematic" or project-based learning gained enormous benefits. "Classrooms Without Walls: A Forgotten Age of Open-Air Schools," Messy Nessy, May 1, 2020, https://www.messynessychic.com/2016/03/15/classrooms-without -walls-a-forgotten-age-of-open-air-schools.

23. Kirsten Grind, "One-Room Schoolhouses Make a Covid-19 Comeback—in Backyards and Garages," *Wall Street Journal,* July 31, 2020, https://www.wsj.com/articles /schoolhouse-backyard-coronavirus-remote-learning-pandemic-pod-11596207290. See also Eilene Zimmerman, "In Pandemic's Wake, Learning Pods and Microschools Take Root," *New York Times,* October 14, 2020, https://www.nytimes.com/2020/10/14/education /learning/pods-microschools-pandemic.html. To be sure, learning pods are not without their challenges. See, e.g., Ronda Kaysen, "Learning Pods Show Their Cracks," *New York Times,* December 22, 2020, updated December 31, 2020, https://www.nytimes.com/2020/12/22 /style/learning-pods-pros-and-cons.html.

24. Robin Cogan, "It Has Taken a Pandemic to Understand the Importance of School Nurses," *American Nurse,* August 17, 2020, https://www.myamericannurse.com/it-has -taken-a-pandemic-to-understand-the-importance-of-school-nurses.

25. Ashley A. Lowe et al., "The Changing Job of School Nurses During the COVID-19 Pandemic: A Media Content Analysis of Contributions to Stress," *Annals of Work Exposures and Health* 67, no. 1 (2023): 101–17, https://www.ncbi.nlm.nih.gov/pmc/articles/ PMC9494455; Rachel Rothstein and Robert P. Olympia, "School Nurses on the Front Lines of Healthcare: The Approach to Maintaining Student Health and Wellness During COVID-19 School Closures," *NASN School Nurse* 35, no. 5 (2020), https://www.ncbi .nlm.nih.gov/pmc/articles/PMC7331109.

26. Rothstein and Olympia, "School Nurses on the Front Lines of Healthcare."

27. Catherine A. Grano, Eileen M. Gavin, and Robin Cogan, "Through the Looking Glass: Reflections From Three School Nurses Amid the COVID-19 Pandemic," *Online Journal of Issues in Nursing* 26, no. 2, manuscript 4 (2021), https://ojin.nursingworld .org/table-of-contents/volume-26-2021/number-2-may-2021/through-the-looking-glass -reflections-from-three-school-nurses-amid-the-covid-19-pandemic-.

28. ASCA Ethics Committee, "School Counseling During a Pandemic," *ASCA School Counselor,* September 1, 2020, https://www.schoolcounselor.org/Magazines/September -October-2020/School-Counseling-During-a-Pandemic; Molly Strear, Helen Duffy, and Ashley Sunde, "When Schools Go Dark, School Counselors Shine: School Counseling During a Global Pandemic," American Institutes for Research, n.d., https://files.eric.ed.gov /fulltext/ED613589.pdf.

29. Virtual Calm Room, https://www.virtualcalmroom.com.

30. Strear, Duffy, and Sunde, *When Schools Go Dark, School Counselors Shine;* "Kids Bouncing off the Walls? These Boredom Busters Fill Time Gaps With Activity,"

ADDitude, September 7, 2022, https://www.additudemag.com/bouncing-off-the-walls
-activities-adhd-kids/?utm_source=eletter&utm_medium=email&utm_campaign=school
_april_2020&utm_cont.

31. School Social Work Association of America (SSWAA), "Resolution Statement:
The Impact of School Social Workers during the COVID-19 Pandemic," SSWAA, 2020,
https://www.socialworkers.org/LinkClick.aspx?fileticket=zc_vj6tH1YI%3D&portalid=0.

32. Fiona May et al., "Perspectives of Practicing School Psychologists During COV-
ID-19: A Multi-Country, Mixed Methods Investigation," *School Psychology International*
44, no. 4 (2022), https://www.ncbi.nlm.nih.gov/pmc/articles/PMC9659691.

33. Katharine Carter, "School Psychologists Adapt to Help Students During COV-
ID-19," American Psychological Association, July 14, 2020, https://www.apa.org/members
/content/school-psychologists-covid-19.

34. David Hoch, "Dealing With the COVID-19 Pandemic," *Coach & A.D.*, March 20,
2020, https://coachad.com/articles/dealing-with-the-covid-19-pandemic; Timothy A. Mc-
Guine et al., "High School Sports During the COVID-19 Pandemic: The Effect of Sport
Participation on the Health of Adolescents," *Journal of Athletic Training* 57, no. 1 (2022):
51–58, https://www.ncbi.nlm.nih.gov/pmc/articles/PMC8775289; "The COVID-19 Pandemic: Tips for Athletes, Coaches, Parents, and the Sport Community," *AASP Blog*, Association for Applied Sport Psychology, March 19, 2020, https://appliedsportpsych.org/blog
/2020/03/the-covid-19-pandemic-tips-for-athletes-coaches-parents-and-the-sport-commu-
nity; Allie Reynolds and Alireza Hamidian Jahromi, "Staying Connected and Prepared for
Collegiate Athletic Competitions During the COVID-19 Pandemic," *Frontiers in Sports
and Active Living* 3 (March 12, 2021), https://doi.org/10.3389/fspor.2021.663918.

35. Loren Ledin, "The COVID Pandemic Shut Down High School Sports for a Year.
Has It Altered Them Forever?" *VC Star*, March 18, 2021, https://www.vcstar.com/story
/sports/high-school/2021/03/18/has-covid-pandemic-changed-high-school-sports-forever
/6783754002; Dan Levin, "Despite Covid Outbreaks, Youth Sports Played On," *New
York Times*, March 13, 2021, https://www.nytimes.com/2021/03/13/us/covid-youth-sports
.html; Vincent Nguyen, "Athletes, Coaches Facing Challenges With College Recruiting During Coronavirus," April 9, 2020, https://www.latimes.com/socal/glendale-news-press/https:
/www.latimes.com/socal/burbank-leader/sports/story/2020-04-09/athletes-coaches-facing
-challenges-with-college-recruitment-during-pandemic; Senerey de los Santos, "California's
Pandemic Shutdowns Cause Local High School Athletes to Be Overlooked for Sports Schol-
arships," News Channel 12, 3, 11, February 26, 2021, https://keyt.com/sports/2021/02/26
/californias-pandemic-shut-downs-cause-local-high-school-athletes-to-be-overlooked-for
-sports-scholarships; Eric Sondheimer, "Lost Year: How High School Athletes Coped During COVID-19 Pandemic," *Los Angeles Times*, March 11, 2021, https://www.latimes.com
/sports/highschool/story/2021-03-11/coronavirus-shutdown-high-schools-negative-impact
-athletes; Nancy Haggerty, "National Signing Day: Schools Recognize College-Bound Athletes in New Ways Amid Pandemic," *Lohud*, November 11, 2020, https://www.lohud.com
/story/sports/high-school/2020/11/11/schools-adapt-pandemic-covid-new-look-national
-signing-day/6247386002.

36. "Celebrating School Food Service Workers," 10 Boston, May 1, 2020, https://www
.nbcboston.com/news/local/celebrating-school-food-service-workers/2116836; Jennifer Gaddis and Amy Rosenthal, "Cafeteria Workers Need Support During the COVID-19 Pandemic," *USA Today*, updated April 6, 2020, https://www.usatoday.com/story/opinion/2020/04
/05/cafeteria-workers-risking-their-health-feed-vulnerable-students-column/2939584001;
Eliza W. Kinsey et al., "School Closures During COVID-19: Opportunities for Innovation in

Meal Service," *American Journal of Public Health* 110, no. 11 (2020): 1635–43, https://www
.ncbi.nlm.nih.gov/pmc/articles/PMC7542295; Ashlea Braun, Joshua D. Hawley, and Jennifer A. Garner, "Maintaining School Foodservice Operations in Ohio During COVID-19:
"This [Was] Not the Time to Sit Back and Watch," *International Journal of Environmental
Research and Public Health* 19, no. 10 (2022): 5991, https://www.ncbi.nlm.nih.gov/pmc
/articles/PMC9141818; Kara Clifford Billings, Sarah A. Donovan, and Sylvia L. Bryan, *The
School Foodservice Workforce: Characteristics and Labor Market Outcomes*, Congressional Research Service, July 27, 2022, https://crsreports.congress.gov/product/pdf/R/R47199;
"Newark Public Schools' Superintendent León Praises Food Service 'Frontline Workers'
Who Have Distributed Over 100,000 Meals to Students," City of Newark, News, April 23,
2020, https://www.newarknj.gov/news/newark-public-schools-superintendent-leon-praises
-food-service-frontline-workers-who-have-distributed-over-100-000-meals-to-students.

37. Gaddis and Rosenthal, "Cafeteria Workers Need Support During the COVID-19
Pandemic."

38. Mandy McLaren and Naomi Martin, "Lost in a World of Words," in The Great
Divide series, *Boston Globe*, October 4, 2023, https://www.bostonglobe.com/metro/literacy.

Chapter 5

1. Jon Marcus, "What Researchers Learned About Online Higher Education During the Pandemic," *Hechinger Report*, October 6, 2022, https://hechingerreport.org/what
-researchers-learned-about-online-higher-education-during-the-pandemic; Cathy Li and
Farah Lalani, "The COVID-19 Pandemic Has Changed Education Forever. This Is How,"
World Economic Forum, April 29, 2020, https://www.weforum.org/agenda/2020/04
/coronavirus-education-global-covid19-online-digital-learning; "Schools Took Immediate
Steps at Beginning of COVID-19 Pandemic to Connect Students to Online Learning, NCES
Report Shows," National Center for Education Statistics, February 22, 2022, https://nces
.ed.gov/whatsnew/press_releases/2_22_2022.asp; "Remote Learning During COVID-19:
Lessons From Today, Principles for Tomorrow," World Bank, n.d., https://www.worldbank
.org/en/topic/edutech/brief/how-countries-are-using-edtech-to-support-remote-learning
-during-the-covid-19-pandemic; Dan Li, "The Shift to Online Classes During the Covid-19
Pandemic: Benefits, Challenges, and Required Improvements From the Students' Perspec-
tive," *Electronic Journal of e-Learning* 20, no. 1 (2022), https://files.eric.ed.gov/fulltext
/EJ1333732.pdf; Tawnell D. Hobbs and Lee Hawkins, "The Results Are in for Remote
Learning: It Didn't Work," *Wall Street Journal*, June 5, 2020, https://www.wsj.com/articles
/schools-coronavirus-remote-learning-lockdown-tech-11591375078; David John Lemay,
Paul Bazelais, and Tenzin Doleck, "Transition to Online Learning During the COVID-19
Pandemic," *Computers in Human Behavior Reports* 4 (August–December 2021), https://
www.sciencedirect.com/science/article/pii/S2451958821000786; Tara Garcia Mathew-
son, "Most Schools Are Completely Unprepared for Coronavirus and Virtual Learning,"
PBS NewsHour, https://www.pbs.org/newshour/education/most-schools-are-completely
-unprepared-for-coronavirus-and-virtual-learning; Teun J. de Vries, "The Pandemic That
Has Forced Teachers to Go Online. Zooming In on Tips for Online Teaching," *Frontiers in
Education* 6 (2021), https://www.frontiersin.org/articles/10.3389/feduc.2021.647445/full.

2. Teresa Haller and Shally Novita, "Parents' Perceptions of School Support During COVID-19: What Satisfies Parents?" *Frontiers in Education* 6 (September 14, 2021),
https://www.frontiersin.org/articles/10.3389/feduc.2021.700441/full; "82% of Parents
Unprepared for at-Home Learning: Homes.com Survey," *PR Newswire*, July 16, 2020,
https://www.prnewswire.com/news-releases/82-of-parents-unprepared-for-at-home

-learning-homescom-survey-301095082.html; Thomais Rousoulioti, Dina Tsagari, and Christina Nicole Giannikas, "Parents' New Role and Needs During the COVID-19 Educational Emergency," *Interchange* 53 (June 1, 2022): 429–55, https://link.springer.com/article /10.1007/s10780-022-09464-6; Sheila Reeves, "The Effect of Virtual Learning on Parents During COVID," master's thesis, Andrews University, 2021, https://digitalcommons .andrews.edu/cgi/viewcontent.cgi?article=1190&context=theses.

3. Beyhan Farhadi and Sue Winton, "Building a Plane While Flying: Crisis Policy Enactment During COVID-19 in Alberta Secondary Schools," *Journal of Teaching and Learning* 15, no. 2 (2021): 117–32, https://eric.ed.gov/?id=EJ1313646; Malcolm Brown, "Education in the Time of the Virus; or, Flying the Plane While Building It," *Educause Review*, April 6, 2020, https://er.educause.edu/blogs/2020/4/education-in-the-time-of-the -virus-or-flying-the-plane-while-building-it.

4. Maddie Martin, "The Advantages and Disadvantages of Learning in Online Classes in 2023," Thinkific, March 31, 2023, https://www.thinkific.com/blog/advantages-and -disadvantages-online-classes; Antonio J. Carrion et al., "Impact of COVID-19 on the Academic Performance and Mental Health of HBCU Pharmacy Students," *Currents in Pharmacy Teaching and Learning* 15, no. 2 (2023): 123–29, https://www.ncbi.nlm.nih.gov /pmc/articles/PMC9977613; "Remote Teaching During the Pandemic Disadvantages Students in New Jersey's Lower-Income School Districts," Rutgers, n.d., https://www.rutgers .edu/news/remote-teaching-during-pandemic-disadvantages-students-new-jerseys-lower -income-school; Andrea Westphal et al., "K–12 Teachers' Stress and Burnout During the COVID-19 Pandemic: A Systematic Review," *Frontiers in Psychology* 13 (September 2, 2022), https://www.ncbi.nlm.nih.gov/pmc/articles/PMC9479001.

For the impact of online learning on English as a Second Language learners, see Leslie Villegas and Amaya Garcia, *Educating English Learners During the Pandemic: Insights From Experts, Advocates, and Practitioners* (New America, April 2022), https://files.eric .ed.gov/fulltext/ED619505.pdf. We also have been struck by, although rarely addressed, how the internet truncated hand gestures, which many educators and students use to communicate. See Susan Goldin-Meadow, *Thinking With Your Hands: The Surprising Science Behind How Gestures Shape Our Thoughts* (Basic Books, 2023).

5. Kalhan Rosenblatt, "High School Students Miss End-of-Year Traditions as Coronavirus Spreads," *NBC News*, March 27, 2020, https://www.nbcnews.com/news/us-news/high -school-students-miss-end-year-traditions-coronavirus-spreads-n1169186; Veda Morgan, "The Unforgettable Class of 2020: Missing Out on Memories, Coping With a Pandemic," *Courier Journal*, May 21, 2020, https://www.courier-journal.com/in-depth/opinion/2020 /05/21/class-2020-coronavirus-caused-graduates-miss-out-memories/5216065002; Taylor Trudon, "'We Feel Lost in Time': Covid Transforms Teen Milestones," *New York Times*, May 3, 2021, https://www.nytimes.com/2021/05/03/well/family/teen-milestones-prom -graduation.html.

6. Heather Hollingsworth and Carolyn Thompson, "Test Scores Show American Students Slipping Further Behind Despite Recovery Efforts," Associated Press, July 11, 2023, https://apnews.com/article/standardized-test-scores-pandemic-school-caf7eb10e5964c 2f654f9621dd4b6648; Sarah Mervosh and Ashley Wu, "Math Scores Fell in Nearly Every State, and Reading Dipped on National Exam," *New York Times*, October 24, 2022, https://www.nytimes.com/2022/10/24/us/math-reading-scores-pandemic.html; Donna St. George, "National Test Scores Plunge, With Still No Sign of Pandemic Recovery," *Washington Post*, June 21, 2023, https://www.washingtonpost.com/education/2023/06/21 /national-student-test-scores-drop-naep.

7. Ashley Abramson, "Capturing the Benefits of Remote Learning," *Monitor on Psychology* 52, no. 6 (2021): 46, https://www.apa.org/monitor/2021/09/cover-remote-learning; Andrew J. Martin, Rebecca J. Collie, and Robin P. Nagy, "Adaptability and High School Students' Online Learning During COVID-19: A Job Demands–Resources Perspective," *Frontiers in Psychology* 12 (August 17, 2021), https://www.frontiersin.org/articles/10.3389/fpsyg.2021.702163/full; Shivangi Dhawan, "Online Learning: A Panacea in the Time of COVID-19 Crisis," *Journal of Educational Technology Systems* 49, no. 1, https://journals.sagepub.com/doi/full/10.1177/0047239520934018.

8. Sergio A. Costa et al., "Moving Education Online During the COVID-19 Pandemic: Thinking Back and Looking Ahead," *Frontiers in Public Health*, October 25, 2021, https://doi.org/10.3389/fpubh.2021.751685; Andrew A. Tawfik et al., "First and Second Order Barriers to Teaching in K–12 Online Learning, *TechTrends* 65, no. 6 (2021): 925–38, https://www.ncbi.nlm.nih.gov/pmc/articles/PMC8372684; Darren Turnbull, Ritesh Chugh, and Jo Luck, "Transitioning to e-Learning During the COVID-19 Pandemic: How Have Higher Education Institutions Responded to the Challenge?" *Education and Information Technologies* 26 (2021): 6401–19, https://link.springer.com/article/10.1007/s10639-021-10633-w; Nancy L. Leech et al., "The Challenges of Remote K–12 Education During the COVID-19 Pandemic: Differences by Grade Level," *Online Learning Journal* 26, no. 1 (2022): 245–67, https://www.cde.state.co.us/educatortalent/remote-teaching-challenges-by-grade-level; "Homework Gap and Connectivity Divide," Federal Communications Commission, n.d., https://www.fcc.gov/about-fcc/fcc-initiatives/homework-gap-and-connectivity-divide; Pew Charitable Trusts, "States Tap Federal CARES Act to Expand Broadband," Pew, November 16, 2020, https://www.pewtrusts.org/en/research-and-analysis/issue-briefs/2020/11/states-tap-federal-cares-act-to-expand-broadband; John Busby, Julia Tanberk, and Tyler Cooper, "BroadbandNow Estimates Availability for All 50 States; Confirms That More Than 42 Million Americans Do Not Have Access to Broadband," BroadbandNow, November 8, 2023, https://broadbandnow.com/research/fcc-broadband-overreporting-by-state; Patrick Wall, "Schools Scale Back Home Internet Help as Remote Learning Fades," Chalkbeat, September 27, 2022, https://www.chalkbeat.org/2022/9/27/23373910/schools-remote-learning-home-internet-access.

9. "The Digital Divide Among Students During COVID-19: Who Has Access? Who Doesn't?" CRPE, ASU, June 2020, https://crpe.org/the-digital-divide-among-students-during-covid-19-who-has-access-who-doesnt; Dania V. Francis and Christian E. Weller, "Economic Inequality, the Digital Divide, and Remote Learning During COVID-19," *Review of Black Political Economy* 49, no. 1 (2021), https://www.ncbi.nlm.nih.gov/pmc/articles/PMC8914302; John Roese, "COVID-19 Exposed the Digital Divide. Here's How We Can Close It," World Economic Forum, January 27, 2021, https://www.weforum.org/agenda/2021/01/covid-digital-divide-learning-education.

10. Here we are not discussing asynchronous learning where educators videotaped themselves and then shared the video with students as a prime delivery system. We have had that technology for years. Some of us used it with older students when we were absent from class before the pandemic but it was rare and suboptimal, as it did not involve student engagement.

11. Shira Ovide, "The Faded but Winning Pandemic Star," *New York Times*, August 18, 2022, https://www.nytimes.com/2022/08/18/technology/chromebooks-pandemic-star.html; Kevin Bushweller, "What the Massive Shift to 1-to-1 Computing Means for Schools, in Charts," *Education Week*, May 17, 2022, https://www.edweek.org/technology/what-the-massive-shift-to-1-to-1-computing-means-for-schools-in-charts/2022/05; Jillian Fellows

and Don Reid, "The Pandemic Brought a Technological Revolution to Schools. Is That a Good Thing?" *Petoskey News-Review*, November 12, 2022, https://www.petoskeynews .com/story/news/education/2022/11/12/the-pandemic-brought-a-technological-revolution -to-schools-is-that-a-good-thing/69620969007.

12. Katherine Reynolds Lewis, "What the Covid-19 Pandemic Revealed About Remote School," *Smithsonian Magazine*, July 14, 2023, https://www.smithsonianmag.com /innovation/what-the-covid-19-pandemic-revealed-about-remote-school-180982530; "COVID-19's Effect on High-Tech and Software M&A Dealmaking," West Monroe, December 8, 2020, https://www.westmonroe.com/perspectives/in-brief/covid-19-effect-on-high -tech-software-merger-acquisition-dealmaking; Sophie Foggin, "5 e-Learning Platforms Assisting Schools During COVID-19," Publicize, April 14, 2020, updated February 17, 2022, https://publicize.co/startup-resources/5-e-learning-platforms-assisting-schools-during-covid -19. See also Denise Ammeraal Furlong, *Voices of Newcomers: Experiences of Multilingual Learners* (EduMatch, 2022).

13. Pew Charitable Trusts, "States Tap Federal CARES Act to Expand Broadband"; Riordan Frost, "Pandemic Highlights Disparities in High-Speed Internet Service," Joint Center for Housing Studies, September 8, 2021, https://www.jchs.harvard.edu/blog/pandemic -highlights-disparities-high-speed-internet-service; Busby, Tanberk, and Cooper, "Broadband-Now Estimates Availability for All 50 States."

14. "Comcast Launches New Internet Essentials Programs as Nation Gears Up for the Academic Year," Comcast, August 13, 2020, https://corporate.comcast.com/press/releases /new-internet-essentials-programs-schools-students-families-connected-academic-year; U.S. Department of Education, "Helping Students, Families, and Communities Access the Internet and Technology-Enabled Learning Opportunities," *HomeRoom* (blog), June 10, 2022, https://blog.ed.gov/2022/06/helping-students-families-and-communities-access-the-internet -and-technology-enabled-learning-opportunities; Martin Giles, "Free Software That Businesses, Schools and Others Can Use During the COVID-19 Crisis," *Forbes*, March 19, 2020, https://www.forbes.com/sites/martingiles/2020/03/19/free-software-for-businesses -and-schools-covid19/?sh=157c6005752d; "Project 10 Million," T-Mobile, n.d., https:// www.t-mobile.com/business/education/project-10-million; "Free Computers to Help Marginalised Children Learn During Coronavirus School Closures," Theirworld, April 23, 2020, https://theirworld.org/news/free-computers-american-children-low-income-homes -coronavirus-schools-shutdown.

15. Matt Zalaznick, "Creativity in Crisis: WiFi Buses Narrow the Digital Divide," District Administration, April 27, 2020, https://districtadministration.com/creativity-in-crisis -wifi-buses-narrow-the-digital-divide; Taylor Ekbatani, "School Bus Wi-Fi Hotspots Aide [*sic*] Student Learning During COVID-19 Closures," *School Transportation News*, April 8, 2020, https://stnonline.com/special-reports/school-bus-wi-fi-hotspots-aide-student-learning -during-covid-19-closures; Nathan Mattise, "In the COVID-19 Era, the Wheels on the Bus Increasingly Bring Wi-Fi," *Ars Technica*, April 15, 2020, https://arstechnica.com/information -technology/2020/04/in-the-covid-19-era-the-wheels-on-the-bus-increasingly-bring-wi-fi; Alaa Elassar, "Austin School District Deployed Over 100 School Buses Equipped With WiFi for Students Without Internet Access," CNN, April 14, 2020, https://www.cnn.com/2020/04 /14/us/austin-wifi-busses-independent-school-district-trnd/index.html.

16. Taylor Ekbatani, "FCC Approves School Bus Wi-Fi Hotspots Under COVID-19 Emergency Connectivity Fund," *School Transportation News*, May 19, 2021, https:// stnonline.com/news/fcc-approves-school-bus-wi-fi-hotspots-under-covid-19-emergency -connectivity-fund.

17. Caroline Parker, "How to Route Wi-Fi for Students Who Need Internet Access," EdNC, June 22, 2020, https://www.ednc.org/how-to-deploy-smart-buses-for-students-who-need-internet-access; "Complete Guide to School Bus WiFi," Kajeet, n.d., https://f.hubspotusercontent10.net/hubfs/367813/Kajeet-SchoolBusWifi-Guide%20(1).pdf.

18. "Wi-Fi-Enabled School Buses Leave No Child Offline," *PBS NewsHour*, January 22, 2016, https://www.pbs.org/newshour/show/wi-fi-enabled-school-buses-leave-no-child-offline; Julia McCandless, "School Buses Equipped With Wi-Fi Help to Bridge the Digital Divide," Government Technology, August 1, 2016, https://www.govtech.com/education/k-12/school-buses-equipped-with-wi-fi-help-to-bridge-the-digital-divide.html; Michael Trucano, "Mobile Internet Buses, Vans, and Classrooms to Support Teachers & Learners in Remote Communities," *World Bank Blogs*, April 27, 2016, https://blogs.worldbank.org/en/education/mobile-internet-buses-vans-and-classrooms; Imran A. Zualkernan, Shirin Lutfeali, and Asad Karim, *Using Tablets and Satellite-Based Internet to Deliver Numeracy Education to Marginalized Children in a Developing Country* (American University of Sharjah, Save the Children, Teletaleem [Pvt] Limited, 2015), https://resourcecentre.savethechildren.net/pdf/using_tablets_and_satellite-based_internet_to_deliver_numeracy_education.pdf; Indrajit Basu, "Internet Connected School Buses Work Wonders," Government Technology, August 2, 2010, https://www.govtech.com/dc/articles/internet-connected-school-buses-work-wonders.html.

19. "Complete Guide to School Bus WiFi"; Lauraine Langreo, "Wi-Fi on School Buses: Smart Move or Stupidest Idea Ever?" *Education Week*, May 18, 2022, https://www.edweek.org/technology/wi-fi-on-school-buses-smart-move-or-stupidest-idea-ever/2022/05; Lexi Lonas and Rebecca Klar, "Republicans Take On FCC Over Proposal to Add Wi-Fi to School Buses," *The Hill*, October 9, 2023, https://thehill.com/homenews/education/4242184-republicans-fcc-wifi-school-buses; Bijay Laxmi, "Digital Divide or Fiscal Misstep? FCC's Proposal to Equip School Buses With Wi-Fi Sparks Political Debate," BNN, [October 2023], https://bnn.network/world/us/digital-divide-or-fiscal-misstep-fccs-proposal-to-equip-school-buses-with-wi-fi-sparks-political-debate.

Chapter 6

1. Both authors have written about change, separately and together. See, e.g., "Karen Gross: Good Things Have Happened in Higher Education During the Pandemic," *New England Diary* (blog), December 2, 2022, https://newenglanddiary.com/blog/y3qnvvpdm67xub6v03hmd39dxz1e02/12/1/2022. Erin Richards et al., "A Year After COVID-19 Shut Schools, Students and Teachers Share What Shook Them—and What Strengthened Them," *USA Today*, March 21, 2021, updated March 23, 2021, https://www.usatoday.com/in-depth/news/education/2021/03/21/covid-online-school-1-year-teachers-kids-share-powerful-quotes/4652348001.

2. For the pace of change in education, see "Lessons Learned #9: Glacial Pace of Change," Ian Symmonds and Associates, July 19, 2016, https://iansymmonds.org/blog/2016/7/19/lessons-learned-9-glacial-pace-of-change; James A. Kadamus, "R.I.'s Glacial Pace of School Reform," *Providence Journal*, February 13, 2018, https://www.providencejournal.com/story/opinion/2018/02/13/my-turn-james-a-kadamus-ris-glacial-pace-of-school-reform/14807402007; Ken Rogoff, "Glacial Universities Need to Reinvent Themselves and Welcome Technology," *Financial Review*, February 12, 2018, https://www.afr.com/opinion/glacial-universities-need-to-reinvent-themselves-and-welcome-technology-20180211-h0vw2a; Karen Gross, "Let's Think Differently About Change to Understand Why It's So Difficult," Aspen Institute, July 12, 2017, https://www

.aspeninstitute.org/blog-posts/lets-think-differently-about-change-to-understand-why-its
-so-difficult; Penny Bauder, "Karen Gross: 'Here Are 5 Things We Should Do to Improve
the US Education System,'" interview with Karen Gross, Medium, December 2, 2019,
https://medium.com/authority-magazine/karen-gross-here-are-5-things-we-should-do-to
-improve-the-us-education-system-b250d2e2510.

3. The term *leapfrog* is taken from Emiliana Vegas and Rebecca Winthrop, "Beyond
Reopening Schools: How Education Can Emerge Stronger Than Before COVID-19," Brookings, September 8, 2020, https://www.brookings.edu/articles/beyond-reopening-schools-how
-education-can-emerge-stronger-than-before-covid-19. See also Karen Gross, "Karen Gross:
Words vs. Action," *VTDigger*, May 27, 2018, https://vtdigger.org/2018/05/27/karen-gross
-words-vs-action.

4. For the score, see Marc-André Hamelin, *Four Perspectives for Cello and Piano*, musical score, 2016 (C. F. Peters, 2018), https://content.alfred.com/catpages/98-EP68615.pdf.
For a review of a concert at which this piece was played, see Lee Eiseman, "Top Soloists
Collaborated With Style and Warmth," *Boston Musical Intelligencer*, October 11, 2023,
https://www.classical-scene.com/2023/10/11/collaborate.

5. For a sampling of the controversies and debates, see Holly Korbey, "Should Textbooks Still Play a Role in Schools?" Edutopia, June 9, 2023, https://www.edutopia.org
/article/should-textbooks-still-play-a-role-in-schools; Katherine Schulten, "Banned Books,
Censored Topics: Teaching About the Battle Over What Students Should Learn," *New York
Times*, September 22, 2022, updated September 24, 2022, https://www.nytimes.com/2022
/09/22/learning/lesson-plans/banned-books-censored-topics-teaching-about-the-battle-over
-what-students-should-learn.html; Akilah Alleyne, "Book Banning, Curriculum Restrictions,
and the Politicization of U.S. Schools," CAP 20, Center for American Progress, September 19,
2022, https://www.americanprogress.org/article/book-banning-curriculum-restrictions-and
-the-politicization-of-u-s-schools; Judith L. Pace, Eric Soto-Shed, and Elizabeth Yeager
Washington, "Teaching Controversial Issues When Democracy Is Under Attack," Brookings, January 31, 2022, https://www.brookings.edu/articles/teaching-controversial-issues
-when-democracy-is-under-attack.

6. Bauder, "Karen Gross: Here Are 5 Things We Should Do"; Allison Dampier, "What
Are the Different Types of Academic Assessment Tests?" *Advantages DLS Education Blog*,
n.d., https://advantages-dls.com/types-academic-assessment-tests.

Some assessment tests are the National Assessment of Educational Progress (NAEP),
Iowa Test of Basic Skills (ITBS), Star, Massachusetts Comprehensive Assessment System
(MCAS), and Colorado Student Assessment Program (CSAP).

7. Valerie Strauss, "Confirmed: Standardized Testing Has Taken Over Our Schools.
But Who's to Blame?" *Washington Post*, October 24, 2015, https://www.washingtonpost
.com/news/answer-sheet/wp/2015/10/24/confirmed-standardized-testing-has-taken-over
-our-schools-but-whos-to-blame; Lyndsey Layton, "Study Says Standardized Testing Is
Overwhelming Nation's Public Schools," *Washington Post*, October 24, 2015, https://www
.washingtonpost.com/local/education/study-says-standardized-testing-is-overwhelming
-nations-public-schools/2015/10/24/8a22092c-79ae-11e5-a958-d889faf561dc_story
.html.

8. Matthew Lynch, "What Debates Are Currently Being Had About Education Assessments?" *Edvocate*, August 22, 2022, https://www.theedadvocate.org/what-debates-are
-currently-being-had-about-education-assessments; Terri S. Wilson and Matthew Hastings,
"Refusing the Test: Debating Assessment and Accountability in Public Education," *Journal
of Cases in Educational Leadership* 24, no. 3 (2021), https://journals.sagepub.com/doi/10

.1177/1555458921993181; Santhosh Areekkuzhiyil, "Issues and Concerns in Classroom Assessment Practices," *Edutracks* 20, no. 8 (2021): 20–23, https://files.eric.ed.gov/fulltext /ED613841.pdf; Gavin T. L. Brown, "The Past, Present, and Future of Educational Assessment: A Transdisciplinary Perspective," *Frontiers in Education* 7 (November 11, 2022), https://www.frontiersin.org/articles/10.3389/feduc.2022.1060633/full; Karen Gross, "We Are Missing Teachable Moments: This Math Example Is but One," LinkedIn, November 3, 2015, https://www.linkedin.com/pulse/we-missing-teachable-moments-math-example-one -karen-gross/?forceNoSplash=true.

9. National Academy of Education, *Educational Assessments in the COVID-19 Era and Beyond* (National Academy of Education, 2021), https://naeducation.org/wp-content /uploads/2021/02/Educational-Assessments-in-the-COVID-19-Era-and-Beyond.pdf; Adam E. Wyse, "The Potential Impact of COVID-19 on Student Learning and How Schools Can Respond," *Educational Measurement* 39, no. 3 (2020): 60–64, https://www.ncbi.nlm .nih.gov/pmc/articles/PMC7405060; Valerie Strauss, "It Looks Like the Beginning of the End of America's Obsession With Student Standardized Tests," *Washington Post*, June 21, 2020, https://www.washingtonpost.com/education/2020/06/21/it-looks-like-beginning-end -americas-obsession-with-student-standardized-tests; "Rethinking Standardized Tests," National Education Association, March 19, 2021, last updated May 26, 2021, https:// www.nea.org/advocating-for-change/new-from-nea/rethinking-standardized-tests; Kelly Field, "To Test or Not to Test? Educators Weigh the Value of Standardized Testing During a Pandemic," *Hechinger Report*, February 12, 2021, https://hechingerreport.org/to-test-or -not-to-test-educators-weigh-the-value-of-standardized-testing-during-a-pandemic.

10. Katie Lannan, "Mass. Standardized Tests Scores Drop in Pandemic," GBH, September 21, 2021, updated August 9, 2023, https://www.wgbh.org/culture/2021-09-21 /mass-standardized-tests-scores-drop-in-pandemic; Sequoia Carrillo, "U.S. Reading and Math Scores Drop to Lowest Level in Decades," NPR, June 21, 2023, https://www.npr.org /2023/06/21/1183445544/u-s-reading-and-math-scores-drop-to-lowest-level-in-decades; Associated Press, "Test Scores Dropped to Lowest Levels in Decades During Pandemic, According to Nationwide Exam," *NBC News*, https://www.nbcnews.com/news/us-news /test-scores-dropped-lowest-levels-decades-pandemic-according-nationwid-rcna53659.

11. Richard Welsh, "Suspending Suspensions: Time to Reexamine Discipline in Schools in the Age of COVID-19," Metropolitan Center for Research on Equity and the Transformation of Schools, New York University/Steinhardt, n.d., https://steinhardt.nyu.edu /metrocenter/suspending-suspensions-time-reexamine-discipline-schools-age-covid-19; Nadia Tamez-Robledo, "There's Still Time to Do School Discipline Differently, Researcher Says," EdSurge, August 11, 2022, https://www.edsurge.com/news/2022-08-11-there-s-still -time-to-do-school-discipline-differently-researcher-says; Eesha Pendharkar, "Here's How the Pandemic Changed School Discipline," *Education Week*, November 28, 2022, https:// www.edweek.org/leadership/heres-how-the-pandemic-changed-school-discipline/2022/11; Claudia G. Vincent et al., "Blending Restorative Practices With Multitiered Support Systems in High Schools Before and During the COVID Pandemic: Successes, Challenges, and Adaptations," *NAASP Bulletin* 107, no. 3 (2023), https://www.ncbi.nlm.nih.gov/pmc /articles/PMC10285470.

For references to data collection on discipline by the federal government, which compiles state data, see "School Climate and Student Discipline Resources: Know the Data," U.S. Department of Education, n.d., https://www2.ed.gov/policy/gen/guid/school-discipline /data.html; "Data on School Disciplinary Actions: Who Collects Data on School Disciplinary Actions and for What Purpose?" Public Health Informatics Institute, n.d., https://phii

.org/module-5/data-on-school-disciplinary-actions; "Race, Discipline, and Safety at U.S. Public Schools," American Civil Liberties Union, n.d., https://www.aclu.org/issues/juvenile -justice/school-prison-pipeline/race-discipline-and-safety-us-public-schools. For state data collection on discipline, see, e.g., "School and District Profiles," DESE, n.d., https://profiles .doe.mass.edu/ssdr/default.aspx?orgcode=00000000&org"ypecode=0&=00000000&.

12. At the collegiate level, one of the coauthors frequently disagreed with her dean of students, who was rule bound with regard to discipline. The coauthor saw the need to contextualize misbehavior, focus on its origins, and then offer restorative justice. She provides concrete examples in Karen Gross, *Trauma Doesn't Stop at the School Door: Strategies and Solutions for Educators, PreK–College* (Teachers College Press, 2020), 131–34. Recalling the suspension of a student who had no home to go to, she wondered how the punishment could be right—even if the student did destroy a window during an outburst.

13. Karen Gross, *Finding Hope Amidst Traumatic Events: Can Trauma Improve Education?* Samuel Dewitt Proctor Institute for Leadership, Equity, and Justice, n.d., https:// proctor.gse.rutgers.edu/sites/default/files/Can%20Trauma%20Improve%20Education%3F .pdf; Karen Gross, "Behavior Is the Language of Trauma," *BBN Times*, September 8, 2022, https://www.bbntimes.com/society/behavior-is-the-language-of-trauma; Karen Gross, "What *Not* to Do When the Principal Is Knocked Unconscious," Medium, November 12, 2021, https://medium.com/age-of-awareness/what-not-to-do-when-the-principal-is-knocked -unconscious-f2360e04a946; Karen Gross, "We Need Fewer School Police Officers and More Trauma Interventionalists," Medium, August 17, 2021, https://medium.com/age -of-awareness/we-need-fewer-school-police-officers-and-more-trauma-interventionalists -e90bbb95b25e.

14. Associated Press, "Schools Face Pressure to Take Harder Line on Discipline," *U.S. News*, January 21, 2023, https://www.usnews.com/news/us/articles/2023-01-21/schools -face-pressure-to-take-harder-line-on-discipline; Carly Graf, "The Newest Form of School Discipline: Kicking Kids out of Class and Into Virtual Learning," *Hechinger Report*, August 7, 2023, https://hechingerreport.org/the-newest-form-of-school-discipline-kicking-kids -out-of-class-and-into-virtual-learning; Elizabeth Heubeck, "Is Virtual Learning a New Form of Exclusionary Discipline?" *Education Week*, September 11, 2023, https://www .edweek.org/leadership/is-virtual-learning-a-new-form-of-exclusionary-discipline/2023/09.

15. On the importance of making mental wellness a priority, see Michele Nealon, "The Pandemic Accelerant: How COVID-19 Advanced Our Mental Health Priorities," *UN Chronicle*, United Nations, October 9, 2021, https://www.un.org/en/un-chronicle/pandemic -accelerant-how-covid-19-advanced-our-mental-health-priorities. HIPAA stands for Health Insurance Portability and Accountability Act. "Telehealth Guidance by State During CO-VID-19," American Psychological Association Services, n.d., https://www.apaservices.org /practice/clinic/covid-19-telehealth-state-summary; "HIPAA and COVID-19," U.S. Department of Health and Human Services, n.d., https://www.hhs.gov/hipaa/for-professionals /special-topics/hipaa-covid19/index.html; "Telehealth in the Pandemic—How Has It Changed Health Care Delivery in Medicaid and Medicare?" *Watchblog: Following the Federal Dollar*, U.S. Government Accountability Office, September 29, 2022, https://www .gao.gov/blog/telehealth-pandemic-how-has-it-changed-health-care-delivery-medicaid-and -medicare.

16. Melissa Boudin, "Answering the Call: The Benefits of Teletherapy for Teens and Young Adults," National Council for Mental Wellbeing, July 4, 2021, https://www .thenationalcouncil.org/answering-the-call-the-benefits-of-teletherapy-for-teens-and -young-adults; "Teletherapy for Kids: Keeping Them Engaged," Therapy Brands, June 7,

2022, https://therapybrands.com/blog/keeping-kids-and-teens-engaged-during-teletherapy; Beverly Ford, "Finding Privacy at Home: 5 Tips for Remote Therapy Visits," *Boston Globe*, n.d., https://sponsored.bostonglobe.com/bcbsma/private-remote-therapy.

17. Hannah Calkins, "Telehealth Is Here to Stay. Psychologists Should Equip Themselves to Offer It," *Monitor on Psychology* 53, no. 7 (2022): 30, https://www.apa.org/monitor/2022/10/future-of-telehealth; Zara Abrams, "How Well Is Telepsychology Working?" *Monitor on Psychology* 51, no. 5 (2020): 46, https://www.apa.org/monitor/2020/07/cover-telepsychology; João Bocas, "5 Key Advantages of Technology in Mental Health Treatments," Digital Salutem, March 22, 2023, https://digitalsalutem.com/technology-in-mental-health-treatments/#:~:text=One%20of%20the%20main%20drawbacks,connection%20as%20in%2Dperson%20therapy; John C. Markowitz et al., "Psychotherapy at a Distance," *American Journal of Psychiatry* 178, no. 3 (2020): 240–46, https://ajp.psychiatryonline.org/doi/10.1176/appi.ajp.2020.20050557; Amy J. L. Baker et al., "Successes, Challenges, and Opportunities in Providing Evidence-Based Teletherapy to Children Who Have Experienced Trauma as a Response to Covid-19: A National Survey of Clinicians," *Children and Youth Services Review* 146 (March 2023), https://www.ncbi.nlm.nih.gov/pmc/articles/PMC9872563; Katherine M. Boydell et al., "Using Technology to Deliver Mental Health Services to Children and Youth: A Scoping Review," *Journal of the Canadian Academy of Child and Adolescent Psychiatry* 23, no. 2 (2014): 87–99, https://www.ncbi.nlm.nih.gov/pmc/articles/PMC4032077.

18. Christina Baker, "School-Based Mental Health Services: What Can the Partnership Look Like?" *Counseling Today*, January 1, 2013; "School and Community Programs," Child Mind Institute, n.d., https://childmind.org/school-and-community.

19. The importance of mental health and social and emotional learning is detailed throughout Parts I and II, including in the discussion in Chapter 3.

20. Karen Gross, "How to Address Student Wellness, Post-Pandemic," *University Business*, May 26, 2020, https://universitybusiness.com/what-is-wellness-post-pandemic.

21. Brent Harger, "A Culture of Aggression: School Culture and the Normalization of Aggression in Two Elementary Schools," *British Journal of Sociology of Education* 40, no. 8 (2019): 1105–1120, https://cupola.gettysburg.edu/cgi/viewcontent.cgi?article=1048&context=socfac.

22. Juliana F. W. Cohen et al., "Implementation of Universal School Meals During COVID-19 and Beyond: Challenges and Benefits for School Meals Programs in Maine," *Nutrients* 14, no. 19 (2022): 4031, https://www.ncbi.nlm.nih.gov/pmc/articles/PMC9571988; "What Works in Schools: Safe and Supportive School Environments," Division of Adolescent and School Health, Centers for Disease Control and Prevention, last reviewed March 13, 2023, https://www.cdc.gov/healthyyouth/whatworks/what-works-safe-and-supportive-environments.htm; "School Support Staff," National Center on Safe Supportive Learning Environments, n.d., https://safesupportivelearning.ed.gov/training-technical-assistance/roles/school-support-staff; Jamie Bussel, "How School Meals Help Families Impacted by the Pandemic," Robert Wood Johnson Foundation, March 16, 2021, https://www.rwjf.org/en/insights/blog/2021/03/how-school-meals-help-families-impacted-by-the-pandemic.html; Scott Jaschik, "'Breakaway Learners': Author Discusses Her New Book About Promoting Success of At-Risk Students," interview with Karen Gross, *Inside Higher Ed*, July 25, 2017, https://www.insidehighered.com/news/2017/07/26/author-discusses-her-new-book-how-colleges-can-help-risk-students-succeed.

23. Pierre Tristam, "Schools Are Safer Than Your Home," FlaglerLive.com, August 13, 2018, https://flaglerlive.com/school-safety-pt/#gsc.tab=0; "When School Is Safer

Than Home During a Pandemic," M Live, September 28, 2020, updated September 29, 2020, https://www.mlive.com/news/2020/09/when-school-is-safer-than-home-during-a -pandemic.html; "Closed Schools Could Be Putting Children at Risk During the COVID-19 Pandemic," *Northeastern Global News*, November 10, 2023, https://news.northeastern .edu/2020/10/13/closed-schools-could-be-putting-children-at-risk-during-the-covid-19 -pandemic; David Schwartz et al., "The Link Between Harsh Home Environments and Negative Academic Trajectories Is Exacerbated by Victimization in the Elementary School Peer Group," *Developmental Psychology* 49, no. 2 (2013): 305–16, https://www.ncbi.nlm .nih.gov/pmc/articles/PMC3470830.

24. Kimberly A. Schonert-Reichl, "Social and Emotional Learning and Teachers," *Future of Children* 27, no. 1 (2017): 137–155, https://files.eric.ed.gov/fulltext/EJ1145076 .pdf; Katherine Bradley, "The Roles of a Teacher Outside the Classroom," Classroom, n.d., https://classroom.synonym.com/info-8127889-teacher-compensation-extracurricular -activities.html; Judith Taack Lanier, "Redefining the Role of the Teacher: It's a Multifaceted Profession," Edutopia, July 1, 1997, https://www.edutopia.org/redefining-role-teacher; Matt Barnum, "The Teaching Profession Is Facing a Post-Pandemic Crisis," Chalkbeat, June 27, 2023, https://www.chalkbeat.org/2023/6/27/23774375/teachers-turnover-attrition-quitting -morale-burnout-pandemic-crisis-covid; Alex T. Valencic, "Teaching Versus Teachering: Extra Duties of Teachers," Teach Better, March 10, 2022, https://teachbetter.com/blog/teaching -versus-teachering-extra-duties-of-teachers.

25. "Breaking the Cycle: Addressing Social Issues in Schools," Budsies, February 3, 2023, https://www.budsies.com/blog/guest-blog/social-issues-in-schools; "What Are Schools Doing to Address Societal Problems?" Teachers Network, n.d., http://teachersnetwork.org /everywhere/Brady/mod_3.6.htm; William Parrett and Kathleen Budge, "What Can Schools Do to Address Poverty?" Edutopia, December 10, 2015, https://www.edutopia.org/blog /what-can-schools-do-to-address-poverty-william-parrett-kathleen-budge.

Others disagree. See David F. Labaree, "The Winning Ways of a Losing Strategy: Educationalizing Social Problems in the United States," *Educational Theory* 58, no. 4 (2008): 447–60, https://onlinelibrary.wiley.com/doi/abs/10.1111/j.1741-5446.2008.00299.x; Valerie Strauss, "Problems That Schools Are Expected to Solve," *Washington Post*, September 16, 2013, https://www.washingtonpost.com/news/answer-sheet/wp/2013/09/16/problems-that -schools-are-expected-to-solve.

26. Mark Anderson and William Johnson, "A New Model: Schools as Ecosystems," Chalkbeat, February 6, 2012, https://ny.chalkbeat.org/2012/2/6/21096801/a-new-model -schools-as-ecosystems; Richard Arum, "Schools and Communities: Ecological and Institutional Dimensions," *Annual Review of Sociology* 26 (August 2000): 395–418, https:// www.jstor.org/stable/223450.

27. Arum, "Schools and Communities."

28. Nirvi Shah, "'Year of School Choice' Promise Collides With Reality of Litigation-Caused Delays," *Education Next*, March 28, 2023, https://www.educationnext.org/year-of -school-choice-promise-collides-with-reality-of-litigation-caused-delays; Tareena Musaddig et al., "The Pandemic's Effect on Demand for Public Schools, Homeschooling, and Private Schools," *Journal of Public Economics* 212 (August 2022), https://www.sciencedirect .com/science/article/abs/pii/S0047272722001128; Jude Schwalbach, "Parents Can Be Satisfied With Public Schools and Also Want More Educational Choices," Reason Foundation, October 4, 2023, https://reason.org/commentary/parents-can-be-satisfied-with-public -schools-and-want-more-educational-choices.

29. Jon Marcus, "What Researchers Learned About Online Higher Education During the Pandemic," *Hechinger Report*, October 6, 2022, https://hechingerreport.org/what -researchers-learned-about-online-higher-education-during-the-pandemic: Ben Kirshner et al., "Students Learned So Much More During the Pandemic Than We Realize. Just Ask Them," EdSurge, October 11, 2021, https://www.edsurge.com/news/2021-10-11-students -learned-so-much-more-during-the-pandemic-than-we-realize-just-ask-them; Nadia Nandlall et al., "Learning Through a Pandemic: Youth Experiences With Remote Learning During the COVID-19 Pandemic," *SAGE Open* 12, no. 3 (2022), https://www.ncbi.nlm.nih .gov/pmc/articles/PMC9511001; Marva Hinton, "Some Students Have Taken to Remote Learning. They're Thriving, in Fact," *School Library Journal*, January 12, 2021, https:// www.slj.com/story/some-students-have-taken-to-remote-learning-theyre-thriving-in-fact -COVID-coronavirus.

30. Daphne Kis, "How COVID-19 Is Ending the Stigma of Online Learning," World Economic Forum, June 1, 2021, https://www.weforum.org/agenda/2021/06/covid-19-is -ending-the-stigma-of-online-learning-higher-education-workplace-candidate-evaluation -future-of-work.

31. Jonathan Smith, "Q&A: Future Pandemics Are Inevitable, but We Can Reduce the Risk," *Horizon*, December 16, 2021, https://ec.europa.eu/research-and-innovation/en /horizon-magazine/qa-future-pandemics-are-inevitable-we-can-reduce-risk; David Heymann, Emma Ross, and Jon Wallace, "The Next Pandemic—When Could It Be?" Chatham House, February 23, 2022, https://www.chathamhouse.org/2022/02/next-pandemic -when-could-it-be; Peter Banacos, "The Great Vermont Flood of 10–11 July 2023: Preliminary Meteorological Summary," National Weather Service, August 5, [2023], https://www.weather.gov/btv/The-Great-Vermont-Flood-of-10-11-July-2023-Preliminary -Meteorological-Summary.

32. "Geostationary Satellites," Hurricanes: Science and Society, University of Rhode Island, n.d., https://hurricanescience.org/science/observation/satellites/geostationary; Marcin Frąckiewicz, "The Use of Satellites in Detecting Natural Disasters," TS2, May 13, 2023.

33. "3 Reasons Why Strategic Plans Are Absolutely a Waste of Time," Core Impact Coaching, July 20, 2020, https://www.coreimpactcoaching.com/why-strategic-business -plan-sits-on-the-shelf; "What Government's Broken Strategic Planning Needs: Evidence," *Government Executive*, July 26, 2018, https://www.govexec.com/management/2018/07 /what-governments-broken-strategic-planning-needs-evidence/150073; "Boost Your Business With a One-Page Strategic Action Plan," Amend, November 10, 2015, https://amendllc .com/building-a-one-page-strategic-action-plan; "Reconsider Active Shooter Drills," Everytown for Gun Safety, n.d., https://www.everytown.org/solutions/active-shooter-drills; Elc Estrera, "Do Active-Shooter Drills Hurt Students?" Urban Institute, May 4, 2023, https:// www.urban.org/research/publication/do-active-shooter-drills-hurt-students; Danielle Myers, "Why Schools Should Rethink the Century-Old Fire Drill Emergency Response Approach," *Security*, November 30, 2021, https://www.securitymagazine.com/articles/96607 -why-schools-should-rethink-the-century-old-fire-drill-emergency-response-approach.

34. Jessica Lau, "Preparing for the Next Pandemic," T. H. Chan School of Public Health, Harvard, July 28, 2022, https://www.hsph.harvard.edu/news/features/preparing -for-next-pandemic-g7-pact; Dalal Alsaeed et al., "Are We Ready for the Next Pandemic? Lessons Learned From Healthcare Professionals' Perspectives During the COVID-19 Pandemic," *Frontiers in Public Health* 11 (March 30, 2023), https://www.frontiersin.org

/articles/10.3389/fpubh.2023.1048283/full; Meagan C. Fitzpatrick, Rachel Nuzum, and Alison P. Galvani, "Lessons From COVID-19 Can Help the U.S. Prepare for the Next Pandemic," *Commonwealth Fund*, July 5, 2023, https://www.commonwealthfund.org/blog /2023/lessons-covid-19-can-help-us-prepare-next-pandemic; Athena Aktipis and Keith G. Tidball, "How Each of Us Can Prepare for the Next Pandemic," *Scientific American*, May 11, 2021, https://www.scientificamerican.com/article/how-each-of-us-can-prepare -for-the-next-pandemic; "How to Prepare for the Next Pandemics?" Epi Guard, n.d., https://epiguard.com/how-to-prepare-for-next-pandemics; Tom Inglesby, "How to Prepare for the Next Pandemic," *New York Times*, March 12, 2023, https://www.nytimes.com /2023/03/12/opinion/pandemic-health-prepare.html.

35. "What Is Military Readiness?" Institute for Defense and Business, n.d., https:// www.idb.org/what-is-military-readiness; "The Army's Vision and Strategy," U.S. Army, n.d., https://www.army.mil/about; "About the US Army War College," U.S. Army, https:// www.armywarcollege.edu/overview.cfm; U.S. Army, *Academic Program Guide: Academic Year 2023* (U.S. Army War College, n.d.), https://www.armywarcollege.edu/documents /Academic%20Program%20Guide.pdf; Nell McCormack Abom, "Peace at the Root of the U.S. Army War College," LinkedIn, June 13, 2016, https://www.linkedin.com/pulse /peace-root-us-army-war-college-nell-mccormack-abom.

36. Caitlynn Peetz, "4 Tips to Help Schools Prepare for the Next Pandemic," *Education Week*, July 17, 2023, https://www.edweek.org/leadership/4-tips-to-help-schools -prepare-for-the-next-pandemic/2023/07; "Preparing for a Pandemic Illness: Guidelines for School Administrators and School Crisis Response Teams," National Association of School Psychologists, 2020, https://www.nasponline.org/resources-and-publications /resources-and-podcasts/school-safety-and-crisis/health-crisis-resources/preparing-for-a -pandemic-illness-guidelines-for-school-administrators-and-school-crisis-response-teams; Westyn Branch-Elliman, Lloyd Fisher, and Shira Doron, "The Next 'Pandemic Playbook' Needs to Prioritize the Needs of Children—and a Clear Roadmap for Opening Schools," *Antimicrobial Stewardship & Healthcare Epidemiology* 3, no. 1 (2023): e82, https://www .ncbi.nlm.nih.gov/pmc/articles/PMC10173290.

Chapter 7

1. See generally Karen Gross, *Breakaway Learners: Strategies for Post-Secondary Success With At-Risk Students* (Teachers College Press, 2016); Karen Gross, *Trauma Doesn't Stop at the School Door: Strategies and Solutions for Educators, PreK–College* (Teachers College Press, 2020). See also Alfie Kohn, "What We Don't Know About Our Students— and Why We Don't Know It," *HuffPost*, September 7, 2011, https://www.huffpost.com /entry/teacher-education-students_b_946575; Karen Gross, "Why It's So Hard to Understand Our Students and Help Them," LinkedIn, May 30, 2018, https://www.linkedin.com /pulse/why-its-so-hard-understand-our-students-help-them-karen-gross.

2. AJE-DC, "Have You Ever Thought About Observing Your Child's Classroom? Or Their Proposed Classroom? You Can!" Advocates for Justice and Education, February 8, 2022, https://www.aje-dc.org/2022/02/08/have-you-ever-thought-about-observing-your -childs-classroom-or-their-proposed-classroom-you-can; "School Preparation," *Achieve Virtual Blog*, n.d., https://achievevirtual.org/blog/parent-resources/a-parents-role-in-virtual -education; Valerie Kirk, "10 Reasons Parents Switched to Virtual School," Connections Academy, September 29, 2021, https://www.connectionsacademy.com/support/resources /article/why-parents-choose-online-school; Amy Roy et al., "A Preliminary Examination

of Key Strategies, Challenges, and Benefits of Remote Learning Expressed by Parents During the COVID-19 Pandemic," *PsyArXiv Reprints*, February 8, 2021, last edited July 13, 2021, https://osf.io/preprints/psyarxiv/5ca4v; Ashley Abramson, "Capturing the Benefits of Remote Learning," *Monitor on Psychology* 52, no. 6 (2021): 46, https://www.apa.org/monitor/2021/09/cover-remote-learning.

3. For more on how teachers can share with students online, see Richard West, "Teacher, Are You There? Being 'Present' in Online Learning," *Educause Review*, February 3, 2021, https://er.educause.edu/blogs/2021/2/teacher-are-you-there-being-present-in-online-learning.

4. For a discussion of the positive impact of pets in classrooms, see Sarah D. Young, "How Do Pets in the Classroom Impact Student Learning?" Consumer Affairs, August 30, 2017, https://www.consumeraffairs.com/news/how-do-pets-in-the-classroom-impact-student-learning-083017.html#:~:text=Improved%20social%20interaction.&text=One%20study%20showed%20kids%20actually,responsibility%2C%20respect%2C%20and%20empathy. For how online learning can humanize educators and others in the workplace, see Olasile Babatunde Adedoyin and Emrah Soykan, "Covid-19 Pandemic and Online Learning: The Challenges and Opportunities," *Interactive Learning Environments* 31, no. 2 (2023): 863–875, https://www.researchgate.net/profile/Olasile-Adedoyin/publication/344146577_Covid-19_pandemic_and_online_learning_the_challenges_and_opportunities/links/5fdd00e8299bf14088228a04/Covid-19-pandemic-and-online-learning-the-challenges-and-opportunities.pdf; Shamontiel L. Vaughn, "Is It Unprofessional for Your Pet to Interrupt a Video Call?" October 3, 2022, https://blackgirlinadoggoneworld.substack.com/p/cats-unprofessional-anti-pet-jobs-managers.

5. In a humorous (or not so humorous) story, a teacher asked a young student why he was wearing a Superman costume. The student replied that his uncle was Superman. The teacher called the mother and stated that her son was lying about knowing Superman and that it was important for students to distinguish facts from fiction and not lie. The mother replied that, well, his uncle actually *was* Superman—he was the actor Henry Cavill, who played Superman in films. As educators, we need to be careful about all the assumptions we make about our students and get to know who they really are—and their stories. "Henry Cavill's Nephew Got in Trouble for Saying Superman Was His Uncle," MediaChomp, June 28, 2021, https://mediachomp.com/henry-cavills-nephew-got-in-trouble-for-saying-superman-was-his-uncle.

6. For examples of strategies, see Karen Gross, "Getting Ready for School: Some Strategies for a Successful Start," LinkedIn, August 6, 2018, https://www.linkedin.com/pulse/getting-ready-school-some-strategies-karen-gross; Karen Gross, "Forced Self-Reflection: Consider These Questions," LinkedIn, February 8, 2018, https://www.linkedin.com/pulse/forced-self-reflection-consider-questions-karen-gross.

7. Alli Lindenberg, "Here's How One Teacher Used Home Visits to Reconnect With Disengaged Students," EdNC, May 6, 2021, https://www.ednc.org/heres-how-one-teacher-used-home-visits-to-reconnect-with-disengaged-students.

8. The benefits of report cards are mixed. See "The Good, the Bad, and the Ugly of Report Cards," Best Brains Learning Centers, December 20, 2017, https://bestbrains.com/article/the-good-the-bad-and-the-ugly-of-report-cards; "Why I Don't Let My Kids Read Their Report Cards (and I'm a Teacher!)," Today's Parent, June 22, 2022, https://www.todaysparent.com/kids/school-age/why-i-dont-let-my-kids-read-their-report-cards-and-im-a-teacher; "What a Report Card Tells Us (and What Doesn't)," Kobi, February 25, 2021, https://kobiapp.io/en/blog/what-a-report-card-tells-us-and-what-doesnt.

9. Alyson Klein, "Pandemic Parents Are More Engaged. How Can Schools Keep It Going?" *Education Week*, September 14, 2021, https://www.edweek.org/leadership /pandemic-parents-are-more-engaged-how-can-schools-keep-it-going/2021/09; Betül Balkar, Filiz Tuncel, and Burcu Demiroğları, "An Investigation of the Changing Structure of Teacher–Parent Communication and Cooperation in Distance Education in the COVID-19 Pandemic," *Educational Research: Theory and Practice* 33, no. 3 (2022): 136–53, https:// files.eric.ed.gov/fulltext/EJ1366309.pdf.

10. The article by which we were and remain troubled is Sarah Chaves, "Parent Diplomacy Is Overwhelming Teachers," *Atlantic*, September 18, 2023, https://www.theatlantic .com/family/archive/2023/09/teacher-parent-relationships-diplomacy-discussions/675362.

11. While the benefits of online learning can be debated, positives in engagement are indisputable. See Alaa AbdElsamie, "7 Innovative Teaching Strategies to Engage Students in Online Learning," eLearning Industry, April 3, 2023, https://elearningindustry.com /innovative-teaching-strategies-to-engage-students-in-online-learning; Marianna Chade, "7 Strategies to Engage Students in Hybrid and Online Learning," Explain Everything, December 6, 2021, https://explaineverything.com/blog/teaching-trends/7-strategies-to-engage -students-in-hybrid-and-online-learning; Emelina Minero, "8 Strategies to Improve Participation in Your Virtual Classroom," Edutopia, August 21, 2020, https://www.edutopia.org /article/8-strategies-improve-participation-your-virtual-classroom.

12. While hybrid learning and its positives are not addressed in detail in this book, literature exists on the topic. It should be stated that for some educators, hybrid learning was exhausting, difficult, and deeply challenging. "COVID-19 Response—Hybrid Learning," UNESCO, December 2020, https://en.unesco.org/sites/default/files/unesco-covid-19 -response-toolkit-hybrid-learning.pdf; Mark Bedoya Ulla and William Franco Perales, "Hybrid Teaching: Conceptualization Through Practice for the Post COVID19 Pandemic Education," *Frontiers in Education* 7 (June 22, 2022), https://www.frontiersin.org/articles /10.3389/feduc.2022.924594/full; Safia Samee Ali, "Educators Teaching Online and in Person at the Same Time Feel Burned Out," *NBC News*, October 18, 2020, https://www .nbcnews.com/news/us-news/educators-teaching-online-person-same-time-feel-burned-out -n1243296.

13. Karen Gross and Ed Wang, *The Feeling Alphabet Activity Set* (Amazon Press, 2022). For a description of box breathing, see "What Is Box Breathing?" WebMD, April 30, 2023, https://www.webmd.com/balance/what-is-box-breathing.

14. Alison Cook-Sather, "Students as Learners and Teachers: Taking Responsibility, Transforming Education, and Redefining Accountability," *Curriculum Inquiry* 40, no. 4 (2010): 555–575, https://repository.brynmawr.edu/cgi/viewcontent.cgi?article=1010& context=edu_pubs; Júlia Llompart, "Students as Teachers, Teacher as Learner: Collaborative Plurilingual Teaching and Learning in Interaction," in *Plurilingual Classroom Practices and Participation* (Routledge, 2021), 54–65, https://www.researchgate.net/publication /362955220_Students_as_teachers_teacher_as_learner; Judith Taack Lanier, "Redefining the Role of the Teacher: It's a Multifaceted Profession," Edutopia, July 1, 1997, https://www .edutopia.org/redefining-role-teacher.

15. Ghislaine Boulanger, "Fearful Symmetry: Shared Trauma in New Orleans After Hurricane Katrina," *Psychoanalytic Dialogues* 23 (2013): 31–44, http://www.pardess.info /wp-content/uploads/Fearful-Symmetry-Shared-Trauma-in-New-Orleans-After-Katerina -2013-Boulanger.pdf; Douglas Stuart Faust, "After the Storm: Katrina's Impact on Psychological Practice in New Orleans," *Professional Psychology Research and Practice* 39,

no. 1 (2008): 1–6, https://www.researchgate.net/publication/232517484_After_the_Storm
_Katrina%27s_Impact_on_Psychological_Practice_in_New_Orleans.

16. Karen Gross, "Behavior Is the Language of Trauma," Medium, July 24, 2022, https://karengrossedu.medium.com/behavior-is-the-language-of-trauma-ab9ba15b7071.

17. Karen Gross and Cynthia Prather, "Well-Being in Classrooms After COVID-19: A '3-D' Approach for Addressing Student Trauma," *Delta Kappa Gamma Bulletin* 88, no. 1 (2021): 6–13.

18. "How to Make Online Learning More Engaging and Interactive," Upjourney, updated March 7, 2023, https://upjourney.com/how-to-make-online-learning-more-engaging-and-interactive; Karen Gross, "Engaging the Disengaged College Student: Whether Learning Is Online or In-Person," *Evolllution*, n.d., https://evolllution.com/programming/teaching-and-learning/engaging-the-disengaged-college-student-whether-learning-is-online-or-in-person; Karen Gross, "Can Online Learning Be Trauma-Responsive?" New England Board of Higher Education, August 18, 2020, https://nebhe.org/journal/can-online-learning-be-trauma-responsive.

19. On student problems with transitions, see Katherine Martinelli, "Why Do Kids Have Trouble With Transitions?" Child Mind Institute, November 6, 2023, https://childmind.org/article/why-do-kids-have-trouble-with-transitions; Thomas J. Stacho, "My Students Have Trouble With Transitions . . . What Can I Do?" (paper presented at the 11th annual NorthWest PBIS Conference, Eugene, Oregon, February 27–March 1, 2013), https://www.behaviorinschools.com/My_Students_Have_a_Hard_Time_with_Transitions.pdf; Emma (Teach Starter), "5 Secrets to Classroom Transitions That Actually Work," Teach Starter, [August 2023], https://www.teachstarter.com/us/blog/the-secret-to-effective-classroom-transitions-us.

20. "Teaching in Flexible Learning Spaces," Columbia Center for Teaching and Learning, n.d., https://ctl.columbia.edu/resources-and-technology/teaching-with-technology/teaching-online/flexible-spaces; Danny Mareco, "How Technology in the Classroom Improves Learning With Flex Spaces," Secure Edge, July 24, 2012, https://www.securedgenetworks.com/blog/how-technology-in-the-classroom-improves-learning-with-flex-spaces; "How Virtual Breakout Rooms for Students Promote Active Learning," Echo360, n.d., https://echo360.com/articles/how-virtual-breakout-rooms-for-students-promote-active-learning; Lamont Moore, "Small-Group Instruction Using Virtual Breakout Rooms," Graduate Programs for Educators, June 26, 2020, https://www.graduateprogram.org/2020/06/small-group-instruction-using-virtual-breakout-rooms.

21. "Chunking, Scaffolding, Pacing," Digital Learning, University of Washington, Tacoma, https://www.tacoma.uw.edu/digital-learning/chunking-scaffolding-pacing; Liam O'Donovan, "The Importance of Content Chunking for Effective e-Learning Development," Firmwater, May 28, 2021, https://firmwater.com/e-learning; Christopher Pappas, "6 eLearning Content Chunking Strategies to Apply in Instructional Design," eLearning Industry, August 28, 2016, https://elearningindustry.com/elearning-content-chunking-strategies-apply-instructional-design.

22. See "Seat Time," The Glossary of Education Reform, updated August 29, 2013, https://www.edglossary.org/seat-time; Esther Wojcicki, "Re-Envisioning the 'Seat-Time' Algorithm in Education," Media at Stanford University, n.d., https://mediax.stanford.edu/program/insights-perspectives/re-envisioning-the-seat-time-algorithm-in-education; "What Is Seat Time?" Colorado Succeeds, March 31, 2021, https://coloradosucceeds.org/what-is-seat-time; Dana Kleinjan, "Movement Matters: The Importance of Incorporating Movement in the Classroom," NW Commons, Northwestern College, Spring 2020,

https://nwcommons.nwciowa.edu/cgi/viewcontent.cgi?article=1209&context=education
_masters; "Structuring a 45 Minute Class Period," *Maneuvering the Middle* (blog), n.d.;
https://www.maneuveringthemiddle.com/structuring-a-45-minute-class-period; Dean Kir-
chick, "Back to 45 Minutes: Why We Should Return to Our Old Schedule Next Year,"
University Student News, November 5, 2020, https://universityschoolnews.com/3837
/oped/back-to-45-why-we-should-return-to-our-old-schedule-next-year.

23. Leonardo Rocker, "6 Signs Your Child Is Overscheduled," Quirky Kid, n.d.,
https://www.childpsychologist.com.au/resources/6-signs-your-child-is-overscheduled; Sid
Kirchheimer, "Overscheduled Child May Lead to a Bored Teen," WebMD, n.d., https://
www.webmd.com/parenting/features/overscheduled-child-may-lead-to-bored-teen; Nicola
Appleton, "How to Help Your 'Overprogrammed' Kids Deal With the Stress and Pressure," Verywell Family, June 21, 2022, https://www.verywellfamily.com/how-to-help-your
-overprogrammed-kids-deal-with-the-stress-and-pressure-5341313.

24. Debates about homework predate the pandemic but arose then in the online context. See Lauren Barack, "How Homework Is Changing During Online Learning," K–12
Dive, December 23, 2020, https://www.k12dive.com/news/how-homework-is-changing
-during-online-learning/592535; Daniel Lempres, "How Has the Pandemic Changed
the Way Educators Think About Homework?" EdSurge, January 19, 2022, https://www
.edsurge.com/news/2022-01-19-how-has-the-pandemic-changed-the-way-educators-think
-about-homework; Sarah D. Sparks, "This One Change From Teachers Can Make Homework More Equitable," *Education Week*, December 5, 2022, https://www.edweek.org
/leadership/this-one-change-from-teachers-can-make-homework-more-equitable/2022/12;
Harris Cooper, Jorgianne Civey Robinson, and Erika A. Patall, "Does Homework Improve Academic Achievement? A Synthesis of Research, 1987–2003," *Review of Educational Research* 76, no. 1 (2006): 1–62, https://assess.ucr.edu/sites/default/files/2019-02
/cooperrobinsonpatall_2006.pdf; Karen Gross, "Homework for Students and Quarterbacks: Often a Mistake," Medium, July 31, 2022, https://medium.com/age-of-awareness
/homework-for-students-and-quarterbacks-often-a-mistake-93b8c92d78cd.

Chapter 8

1. Enriqueta C. Bond, Kenne Dibner, and Heidi Schweingruber, eds., *Reopening
K–12 Schools During the COVID-19 Pandemic: Prioritizing Health, Equity, and Communities* (National Academies, 2020), https://nap.nationalacademies.org/catalog/25858
/reopening-k-12-schools-during-the-covid-19-prioritizing; "Glimpses of How
Pandemic America Went Back to School," *New York Times*, September 17, 2021, updated
September 22, 2021, https://www.nytimes.com/2021/09/17/education/learning/schools
-reopening-united-states.html; Karen Gross, "My Blood Is Boiling: We Are Missing Key Lessons in Education Post-Pandemic," Medium, August 11, 2022, https://medium.com/age-of
-awareness/my-blood-is-boiling-we-are-missing-key-lessons-in-education-post-pandemic
-675148fe6689; "Back to School and Back to Normal. Or at Least Close Enough," *New
York Times*, October 6, 2022, updated October 19, 2022, https://www.nytimes.com/2022
/10/06/education/learning/students-schools-colleges-pandemic-life.html.

Reopening also was accompanied by protests. Rachel M. Cohen and Paul Abowd,
"As Schools Reopen, Teachers, Parents, and Students Are Pushing Back," *Intercept*, August 3, 2020, https://theintercept.com/2020/08/03/reopening-schools-coronavirus.

2. Bianca Vázquez Toness and Sharon Lurye, "Thousands of Kids Are Missing From
School. Where Did They Go?" Associated Press, February 9, 2023, https://projects.apnews
.com/features/2023/missing-children/index.html; Brian Flood, "School Avoidance Alliance

Founder Says Cutting Class Isn't Always Truancy, Mental Health Issues Could Be Cause,"
Fox News, October 8, 2023, https://www.foxnews.com/media/school-avoidance-alliance
-founder-cutting-class-truancy-mental-health-issues-cause.amp; Libby Stanford, "Students
Are Missing School Because They're Too Anxious to Show Up," *Education Week,* October 6, 2023, https://www.edweek.org/leadership/students-are-missing-school-because
-theyre-too-anxious-to-show-up/2023/10; "Fast Facts," National Center for Education
Statistics, n.d., https://nces.ed.gov/fastfacts/display.asp?id=372; James Vaznis and Deanna
Pan, "Asian American Families Overwhelmingly Reject Full-Time Return to BPS Classrooms This Month," *Boston Globe,* updated April 14, 2021, https://www.bostonglobe
.com/2021/04/14/metro/asian-american-families-overwhelmingly-reject-full-time-return
-bps-classrooms-this-month.

3. Adriana Gomez Licon and Adam Geller, "US Debates School Reopening, WHO
Warns 'No Return to Normal,'" *Medical Press,* July 14, 2020, https://medicalxpress.com
/news/2020-07-debates-school-reopening.html; "As California Schools Reopen to In-Person
Instruction, Students and Families Decide If It's Right for Them," EdSource, April 22, 2021,
https://edsource.org/2021/as-california-schools-reopen-to-in-person-instruction-students
-and-families-decide-if-its-right-for-them/652944; Donna St. George, "How the Pandemic
Is Reshaping Education," *Washington Post,* March 15, 2021, https://www.washingtonpost
.com/education/2021/03/15/pandemic-school-year-changes.

4. Anya Kamenetz, "When It Comes to Reopening Schools, 'the Devil's in the Details,'
Educators Say," NPR, July 9, 2020, https://www.npr.org/2020/07/09/888878030/when-it
-comes-to-reopening-schools-the-devil-s-in-the-details-educators-say; "School Reopening
Data," Washington Office of Superintendent of Public Instruction, n.d., https://ospi.k12
.wa.us/about-ospi/news-releases-and-statements/novel-coronavirus-covid-19-guidance
-resources/school-reopening-data; "In Their Own Words, Americans Describe the Struggles and Silver Linings of the COVID-19 Pandemic," Pew Research Center, March 5,
2021, https://www.pewresearch.org/2021/03/05/in-their-own-words-americans-describe
-the-struggles-and-silver-linings-of-the-covid-19-pandemic.

5. Nicole Chavez, "Some Students Already Started Classes. Here's What We Have
Learned So Far About America's Schools in the Pandemic," CNN, August 15, 2020,
https://www.cnn.com/2020/08/14/us/schools-reopening-pandemic-lessons/index.html; Cohen and Abowd, "As Schools Reopen, Teachers, Parents, and Students Are Pushing Back."

6. Colette Davidson, "Behind the Masks, Teachers and Students Struggle to Communicate," *Christian Science Monitor,* September 30, 2020, https://www.csmonitor.com/World
/Europe/2020/0930/Behind-the-masks-teachers-and-students-struggle-to-communicate;
"Communicating Effectively While Wearing Masks," American Speech-Language-Hearing
Association, n.d., https://www.asha.org/public/communicating-effectively-while-wearing
-masks-and-physical-distancing; "How Mask Mandates Are Impacting Students' Ability
to Learn," Safe 'n' Clear, April 30, 2021, https://safenclear.com/how-mask-mandates-are
-impacting-students-ability-to-learn.

While not addressed here, the difficulties for students and educators with hearing loss
were profound. See, e.g., "Why People With a Hearing Loss Struggle With Face Masks,"
A&HAA, September 15, 2021, https://lagrandehearing.org/patient-resources/news/why
-people-with-a-hearing-loss-struggle-with-face-masks.

7. See generally Karen Gross, *Trauma Doesn't Stop at the School Door: Strategies
and Solutions for Educators, PreK–College* (Teachers College Press, 2020); Maria Salas,
"Recognizing Trauma in Students as Kids Head Back to School," *Texas A&M Today,*
August 15, 2022, https://today.tamu.edu/2022/08/15/recognizing-trauma-in-students-as

-kids-head-back-to-school; Roisleen Todd, "Recognizing the Signs of Trauma," Edutopia, October 27, 2021, https://www.edutopia.org/article/recognizing-signs-trauma; Cindy Long, "Educators Use Own Trauma to Support Students in Crisis," National Education Association, May 4, 2023, https://www.maetoday.org/new-from-mae/educators-use-own -trauma-support-students-crisis; Autumn Jones, "I'm a Teacher Headed Back to School Next Month. It's Going to Be Traumatic," Chalkbeat Colorado, July 29, 2020, https://co .chalkbeat.org/2020/7/29/21345927/im-a-teacher-headed-back-to-school-next-month-its -going-to-be-traumatic.

8. Deborah McMakin, Amy Ballin, and Diana Fullerton, "Secondary Trauma, Burn-out, and Teacher Self-Care During COVID19: A Mixed-Methods Case Study," *Psychology in the Schools* 60, no. 5 (2023): 1442–58, https://www.ncbi.nlm.nih.gov/pmc/articles /PMC9349654; Glenys Oberg, Annemaree Carroll, and Stephanie Macmahon, "Compassion Fatigue and Secondary Traumatic Stress in Teachers: How They Contribute to Burnout and How They Are Related to Trauma-Awareness," *Frontiers in Education* 8 (March 14, 2023), https://www.frontiersin.org/articles/10.3389/feduc.2023.1128618/full; Sarah Gonser, "What to Do About Increasing Dysregulation in the Early Grades," Edutopia, August 25, 2023, https://www.edutopia.org/article/tackling-misbehavior-in-the-early -grades. Trauma in students predated the pandemic for sure. See Emelina Minero, "When Students Are Traumatized, Teachers Are Too," Edutopia, October 4, 2017, https://www .edutopia.org/article/when-students-are-traumatized-teachers-are-too.

9. Jim Geraghty, "How Covid Closures Took a Toll on Kids," *National Review*, April 22, 2022, https://www.nationalreview.com/the-morning-jolt/how-covid-closures-took -a-toll-on-kids; Ellen Almer Durston, Dan Levin, and Juliana Kim, "'I Was So Nervous': Back to Class After a Year Online," *New York Times*, March 9, 2021, updated August 13, 2021, https://www.nytimes.com/2021/03/09/us/schools-reopen-covid.html; Heather Hollingsworth, "This School Reopened Quickly After COVID. Kids' Reading Was Still Behind," *The Hill*, June 10, 2023, https://thehill.com/news/education/this-school-reopened-quickly-after -covid-kids-reading-was-still-behind.

10. Emma Dorn et al., "COVID-19 and Education: The Lingering Effects of Unfinished Learning," Kinsey, July 27, 2021, https://www.mckinsey.com/industries/education /our-insights/covid-19-and-education-the-lingering-effects-of-unfinished-learning; "New Data Show How the Pandemic Affected Learning Across Whole Communities," Harvard Graduate School of Education, May 11, 2023, https://www.gse.harvard.edu/ideas/news/23 /05/new-data-show-how-pandemic-affected-learning-across-whole-communities; Per Engzell, Arun Frey, and Mark D. Verhagen, "Learning Loss due to School Closures During the COVID-19 Pandemic," *PNAS* 118, no. 17 (2021): e2022376118, https://www.pnas .org/doi/10.1073/pnas.2022376118; Valeria Olivares, "Students' Social–Emotional Skills Have Suffered Since the Pandemic Started and Some Predict It Will Only Worsen," *Dallas Morning News*, February 11, 2021, https://www.dallasnews.com/news/education/2021/02 /11/students-social-emotional-skills-have-suffered-since-the-pandemic-started-and-some -predict-it-will-only-worsen; Avi Wolfman-Arent, "A Year Without Play: Parents and Experts Worry About Loss of Social Skills During Pandemic," WHYY PBS, April 21, 2021, https://whyy.org/articles/a-year-without-play-parents-and-experts-worry-about-loss-of -social-skills-during-pandemic.

11. Michelle Fox, "The Coronavirus Pandemic, Nearly a Year Long, Is Hitting Students of Color the Worst," CNBC, February 23 2021, https://www.cnbc.com/2021/02/23 /the-covid-19-pandemic-is-hitting-students-of-color-the-worst.html; Emma Dorn et al., "COVID-19 and Learning Loss—Disparities Grow and Students Need Help," McKinsey,

December 8, 2020, https://www.mckinsey.com/industries/public-sector/our-insights/covid
-19-and-learning-loss-disparities-grow-and-students-need-help; "New Data Show How
the Pandemic Affected Learning Across Whole Communities," https://www.gse.harvard
.edu/ideas/news/23/05/new-data-show-how-pandemic-affected-learning-across-whole
-communities; Cory Turner, "6 Things We've Learned About How the Pandemic Disrupted
Learning," NPR, June 22, 2022, https://www.npr.org/2022/06/22/1105970186/pandemic
-learning-loss-findings.

The calculation of the number of deaths is complex and highly dependent on the date
used and the definitions employed, among other issues such as cause of death. Dan Treglia
et al., "Parental and Other Caregiver Loss due to COVID-19 in the United States: Prevalence by Race, State, Relationship, and Child Age," *Journal of Community Health* 48 (December 14, 2022): 390–397, https://link.springer.com/article/10.1007/s10900-022-01160-x;
"Children's Collaborative for Healing and Support," Covid Collaborative, n.d., https://
www.covidcollaborative.us/initiatives/hidden-pain. However we calculate the number,
students were, and still are, experiencing grief. Tori DeAngelis, "Thousands of Kids Lost
Loved Ones to the Pandemic. Psychologists Are Teaching Them How to Grieve, and Then
Thrive," *Monitor on Psychology* 53, no. 7 (2022, updated 2023): 69, https://www.apa.org
/monitor/2022/10/kids-covid-grief.

12. Frieda Wiley, "How to Make Black Lives Matter During COVID-19," *Yes!*
May 5, 2020, https://www.yesmagazine.org/social-justice/2020/05/05/coronavirus
-black-lives-matter; Madeleine Schachter, "Black Lives Matter and COVID-19: Lessons in Coincidence, Confluence, and Compassion," *International Journal of Information, Diversity & Inclusion* 4, no. 3/4 (2020): 81–86, https://www.jstor.org/stable
/48645287; Black Lives Matter, https://blacklivesmatter.com; Bisola Ojikutu, "Saving
Black Lives During COVID-19: Vaccines Matter," Association of American Medical
Colleges, October 13, 2020, https://www.aamc.org/news/saving-black-lives-during
-covid-19-vaccines-matter.

13. For an understanding of lasticity, see Karen Gross, *Breakaway Learners: Strate-
gies for Post-Secondary Success With At-Risk Students* (Teachers College Press, 2016).
For an overview of resiliency in the context of the pandemic, see Mohammad Javed Ali,
"Innate Human Resilience and COVID-19: Help From an Old Friend to Beat the New
Enemy," *Indian Journal of Ophthalmology* 68, no. 10 (2020): 2061, https://www.ncbi
.nlm.nih.gov/pmc/articles/PMC7727935.

14. See Gross, *Finding Hope Amidst Traumatic Events*; Karen Gross, "Intergenera-
tional Transmission of Trauma: It Is Time to Worry," LinkedIn, October 30, 2020, https://
www.linkedin.com/pulse/intergenerational-transmission-trauma-time-worry-karen-gross;
Karen Gross, "Trauma in the Time of Coronavirus and Beyond: A *NEJHE* Q&A With
Karen Gross," interview by John O. Harney, New England Board of Higher Education,
April 21, 2020, https://nebhe.org/journal/trauma-in-the-time-of-coronavirus-and-beyond
-a-nejhe-qa-with-karen-gross.

15. Ethan Forman, "White Board Has Gloucester High Students Talking," *Gloucester
Daily Times*, December 21, 2023 (e-edition, January 4, 2024), https://www.gloucestertimes
.com/news/local_news/white-board-has-gloucester-high-students-talking/article_759cf92a
-9f7b-11ee-8d7c-ef76a0abfc31.html.

16. "Teacher Has Personalized Handshakes With Every One of His Students," *ABC
News*, February 1, 2017, https://abcnews.go.com/Lifestyle/teacher-personalized-handshakes
-students/story?id=45190825; Dustin Nelson, "This Teacher Has a Special Handshake for

Every Student and It's Fantastic," *Thrillist*, February 1, 2017, https://www.thrillist.com/news/nation/teacher-barry-white-jr-has-handshake-for-every-student.

17. Rhitu Chatterjee, "As School Starts, Teachers Add a Mental-Health Check-In to Their Lesson Plans," NPR, September 2, 2022, https://www.npr.org/sections/health-shots/2022/09/02/1120077364/with-kids-back-in-school-educators-brace-to-help-with-ongoing-mental-health-trou; Jena Brooker, "Schools Bring Mindfulness to the Classroom to Help Kids in the Covid-19 Crisis," *Hechinger Report*, November 23, 2020, https://hechingerreport.org/schools-bring-mindfulness-to-the-classroom-to-help-kids-in-the-covid-19-crisis; Iyus Yosep, Ai Mardhiyah, and Aat Sriati, "Mindfulness Intervention for Improving Psychological Wellbeing Among Students During COVID-19 Pandemic: A Scoping Review," *Journal of Multidisciplinary Healthcare* 16 (2023): 1425–37, https://www.ncbi.nlm.nih.gov/pmc/articles/PMC10224675.

18. Nick Walker, "Curriculum Integration: How to Use Musical Instruments in Cross-Disciplinary Learning," September 15, 2023, Normans Education, https://www.normans.co.uk/blogs/blog/how-to-use-musical-instruments-in-cross-disciplinary-learning; Karen Gross, "Engaging the Disengaged College Student: Whether Learning Is Online or In-Person," *Evolllution*, n.d., https://evolllution.com/programming/teaching-and-learning/engaging-the-disengaged-college-student-whether-learning-is-online-or-in-person.

19. Lori Desautels, "Connections Go a Long Way for Students With Trauma," Edutopia, July 18, 2018, https://www.edutopia.org/article/connections-go-long-way-students-trauma; Nancy Perez, "Classroom Strategies to Support Students Experiencing Trauma," Regional Educational Laboratory Appalachia, December 8, 2021, https://ies.ed.gov/ncee/edlabs/regions/appalachia/blogs/blog51_strategies-to-support-students-experiencing-trauma.asp; Eujeana Starr Hinkle, "Trauma: How the Student Teacher Relationship Impacts Student Success" (master's thesis, Bethel University, 2022), https://spark.bethel.edu/cgi/viewcontent.cgi?article=1836&context=etd; "More Important Than Ever: Trauma-Informed Adult Education," World Education, January 5, 2022; https://worlded.org/more-important-than-ever-trauma-informed-adult-education; Karen Gross, "Stress Abounds: What Can We Do to Help Youth?" Forest of the Rains Productions, October 4, 2022, https://www.forestoftherain.net/click-our-blog-your-voice/stress-abounds-what-can-we-do-to-help-youth-karen-gross-karengrossedu; Karen Gross, "Role-Modeling by Adults Too Often Lacking in COVID-19 Crisis," *New England Diary* (blog), November 25, 2020, https://newenglanddiary.com/blog/v4ooupfyly09ybb3bbo52tigyi4r8m/11/25/2020; Gross, "Behavior Is the Language of Trauma."

20. "How Do I Chunk Content to Increase Learning?" Center for Teaching and Learning, University of Massachusetts Amherst, n.d., https://www.umass.edu/ctl/resources/how-do-i/how-do-i-chunk-content-increase-learning; "Chunking Strategy," Peak Performance Center, n.d., https://thepeakperformancecenter.com/educational-learning/thinking/chunking/chunking-as-a-learning-strategy; Kate Moran, "How Chunking Helps Content Processing," Nielsen Norman Group, March 20, 2016, https://www.nngroup.com/articles/chunking; Dave Cornell, "15 Chunking Examples (Memory Psychology)," HelpfulProfessor.com, August 24, 2023, https://helpfulprofessor.com/chunking-examples-psychology.

21. Gross, "Engaging the Disengaged College Student"; Shaheena Chowdhury, "Red, Yellow and Green: Tell Me What My Learners Mean," Medium, March 11, 2021, https://medium.com/age-of-awareness/red-yellow-and-green-586d26161dba; "Active Engagement Strategies for Each Direct Instruction Component," https://www.shastacoe.org/uploaded/Dept/is/District_Support/Active_Engagement_Strategies_3-17-09.pdf.

22. Holly Korbey, "Should Textbooks Still Play a Role in Schools?" Edutopia, June 9, 2023, https://www.edutopia.org/article/should-textbooks-still-play-a-role-in-schools; Dana Goldstein, "Two States. Eight Textbooks. Two American Stories," *New York Times*, January 12, 2020, https://www.nytimes.com/interactive/2020/01/12/us/texas-vs-california -history-textbooks.html; Grace Chen, "Public Classrooms Say Goodbye Textbooks, Hello e-Texts," *Public School Review*, July 13, 2023, https://www.publicschoolreview.com/blog /public-classrooms-say-goodbye-textbooks-hello-e-texts.

23. Larry Ferlazzo, "Making Current Events Connections to Lessons," *Education Week*, January 29, 2020, https://www.edweek.org/teaching-learning/opinion-making -current-events-connections-to-lessons/2020/01; Kat St. Pierre, "How to Teach With Current Events," *Montessori Life*, American Montessori Society, November 12, 2021, https:// amshq.org/Blog/2021_11_3-How-to-Teach-with-Current-Events; "5 Ways to Incorporate Current Events in the Classroom," The Juice, April 2, 2021, https://thejuicelearning.com /blog/incorporate-current-events-classroom; Karen Gross, "Seizing the Teachable Moment," *Inside Higher Ed*, October 14, 2018, https://www.insidehighered.com/views/2018 /10/15/colleges-should-use-recent-us-supreme-court-confirmation-hearings-teachable-moment; Karen Gross, "Life Lessons From Game 1 of NBA Finals," LinkedIn, June 1, 2018, https://www.linkedin.com/pulse/life-lessons-from-lebron-karen-gross.

24. Karen Gross, "Desire and Will, Not Resources, Are the Main Stumbling Blocks to Change," *Evolllution*, October 25, 2016, https://evolllution.com/managing-institution /higher_ed_business/desire-and-will-not-resources-are-the-main-stumbling-blocks-to -change; Makayla McGeeney, "Molly Stark to Use Karen Gross' 'Lady Lucy's Quest' for Year-Long Study," *Bennington Banner*, August 30, 2016, https://www.benningtonbanner .com/archives/molly-stark-to-use-karen-gross-lady-lucys-quest-for-year-long-study/article _275d4984-d745-5689-b305-635b84faacea.html.

25. Karen Gross, "Mourning and Missing: A Price of Love," Medium, July 15, 2022, https://medium.com/age-of-awareness/mourning-and-missing-a-price-of-love-8728cfc-ca5a. The models of mood swings are available online through Etsy at https://www.etsy .com/listing/1168610663/mood-swings-mini-fairy-garden-swing-set.

26. "Self-regulation is the ability to monitor and manage one's behavior, emotions, or thoughts effectively, adapting to the stressful demands triggered by the environment. Co-regulation is with the support, nurturance, and coaching of others; one monitors and manages one's behavior, emotions, or thoughts effectively, adapting to the stressful demands triggered by the environment," in Desiree W. Murray et al., *Self-Regulation and Toxic Stress Report 1: Foundations for Understanding Self-Regulation From an Applied Perspective*, OPRE Report # 2015-21 (Center for Child and Family Policy, Duke University, January 2015); "Children's Social and Emotional Development Starts With Co-Regulation," National Institute for Children's Health Quality, https://nichq.org/insight/childrens-social -and-emotional-development-starts-co-regulation; Camile Earle-Dennis, "Emotional Self-Management: 8 Tips for Educators to Self-Regulate and Co-Regulate Emotions and Behaviors," Learning Sciences International, January 6, 2021, https://www.learningsciences .com/blog/emotional-self-management-self-regulation-co-regulation; Pamela Li, "How Co-regulation With Parents Develops Into Self-Regulation in Children," Parenting for Brain, last updated October 28, 2023, https://www.parentingforbrain.com/co-regulation; "3 Ways Coregulation Is the Key to Raising an Emotionally Healthy Child," American Society for the Positive Care of Children, n.d., https://americanspcc.org/coregulation; Jenna Elgin and Shanna Alvarez, "Three Pillars of Co-Regulation," Helping Families Thrive, n.d., https://helpingfamiliesthrive.com/three-pillars-of-coregulation.

27. One of the coauthors uses this mitt and has recommended it to others. "Handy Brain Model B-2," Amazon, n.d., https://www.amazon.com/Handy-Brain-Model-B-2-large/dp/B01A3DIRTY.

28. *Dr Dan Siegel's Hand Model of the Brain* (video), YouTube, n.d., https://www.youtube.com/watch?v=LdaUZ_wbD1c; bbbaustralia, "Our Reaction to Stress Explained: How to Use 'The Hand Model of the Brain,'" Building Better Brains, December 24, 2019, https://buildingbetterbrains.com.au/hand-model-of-the-brain.

29. Sarah Hart, *Once Upon a Prime: The Wondrous Connections Between Mathematics and Literature* (Macmillan, 2023). See Cindy Long, "Express Yourself! Arts Integration in the Classroom," *NEA News*, October 12, 2022, https://www.nea.org/nea-today/all-news-articles/express-yourself-arts-integration-classroom; "What Is Arts Integration: An Educators [*sic*] Guide," Institute for Arts Integration and Steam, n.d., https://artsintegration.com/what-is-arts-integration-in-schools.

30. Ashley Taplin, "How to Embed SEL Into Your Instruction," Edutopia, April 8, 2021, https://www.edutopia.org/article/how-embed-sel-your-instruction; "Integration of SEL and Academic Instruction," CASEL Guide to Schoolwide SEL, n.d., https://schoolguide.casel.org/focus-area-3/classroom/integration-of-sel-and-instruction; Meena Srinivasan, "Three Keys to Infusing SEL Into What You Already Teach," *Greater Good Magazine*, June 21, 2019, https://greatergood.berkeley.edu/article/item/three_keys_to_infusing_sel_into_what_you_already_teach.

31. "Beginning Sounds STOMP Game," Forward With Fun, May 7, 2021, https://forwardwithfun.com/beginning-sounds-game-stomp; Andrew E. Budson, "Why Is Music Good for the Brain?" *Harvard Health Blog*, October 7, 2020, https://www.health.harvard.edu/blog/why-is-music-good-for-the-brain-2020100721062; Mitzi Baker, "Music Moves Brain to Pay Attention, Stanford Study Finds," Stanford Medicine News Center, August 1, 2007, https://med.stanford.edu/news/all-news/2007/07/music-moves-brain-to-pay-attention-stanford-study-finds.html; Jena Minnick-Bull, "How Tap Dance Helps Your Child's Education," South Coast Conservatory, May 27, 2022, https://scconservatory.com/blog/2022/05/27/how-tap-dance-helps-your-childs-education.

32. See Part III.

33. Lauren Bromley-Bird, "What Are the Wonderful Wellbeing Benefits of Lego Play as an Adult?" Happiful, updated January 6, 2023, https://happiful.com/what-are-the-wonderful-wellbeing-benefits-of-lego-play-as-an-adult; "Mindfulness and LEGO Bricks," LEGO, n.d., https://www.lego.com/en-us/categories/adults-welcome/article/mindfulness; "8 Relaxing LEGO Sets to Build for Adults," LEGO, n.d., https://www.lego.com/en-us/categories/adults-welcome/article/relaxing-lego-sets-to-build-for-adults.

34. "The Science Behind Fidget Toys," Sensory Edge, September 7, 2021, https://blog.sensoryedge.com/the-science-behind-fidget-toys; "4 Reasons Why Fidget Toys Are Helpful for Kids," Fundemonium, May 17, 2021, https://www.fundemoniumtoys.com/4-reasons-why-fidget-toys-are-helpful-for-kids; Alexia Dellner, "Why All Kids Need a Trauma Toolbox, According to This Educator," Pure Wow, July 20, 2021, https://www.purewow.com/family/trauma-toolbox; "Magnetic Marble Maze Challenge," Hands on as We Grow, n.d., https://handsonaswegrow.com/magnetic-marble-maze; Karen Gross, "Missing Pieces and Filling Holes: Finding Solutions to Enable Student Success," Medium, January 16, 2020, https://medium.com/age-of-awareness/missing-pieces-and-filling-holes-finding-solutions-to-enable-student-success-a31f0475592d.

35. "The Benefits of Play for Adults," *The Beacon* (blog), Luminis Health, May 27, 2019, https://living.aahs.org/behavioral-health/the-benefits-of-play-for-adults; "How Play

Helps Children's Development," NI Direct, n.d., https://www.nidirect.gov.uk/articles/how
-play-helps-childrens-development; "How Play Strengthens Your Child's Mental Health,"
UNICEF, n.d., https://www.unicef.org/parenting/child-development/how-play-strengthens
-your-childs-mental-health; Jackie Mader, "Want Resilient and Well-Adjusted Kids? Let
Them Play," *Hechinger Report*, November 14, 2022, https://hechingerreport.org/want
-resilient-and-well-adjusted-kids-let-them-play; James Calder, "The Importance of Playing With Your Kids," *BBN Times*, July 5, 2020, https://www.bbntimes.com/society/the
-importance-of-playing-with-your-kids; Kimberly Zapata, "The Importance of Play: How
Kids Learn by Having Fun," *Healthline*, September 28, 2020, https://www.healthline.com
/health/the-importance-of-play; "Play Therapy Activities for a Child With Trauma," FCA,
n.d., https://www.thefca.co.uk/what-is-trauma/play-therapy-for-trauma; Rebecca van der
Weij, "Play Is the Natural Expression of Learning, Growing, and Healing," Trauma Research Foundation, August 22, 2022, https://traumaresearchfoundation.org/play-is-the
-natural-expression-of-learning-growing-and-healing; Karen Gross, "Learning to Play
Again in a World Filled With Trauma," Medium, October 7, 2021, https://medium.com
/age-of-awareness/learning-to-play-again-in-a-world-filled-with-trauma-689d09824406.
For many references to play, including play tables and play for adults, see Gross, *Trauma*.

36. "Brain-Building Through Play: Activities for Infants, Toddlers, and Children,"
Center on the Developing Child, Harvard University, n.d., https://developingchild.harvard
.edu/resources/brainbuildingthroughplay; see particularly "6 Games to Play with Toddlers
(2–3 years)," "5 Games and Activities for Children (4–7 years)," "Games and Activities
for Children (8–12 years)," and "6 Playful Activities for Teens (13–17 years)."

37. "7 Writing Prompts for Processing Trauma," Surviving Childhood Trauma, n.d.,
https://survivingchildhoodtrauma.com/2020/05/11/7-writing-prompts-for-processing
-trauma; "30+ Journal Prompts for Trauma Healing: Write to Heal From Trauma," Calm
Sage, August 9, 2022, https://www.calmsage.com/journal-prompts-for-trauma-healing;
Melissa Tayles, "Trauma-Informed Writing Pedagogy: Ways to Support Student Writers Affected by Trauma and Traumatic Stress," National Council of Teachers of English,
May 21, 2021, https://ncte.org/blog/2021/05/trauma-informed-writing-pedagogy-ways
-support-student-writers-affected-trauma-traumatic-stress. Karen Gross was inspired by a
workshop on this topic conducted at Bridgewater College in 2022 by Professor Elizabeth
Lehman, whose work is thoughtful and useful. Louise Chunn, "The Psychology of the To-
Do List—Why Your Brain Loves Ordered Tasks," *Guardian*, May 10, 2017, https://www
.theguardian.com/lifeandstyle/2017/may/10/the-psychology-of-the-to-do-list-why-your
-brain-loves-ordered-tasks; Lauren Kent, "The Psychology Behind To-Do Lists and How
They Can Make You Feel Less Anxious," *CNN Health*, July 14, 2020, https://www.cnn
.com/2020/07/14/health/to-do-lists-psychology-coronavirus-wellness/index.html. There are
even books of lists. See Sandra Choron and Harry Choron, *The Book of Lists for Kids*
(Houghton Mifflin, 1995); Gary Robert Muschla, Judith A. Muschla, and Erin Muschla-
Berry, *The Elementary Teacher's Book of Lists* (John Wiley & Sons, 2010).

38. Jeremy Sutton, "Mirror Neurons and the Neuroscience of Empathy," Positive Psy-
chology.com, September 7, 2023, https://positivepsychology.com/mirror-neurons; Luca
Bonini et al., "Mirror Neurons 30 Years Later: Implications and Applications," *Trends
in Cognitive Sciences* 26, no. 9 (2022), 767–81, https://www.sciencedirect.com/science
/article/pii/S1364661322001346; Karen Gross, "The New Pandas in DC: Why We Can't
and Shouldn't Stop Gawking," LinkedIn, August 23, 2015, https://www.linkedin.com
/pulse/new-pandas-dc-why-we-cant-shouldnt-stop-gawking-karen-gross; Karen Gross,

"Stress Abounds: What Can We Do to Help Youth?" Medium, October 3, 2022, https://medium.com/age-of-awareness/stress-abounds-what-can-we-do-to-help-youth-e8b6ad-c06b5d; Carol S. Jeffers, "On Empathy: The Mirror Neuron System and Art Education," *International Journal of Education & the Arts* 10, no. 15 (2009), https://files.eric.ed.gov/fulltext/EJ859046.pdf.

39. Karen Gross, "Kindness Rock Projects: They're Needed More Than Ever," Medium, July 5 [no year], https://medium.com/age-of-awareness/kindness-rock-projects-theyre-needed-more-than-ever-c7dc08ae819b; Kindness Rocks Project, https://www.thekindnessrocksproject.com; "A Complete Guide to Rock Painting and Spreading a Little Kindness Through Art," Inspire Kindness, n.d., https://inspirekindness.com/blog/rock-painting.

40. Jura Koncius, "What We Kept, What We Ditched, What We Cooked: How Covid Changed the Holidays," *Washington Post*, December 15, 2021, https://www.washingtonpost.com/lifestyle/home/covid-effects-on-holiday-traditions/2021/12/14/ce2e11d0-464c-11ec-95dc-5f2a96e00fa3_story.html; "Culture in 2020: What We Lost and Found in the Year of COVID," *Los Angeles Times*, December 14, 2020, https://www.latimes.com/entertainment-arts/story/2020-12-14/culture-2020-what-we-lost-and-found-in-the-year-of-covid; Kateri Hartman Braithwaite, "Pandemic Rewriting, Strengthening Family Traditions," *Nebraska Today*, December 21, 2021, https://news.unl.edu/newsrooms/today/article/braithwaite-pandemic-rewriting-strengthening-family-traditions; Alyson Krueger, "Not Home for the Holidays," *New York Times*, December 9, 2021, https://www.nytimes.com/2021/12/09/style/new-holiday-traditions-covid.html; Karen Gross, "Thanksgiving This Year (and Others) Won't Be a Hallmark Card . . . and That's OK. . . . . ," Medium, November 22, 2021, https://medium.com/age-of-awareness/thanksgiving-this-year-and-others-wont-be-a-hallmark-card-and-that-s-ok-4a3598ed8df9; Karen Gross, "11 Ways to Create New Holiday Traditions," Upjourney, November 16, 2020, https://upjourney.com/ways-to-create-new-holiday-traditions.

41. Cath Noakes and Henry Burridge, "Attendance Focus Shows Why Good Ventilation in Schools Still Matters," *Tes Magazine*, May 25, 2022, https://www.tes.com/magazine/analysis/general/attendance-focus-shows-why-good-ventilation-schools-still-matters; "Improving Ventilation in Schools, Colleges, and Universities to Prevent COVID-19," U.S. Department of Education, n.d., https://www.ed.gov/improving-ventilation-schools-colleges-and-universities-prevent-covid-19; "Ventilation in Schools and Childcare Programs," Centers for Disease Control and Prevention, updated February 26, 2021, https://www.cdc.gov/coronavirus/2019-ncov/community/schools-childcare/ventilation.html.

42. Mary Filardo, *State of Our Schools: America's K–12 Facilities* (21st Century School Fund, 2016), https://files.eric.ed.gov/fulltext/ED581630.pdf; Amanda Menas, "Educators Speak Out: In Decaying Buildings, We Cannot Keep Students Safe," National Education Association, October 8, 2021, https://www.nea.org/advocating-for-change/new-from-nea/educators-speak-out-decaying-buildings; Erin McIntyre, "Decaying School Buildings Have Physical, Psychological Consequences," K–12 Dive, April 13, 2016, https://www.k12dive.com/news/decaying-school-buildings-have-physical-psychological-consequences/417119; "The Effects of Classroom Temperature on Students' Performance," sitelogiq, May 13, 2021, https://www.sitelogiq.com/blog/effect-classroom-temperature-student-performance; Tim Walker, "It's Getting Hot in Here: Without Air Conditioning, Students and Staff Suffer," *NEA Today*, June 9, 2023, https://www.nea.org/nea-today/all-news-articles/its-getting-hot-here-without-air-conditioning-students-and-staff-suffer.

43. Maria Godoy, "Better Air in Classrooms Matters Beyond COVID. Here's Why Schools Aren't There Yet," NPR, March 14, 2022, https://www.npr.org/sections/health-shots/2022/03/14/1086125626/school-air-quality.

44. Noakes and Burridge, "Attendance Focus Shows Why Good Ventilation in Schools Still Matters"; "Improving Ventilation in Schools, Colleges, and Universities to Prevent COVID-19"; "Ventilation in Schools and Childcare Programs."

45. Environmental Law Institute, Ventilation in Schools: A Review of State Policy Strategies (Environmental Law Institute, January 2023), https://www.eli.org/sites/default/files/files-pdf/Vent%20in%20Schools%20Report_Jan%202023.pdf; Miguella Mark-Carew et al., "Ventilation Improvements Among K–12 Public School Districts—United States, August–December 2022," Morbidity and Mortality Weekly Report 72, no. 14 (2023): 372–76, https://www.cdc.gov/mmwr/volumes/72/wr/mm7214a4.htm (contains specific data referenced in this paragraph).

46. Mark-Carew et al., "Ventilation Improvements Among K–12 Public School Districts"; "Open and Shut Case—The Benefits of Good Ventilation in Schools," Health News, University of Leeds, May 25, 2022, https://www.leeds.ac.uk/news-health/news/article/5088/open-and-shut-case-the-benefits-of-good-ventilation-in-schools.

47. Shihan Deng et al., "Associations Between Illness-Related Absences and Ventilation and Indoor $PM_{2.5}$ in Elementary Schools of the Midwestern United States," Environment International 176 (June 2023), https://www.sciencedirect.com/science/article/pii/S0160412023002179; "School Air Filtration and Ventilation Strategies to Improve Health, Education, Equity, and Environmental Outcomes," CAP 20, August 31, 2022, https://www.americanprogress.org/article/school-air-filtration-and-ventilation-strategies-to-improve-health-education-equity-and-environmental-outcomes; "The Air We Breathe: Why Good HVAC Systems Are an Essential Resource for Our Students and School Staff," Learning Policy Institute, December 8, 2020, https://learningpolicyinstitute.org/blog/covid-hvac-systems-essential-resource.

48. Noakes and Burridge, "Attendance Focus Shows Why Good Ventilation in Schools Still Matters."

Chapter 9

1. Larry DeWitt, "Research Note #1: Origins of the Three-Legged Stool Metaphor for Social Security," Social Security Administration, May 1996, https://www.ssa.gov/history/stool.html; C. Michael Watson, "The 3-Legged Stool," Ohio Beacon, n.d., https://theohiobeacon.com/articles/3-legged-stool; Veryan Johnston, "Digging Up Memories—Making Connections: The Milking School?" Vindolanda Charitable Trust, n.d., https://www.vindolanda.com/milking-stool; Kris Cosca and Lori Schwartz Reichl, "The Three-Legged Stool: Creating and Maintaining Stability in Education," National Association for Music Education, May 9, 2023, https://nafme.org/blog/the-three-legged-stool-creating-and-maintaining-stability-in-education; Laurie Ann Stetzer, "Coaching the Whole Person: The Secret of the Three-Legged Stool," LinkedIn, June 5, 2020, https://www.linkedin.com/pulse/coaching-whole-person-secret-three-legged-stool-laurie-ann-stetzer; Brent Hultman, "The 3-Legged Stool of Business Success," LinkedIn, February 18, 2019, https://www.linkedin.com/pulse/3-legged-stool-business-success-brent-hultman.

2. Kevin J. Bernstein, "Erosion of Trust," LinkedIn, April 20, 2019, https://www.linkedin.com/pulse/erosion-trust-kevin-j-bernstein/?trk=articles_directory; "PwC's 2023 Trust Survey," PwC, n.d., https://www.pwc.com/us/en/library/trust-in-business-survey.html?utm_leadsource=dynamicsignal&userid=25928&userchannelid=9899&channeltype

=LinkedIn&postid=fcd442f4-2af6-4308-9e90-ed51b4871dee; Tracy Brower, "Trust Is Eroding: 2 Ways Leaders Can Rebuild It," *Forbes*, February 5, 2023, https://www.forbes .com/sites/tracybrower/2023/02/05/trust-is-eroding-2-ways-leaders-can-rebuild-it/?sh =4c0728966633; Robert Pondiscio, "Americans Have Lost Trust in Public Schools," Thomas B. Fordham Institute, January 27, 2022, https://fordhaminstitute.org/national /commentary/americans-have-lost-trust-public-schools.

3. Scott Souza, "'Building That Trust': New Danvers Superintendent Eyes Positive Future," *Patch*, August 30, 2023, https://patch.com/massachusetts/danvers/building-trust -new-danvers-superintendent-eyes-positive-future.

4. "Ben Orlin, Quotes, Quotable Quote," Goodreads, n.d., https://www.goodreads .com/quotes/9721938-creativity-is-what-happens-when-a-mind-encounters-an-obstacle; Stephen DeAngelis, "No Better Time to Consider the Theory of Constraints," Innovation Constraints," February 18, 2022, https://enterrasolutions.com/no-better-time-to-consider -the-theory-of-constraints.

5. "Reciprocity," chap. 8 in *Fundamentals of Community Engagement: A Sourcebook for Students* by ExCel Faculty Group (McMaster Office of Community Engagement, 2022), https://ecampusontario.pressbooks.pub/communityengagedlearningatmcmaster/chapter/ reciprocity; David A. Delaine et al., "Factors That Promote Reciprocity Within Community–Academic Partnership Initiation," *International Journal of Research on Service-Learning and Community Engagement* 10, no. 1, article 7 (2022), https://doi.org/10.37333/001c .66271; Emily Janke et al., "Presenter Q&A: Operationalizing Reciprocity in Community Engagement and Public Service Activities," Collaboratory, February 5, 2020, https:// cecollaboratory.com/presenter-qa-operationalizing-reciprocity-in-community-engagement -and-public-service-activities.

6. Emily Lubin Woods, *The Path to Successful Community School Policy Adoption: A Comparative Analysis of District-Level Policy Reform Processes*, Routledge Research in Education Policy and Politics (Routledge, 2022), https://doi.org/10.4324/9781003255611; Emily Woods, "Opinion: Community Schools Promote Equity: We Need More of Them," *Hechinger Report*, August 15, 2022, https://hechingerreport.org/opinion-community-schools -promote-equity-we-need-more-of-them; Coalition for Community Schools at the Institute for Educational Leadership, https://www.communityschools.org.

7. Emiliana Vegas and Rebecca Winthrop, "Beyond Reopening Schools: How Education Can Emerge Stronger Than Before COVID-19," Brookings, September 8, 2020, https://www.brookings.edu/articles/beyond-reopening-schools-how-education-can-emerge -stronger-than-before-covid-19.

8. Patricia Hunt, "Americans Are Slaves to Short-Term Thinking," *News Leader*, July 16, 2016, https://www.newsleader.com/story/opinion/columnists/2016/07/16/americans-slaves -short-term-thinking/87189152; Richard Fisher, "Humanity Is Stuck in Short-Term Thinking. Here's How We Escape," *MIT Technology Review*, October 21, 2020, https://www .technologyreview.com/2020/10/21/1009443/short-term-vs-long-term-thinking; "Long-Term Thinking Is Your Best Short-Term Strategy," *Wharton @ Work* (blog), Wharton School, University of Pennsylvania, August 2018, https://executiveeducation.wharton .upenn.edu/thought-leadership/wharton-at-work/2018/08/long-term-thinking.

9. Roman Krznaric, *The Good Ancestor: A Radical Prescription for Long-Term Thinking* (The Experiment, 2021), https://theexperimentpublishing.com/catalogs/fall-2021 /the-good-ancestor; Tristan Bove, "The Good Ancestor by Roman Krznaric," Earth.org, June 29, 2021, https://earth.org/book-reviews/book-review-the-good-ancestor-by-roman -krznaric.

Chapter 10

1. Beth A. Stroul and Gary M. Blau, eds., *The System of Care Handbook: Transforming Mental Health Services for Children, Youth, and Families* (Brookes, 2008); Mareasa R. Issacs et al., "Cultural and Linguistic Competence and Eliminating Disparities," in *The System of Care Handbook: Transforming Mental Health Services for Children, Youth, and Families*, ed. Beth A. Stroul and Gary M. Blau (Brookes, 2008), 301–28; Edward K. Wang, "A Journey of Public Stewardship on Asian American and Pacific Islander Mental Health: Massachusetts's Approach to Addressing Disparities," *Asian American Policy Review* 29 (Spring 2019), https://www.proquest.com/docview/2317571852?pq-origsite=summon&sourcetype=Scholarly%20Journals.

2. Will Kenton, "Game-Changer: Definition and Examples in Business," Investopedia, May 2, 2023, https://www.investopedia.com/terms/g/game-changer.asp; "Game Changer," *Merriam Webster Dictionary*, n.d., https://www.merriam-webster.com/dictionary/game%20changer; "Game Changer—Definition and Meaning," *Market Business News*, n.d., https://marketbusinessnews.com/financial-glossary/game-changer. This author uses the term *game changer* in the context of education in his examples, topics to which we return in Chapter 11. Utkarsh Marwaha, "The COVID-19 Pandemic: A Game-Changer for Education," Medium, December 19, 2022, https://medium.com/@Utkarsh_Marwaha/the-covid-19-pandemic-a-game-changer-for-education-9588b513da8a.

3. What are deemed game changers is not uniform. Ulrich A. K. Betz et al., "Game Changers in Science and Technology—Now and Beyond," *Technological Forecasting and Social Change* 193 (August 2023), https://www.sciencedirect.com/science/article/pii/S0040162523002731; "The Stories Behind 20 Inventions That Changed the World," Mental Floss, September 20, 2021, updated March 30, 2023, https://www.mentalfloss.com/article/648542/inventions-changed-world.

4. Suzanne McGee, "6 Inventions That Transformed Housework," History, August 20, 2021, updated May 5, 2023, https://www.history.com/news/inventions-that-transformed-housework; "From Edison to LEDs: Tracing the Evolution of the Light Bulb," Yeelight, June 23, 2023, https://store.yeelight.com/blogs/everything-about-lights-2/from-edison-to-leds-tracing-the-evolution-of-the-light-bulb; John C. Alverdy, "Microbiome Medicine: This Changes Everything," *Journal of the American College of Surgeons* 226, no. 5 (2018): 719–29, https://www.ncbi.nlm.nih.gov/pmc/articles/PMC5924601; "Game Changers: 5 Global Vaccine Innovations on the Horizon," Johns Hopkins, Bloomberg School of Public Health, n.d., https://publichealth.jhu.edu/2023/game-changing-vaccine-developments; "Why the New COVID Shot Is a Game-Changer (and Why the Term 'Booster' Is Obsolete)," *National Geographic*, October 3, 2023, https://www.nationalgeographic.com/science/article/covid-flu-vaccine-questions.

The literature on the use of proning is large. See, e.g., "Proning During COVID-19," *Penn Medicine Physician Blog*, March 10, 2021, https://www.pennmedicine.org/updates/blogs/penn-physician-blog/2020/may/proning-during-covid19; Chad H. Hochberg et al., "Comparing Prone Positioning Use in COVID-19 Versus Historic Acute Respiratory Distress Syndrome," *Critical Care Explorations* 4, no. 5 (2022): e0695, https://www.ncbi.nlm.nih.gov/pmc/articles/PMC9243245; Rachel Hosie, "Damar Hamlin Was Being Treated in the Prone Position on a Ventilator, His Uncle Said. Here's Why Lying Face Down Can Help Patients Recover," *Business Insider*, n.d., https://www.insider.com/damar-hamlin-update-status-prone-position-ventilator-cardiac-arrest-2023-1.

5. "The Printing Press and Its Impact on Literacy," Brewminate, August 21, 2018, https://brewminate.com/the-printing-press-and-its-impact-on-literacy; Dave Roos, "7 Ways

the Printing Press Changed the World," History, August 28, 2019, updated March 27, 2023, https://www.history.com/news/printing-press-renaissance.

6. Richard P. Hallion, "Airplanes That Transformed Aviation," *Smithsonian Magazine*, July 2008, https://www.smithsonianmag.com/air-space-magazine/airplanes-that-transformed-aviation-46502830; Nora McGreevy, "How the Automobile Changed the World, for Better or Worse," *Smithsonian Magazine*, July 6, 2021, https://www.smithsonianmag.com/smart-news/how-automobile-changed-world-cars-history-art-design-vehicles-180978109.

7. "Breaking Down the Stigma: Women and Cancer Care," Union for International-al Cancer Control, March 9, 2023, https://www.uicc.org/news/breaking-down-stigma-women-and-cancer-care; Medine Yılmaz et al., "Cancer-Related Stigma and Depression in Cancer Patients in a Middle-Income Country," *Asia-Pacific Journal of Oncology Nursing* 7, no. 1 (2020): 95–102, https://www.ncbi.nlm.nih.gov/pmc/articles/PMC6927157; "Lung Cancer and Stigma," Canadian Cancer Society, last medical review March 2020, https://cancer.ca/en/cancer-information/cancer-types/lung/supportive-care/lung-cancer-and-stigma; "Survivor Strives to Break the Lung Cancer Stigma," *Each Breath* (blog), American Lung Association, August 31, 2020, https://www.lung.org/blog/breaking-lung-cancer-stigma; Elizabeth O. Akin-Odanye and Anisah J. Husman, "Impact of Stigma and Stigma-Focused Interventions on Screening and Treatment Outcomes in Cancer Patients," *Ecancermedicalscience* 15 (2021): 1308, https://www.ncbi.nlm.nih.gov/pmc/articles/PMC8580722; Samar J. Melhem, Shereen Nabhani-Gebara, and Reem Kayyali, "Latency of Breast Cancer Stigma During Survivorship and Its Influencing Factors: A Qualitative Study," *Frontiers in Oncology* 13 (March 2023), https://www.frontiersin.org/journals/oncology/articles/10.3389/fonc.2023.1075298/full.

8. Cultural norms and types of cancer affect stigma, adding to the complexity of lessening it. It is also dependent on the economic development of nations: The more developed, the less cancer stigma there is. Charlotte Vrinten et al., "Cancer Stigma and Cancer Screening Attendance: A Population Based Survey in England," *BMC Cancer* 19, article no. 566 (2019), https://bmccancer.biomedcentral.com/articles/10.1186/s12885-019-5787-x; Sarah Knapp, Allison Marziliano, and Anne Moyer, "Identity Threat and Stigma in Cancer Patients," *Health Psychology Open* 1, no. 1 (2014), https://www.ncbi.nlm.nih.gov/pmc/articles/PMC5193175; "Niyati's Story: Overcoming Cultural Cancer Stigma to Become an Advocate," Breastcancer.org, n.d., https://www.breastcancer.org/personal-stories/overcoming-cultural-cancer-stigma.

9. Maria Clark, "30 Disheartening Statistics on Mental Health Stigma," Etactics, July 1, 2021, https://etactics.com/blog/statistics-on-mental-health-stigma; Noam Shpancer, "Is Mental Health Stigma Decreasing? It's Complicated," *Psychology Today*, January 1, 2022, https://www.psychologytoday.com/us/blog/insight-therapy/202201/is-mental-health-stigma-decreasing-its-complicated; "Stigma, Prejudice, and Discrimination Against People With Mental Illness," American Psychiatric Association, n.d., https://www.psychiatry.org/patients-families/stigma-and-discrimination.

For the resemblance between the stigma of mental illness and that of trauma, see Karen Gross, "We Have Trouble Using the Word 'Trauma': And That's Not Good," Medium, February 9, 2020, https://medium.com/age-of-awareness/we-have-trouble-using-the-word-trauma-and-thats-not-good-c2f20c2548ce.

10. Luna Greenstein, "9 Ways to Fight Mental Health Stigma," National Alliance on Mental Illness, October 11, 2017, https://www.nami.org/Blogs/NAMI-Blog/October-2017/9-Ways-to-Fight-Mental-Health-Stigma; "Stigma of Mental Illnesses Decreasing,

Survey Shows," HealthPartners, February 24, 2020, https://www.healthpartners.com/hp/about/press-releases/stigma-of-mental-illnesses-decreasing.html; Kathy Powell, "Breaking the Stigma of Mental Illness, One Song at a Time," *National Catholic Reporter*, October 14, 2023, https://www.ncronline.org/culture/breaking-stigma-mental-illness-one-song-time; "The Destigmatization of Mental Health," Elevate Psychiatry, n.d., https://elevatepsychiatry.com/the-destigmatization-of-mental-health; Blake Erickson, "Deinstitutionalization Through Optimism: The Community Mental Health Act of 1963," *American Journal of Psychiatry* 16, no. 4 (2021), https://ajp.psychiatryonline.org/doi/10.1176/appi.ajp-rj.2021.160404.

    11. Scott Bregman, "Exclusive! Simone Biles on Sparking Mental Health Conversation: 'We're Going Through It Together,'" Olympics, October 10, 2021, https://olympics.com/en/news/simone-biles-exclusive-mental-health-advice-future; Kara Gavin, "A Game-Changer for Mental Health: Sports Icons Open Up," Michigan Medicine, University of Michigan, July 29, 2021, https://www.michiganmedicine.org/health-lab/game-changer-mental-health-sports-icons-open; Molly Ball, "How John Fetterman Came out of the Darkness," *Time*, July 20, 2023, https://time.com/6296038/john-fetterman-depression-cover-story.

    For some poignant memoirs on this topic, see Susannah Cahalan, *Brain on Fire: My Month of Madness* (Simon and Schuster, 2013).

    12. Issacs et al., "Cultural and Linguistic Competence and Eliminating Disparities"; Beth A. Stroul and Gary M. Blau, eds., *The System of Care Handbook: Transforming Mental Health Services for Children, Youth, and Families* (Brookes, 2008), abstract, https://psycnet.apa.org/record/2008-11975-000; "Communities in DSpace," State Library of Massachusetts Digital Collections, n.d., https://archives.lib.state.ma.us/home; Crystal L. Barksdale et al., "System-Level Change in Cultural and Linguistic Competence (CLC): How Changes in CLC Are Related to Service Experience Outcomes in Systems of Care," *American Journal of Community Psychology* 49, no. 3–4 (2012): 483–93, https://www.ncbi.nlm.nih.gov/pmc/articles/PMC3182295; National Technical Assistance Center for State Mental Health Planning (NTAC) and National Association of State Mental Health Program Directors (NASMHPD), *Cultural Competency: Measurement as a Strategy for Moving Knowledge Into Practice in State Mental Health Systems* (NTAC and NASMHPD, 2004), https://www.nasmhpd.org/sites/default/files/cult%20comp_0.pdf.

    13. Issacs et al., "Cultural and Linguistic Competence and Eliminating Disparities"; U.S. Department of Health and Human Services, *Mental Health: Culture, Race, and Ethnicity—a Supplement to Mental Health; A Report of the Surgeon General* (U.S. Department of Health and Human Services, Substance Abuse and Mental Health Services Administration, Center for Mental Health Services, 2001); Center for Mental Health Services, *Cultural Competence Standards in Managed Mental Health Care Services: Four Underserved/Underrepresented Racial/Ethnic Groups* (U.S. Department of Health and Human Services, Substance Abuse and Mental Health Services Administration, 2000).

    14. Issacs et al., "Cultural and Linguistic Competence and Eliminating Disparities."

    15. Issacs et al., "Cultural and Linguistic Competence and Eliminating Disparities."

    16. Janice L. Cooper et al., *Unclaimed Children Revisited: The Status of Children's Mental Health Policy in the United States* (National Center for Children in Poverty, 2008), http://www.nccp.org/publications/pub_853.html; NTAC and NASMHPD, *Cultural Competency*; Agency for Healthcare Research and Quality, Effective Health Care Program, *Improving Cultural Competence to Reduce Health Disparities for Priority Populations* (Agency for Healthcare Research and Quality, July 8, 2014), https://effectivehealthcare

.ahrq.gov/products/cultural-competence/research-protocol; "Asian American, Native Hawaiian, and Pacific Islander (AA and NHPI)," Substance Abuse and Mental Health Services Administration, last updated May 25, 2023, https://www.samhsa.gov/behavioral-health-equity/aa-nhpi.

17. U.S. Department of Health and Human Services, *Mental Health: Culture, Race, and Ethnicity*; "Prioritizing Minority Mental Health," Centers for Disease Control and Prevention, June 27, 2023, https://www.cdc.gov/healthequity/features/minority-mental-health/index.html; Wang, "A Journey of Public Stewardship"; Danica Richards, "Incorporating Racial Equity Into Trauma-Informed Care," Center for Health Care Strategies, September 2021, https://www.chcs.org/media/Brief-Incorporating-Racial-Equity-into-Trauma-Informed-Care.pdf; Institute of Medicine, *Race, Ethnicity, and Language Data: Standardization for Health Care Quality Improvement* (National Academies Press, 2009); "Vivek Murthy Distinguished Lecture: Addressing COVID-19 Health Disparities, Root Causes, Mental Health Impacts, Lessons Learned, and Future Opportunities," Office of Research on Women's Health, National Institutes of Health, n.d., https://orwh.od.nih.gov/about/newsroom/events/vivek-murthy-distinguished-lecture-addressing-covid-19-health-disparities.

18. Wang, "A Journey of Public Stewardship"; Matt Compton, "The National Conference on Mental Health," The White House, President Barack Obama, June 3, 2013, https://obamawhitehouse.archives.gov/blog/2013/06/03/national-conference-mental-health; "Community Conversations About Mental Health: Discussion Guide," Substance Abuse and Mental Health Services Administration, n.d., https://store.samhsa.gov/product/community-conversations-about-mental-health-discussion-guide/sma13-4764; "Mental Health Disparities: Diverse Populations," American Psychiatric Association, n.d., https://www.psychiatry.org/psychiatrists/diversity/education/mental-health-facts.

19. Wang, "A Journey of Public Stewardship"; "Mental and Behavioral Health—Asian Americans," U.S. Department of Health and Human Services Office of Minority Health, n.d., https://minorityhealth.hhs.gov/mental-and-behavioral-health-asian-americans; Compton, "The National Conference on Mental Health"; "Community Conversations About Mental Health"; Vivek H. Murthy, "Surgeon General's Perspectives," *Public Health Reports* 130, no. 3 (2015): 193–95, https://www.ncbi.nlm.nih.gov/pmc/articles/PMC4388212.

20. Committee on Quality of Health Care in America, Institute of Medicine, *Crossing the Quality Chasm: A New Health System for the 21st Century* (National Academies Press; 2001), https://www.ihi.org/resources/Pages/Publications/CrossingtheQualityChasmANewHealthSystemforthe21stCentury.aspx; Caroline Goon, "A Virtual Conversation With Surgeon General Vivek H. Murthy and Boston Mayor Michelle Wu: Addressing Systemic Racism, Mental Health Stigma, and Community Resilience to Achieve Health Equity," National Institutes of Health, Office of Equity, Diversity, and Inclusion, May 3, 2022, https://www.edi.nih.gov/blog/events/virtual-conversation-surgeon-general-vivek-h-murthy-and-boston-mayor-michelle-wu; U.S. Department of Health and Human Services, *Mental Health: Culture, Race, and Ethnicity*.

21. See L. Rosi and E. K. Wang, "The Project One Billion Global Mental Health Survey," in *Textbook of Global Mental Health: Trauma and Recovery; A Companion Guide for Field and Clinical Care of Traumatized People Worldwide*, ed. Richard F. Mollica (Harvard Program in Refugee Trauma, 2011), 61–88; Richard L. Wiener et al., "Debtor Education, Financial Literacy, and Pending Bankruptcy Legislation," *Behavioral Sciences & the Law* 23, no. 3 (2005): 347–66, https://pubmed.ncbi.nlm.nih.gov/15968706.

22. Ragy Girgis, "Is There a Link Between Mental Health and Mass Shootings?" Columbia University Department of Psychiatry, July 6, 2022, https://www.columbiapsychiatry.org/news/mass-shootings-and-mental-illness; Julianna Goldman, "Why America Doesn't Know How to Stop School Shootings," *Japan Times*, January 13, 2023, https://www.japantimes.co.jp/opinion/2023/01/13/commentary/world-commentary/u-s-gun-control.

23. Karen Gross, *Trauma Doesn't Stop at the School Door: Strategies and Solutions for Educators, PreK–College* (Teachers College Press, 2020); Karen Gross, *Breakaway Learners: Strategies for Post-Secondary Success With At-Risk Students* (Teachers College Press, 2016); Andy Blackstone, *The Principles of Sociological Inquiry: Qualitative and Quantitative Methods* (Saylor Academy, 2012), table of contents, https://open.umn.edu/opentextbooks/textbooks/139.

24. John E. Tropman, "Micro, Mezzo, and Macro: A Guide to the Levels of Social Work," MSW Online, last updated December 22, 2022, https://mastersinsocialworkonline.org/resources/levels-of-social-work; "Social Change: Macro, Meso, Micro Perspectives," Emerald Publishing, n.d., https://www.emeraldgrouppublishing.com/archived/products/journals/call_for_papers.htm%3Fid%3D5717; Petra Molthan-Hill et al., "Reducing Carbon Emissions in Business Through Responsible Management Education: Influence at the Micro-, Meso-, and Macro-Levels," *International Journal of Management Education*, 18, no. 1 (2020), https://nrl.northumbria.ac.uk/id/eprint/41397/1/Scales%20of%20Influence-final%20submitted0907.pdf.

25. Kevin Roose, "How Schools Can Survive (and Maybe Even Thrive) With A.I. This Fall," *New York Times*, August 24, 2023, https://www.nytimes.com/2023/08/24/technology/how-schools-can-survive-and-maybe-even-thrive-with-ai-this-fall.html; Abreanna Blose, "As ChatGPT Enters the Classroom, Teachers Weigh Pros and Cons," *NEA Today*, April 12, 2023, https://www.nea.org/nea-today/all-news-articles/chatgpt-enters-classroom-teachers-weigh-pros-and-cons.

26. Takahiro Kurashima, *Poemotion 1* (Lars Muller, 2013). For interested readers, there are also *Poemotion 2* and *3*.

27. Betty Chandy, "Five Ways Teachers Can Integrate ChatGPT Into Their Classrooms Today," *Educator's Playbook*, Penn Graduate School of Education, February 2, 2023, https://www.gse.upenn.edu/news/educators-playbook/five-ways-teachers-can-integrate-chatgpt-their-classrooms-today; Tracy Wilichowski and Cristóbal Cobo, "How to Use ChatGPT to Support Teachers: The Good, the Bad, and the Ugly," *World Bank Blogs*, May 2, 2023, https://blogs.worldbank.org/education/how-use-chatgpt-support-teachers-good-bad-and-ugly; Roose, "How Schools Can Survive and Maybe Even Thrive With A.I. This Fall."

28. Kevin Roose, "Don't Ban ChatGPT in Schools. Teach With It," *New York Times*, January 12, 2023, https://www.nytimes.com/2023/01/12/technology/chatgpt-schools-teachers.html; Jill Staake, " ChatGPT for Teachers: 20+ Tips, Ideas, Prompts, and More," We Are Teachers, April 5, 2024, https://www.weareteachers.com/chatgpt-for-teachers.

For a thoughtful essay on both the difficulties of ChatGPT and the essential questions this technology forces us to ask, see Jasmine Palma and Austin H. Wang, "Harvard Sciences Dean Stubbs Says Generative AI Is 'Top of the List' of Challenges," *Harvard Crimson*, October 16, 2023, https://www.thecrimson.com/article/2023/10/16/stubbs-october-interview.

29. Alyson Klein, "Teachers Turn to Pen and Paper Amid AI Cheating Fears, Survey Finds," *Education Week*, October 6, 2023, https://www.edweek.org/technology/teachers-turn-to-pen-and-paper-amid-ai-cheating-fears-survey-finds/2023/10; Arianna Johnson, "ChatGPT in Schools: Here's Where It's Banned—and How It Could Potentially Help

Students," *Forbes*, January 18, 2023, https://www.forbes.com/sites/ariannajohnson/2023/01/18/chatgpt-in-schools-heres-where-its-banned-and-how-it-could-potentially-help-students/?sh=29539ada6e2c; Evan Castillo, "These Schools and Colleges Have Banned Chat GPT and Similar AI Tools," BC Best Schools, March 27, 2023, https://www.bestcolleges.com/news/schools-colleges-banned-chat-gpt-similar-ai-tools.

30. Jonathan Zimmerman, "Here's My AI Policy for Students: I Don't Have One," *Washington Post*, August 29, 2023, https://www.washingtonpost.com/opinions/2023/08/29/ai-student-policy-chatgpt-college.

31. Paul Browning, "Why Schools Shouldn't Be Scared of ChatGPT," *Financial Review*, January 30, 2023, https://www.afr.com/work-and-careers/education/why-schools-shouldn-t-be-scared-of-chatgpt-20230125-p5cfbz; Samantha Murphy Kelly, "Schools Are Teaching ChatGPT, So Students Aren't Left Behind," CNN Business, August 19, 2023, https://www.cnn.com/2023/08/19/tech/schools-teaching-chagpt-students/index.html; Sarah Dillard, "Schools Must Embrace the Looming Disruption of ChatGPT," The 74, January 4, 2023, https://www.the74million.org/article/schools-must-embrace-the-looming-disruption-of-chatgpt.

Chapter 11

1. Chip Heath and Dan Heath, *Made to Stick: Why Some Ideas Survive and Others Die* (Random House, 2007); Malcolm Gladwell, *The Tipping Point: How Little Things Can Make a Big Difference* (Little, Brown, 2000).

2. National Research Council, *High-School Biology Today and Tomorrow* (National Academies Press, 1989), https://nap.nationalacademies.org/catalog/1328/high-school-biology-today-and-tomorrow; Naomi Thiers, "To Spur True Change, Know Your Barriers," review of *How to Change: The Science of Getting From Where You Are to Where You Want to Be* by Katy Milkman, ASCD, March 1, 2023, https://www.ascd.org/el/articles/to-spur-true-change-know-your-barriers; "10 Barriers to Education and How to Overcome Them," LearningOnline.xyz, June 13, 2023, https://learningonline.xyz/something-good/10-barriers-to-education-and-how-to-overcome-them.

3. Karen Gross, *Trauma Doesn't Stop at the School Door: Strategies and Solutions for Educators, PreK–College* (Teachers College Press, 2020).

4. Gross, *Trauma*, part 1; *Change Management—Understanding Change*, University of Washington Professional and Organizational Development, n.d., https://hr.uw.edu/leadershipcafe/wp-content/uploads/sites/20/2019/01/Change-Management-Understanding-Change.pdf; "Lewin's Change Management Model," Mind Tools, n.d., https://www.mindtools.com/ajm911e/lewins-change-management-model (suggesting the idea of using shapes in thinking about change; that helps us realize where we are and where we are going).

5. Zhongfang Yang et al., "How Patients With an Uncertain Diagnosis Experience Intolerance of Uncertainty: A Grounded Theory Study," *Psychology Research and Behavior Management* 14 (August 12, 2021): 1269–79, https://www.ncbi.nlm.nih.gov/pmc/articles/PMC8367199; Rebecca C. Spillmann et al., "A Window Into Living With an Undiagnosed Disease: Illness Narratives From the Undiagnosed Diseases Network," *Orphanet Journal of Rare Diseases* 12, no. 1 (2017): 71, https://www.ncbi.nlm.nih.gov/pmc/articles/PMC5392939.

6. Ryan McCarthy, "COVID Vaccines and Weight Loss Medications: A Tale of 2 Needles," Kevin MD.com, October 12, 2023, https://www.kevinmd.com/2023/10/covid-vaccines-and-weight-loss-medications-a-tale-of-2-needles.html.

7. "Stages of Change Model," Loma Linda University School of Medicine, n.d., https://medicine.llu.edu/academics/resources/stages-change-model; "Stages of Change #2: Planning and Preparing for Change," *Adobe Experience Cloud Blog*, n.d., https://business .adobe.com/blog/perspectives/stages-of-change-2-planning-and-preparing-for-change; Tim Creasey, "Why Change Management," Prosci, May 20, 2021, updated April 6, 2024, https://www.prosci.com/resources/articles/why-change-management.

Change isn't easy, even if you have a manual. See Karen Gross, "Changing Time Isn't So Easy: My Car Story Explains Why," LinkedIn, November 8, 2018, https://www .linkedin.com/pulse/changing-time-isnt-so-easy-my-car-story-explains-why-karen-gross.

8. Think about it as echoing the invisible backpack of trauma many students carry with them. Adults carry them too, to be sure. As demonstrated in both Gross, *Breakaway Learners* and Gross, *Trauma*, both those carrying the backpack and the people working with them need to reverse their invisibility for improvement to happen. And, importantly, it is not just that students need to "own" their backpack; educators, parents and caregivers, and communities must be able to create a culture in which those with a backpack can thrive. Transmuting this idea to pandemic positives, these developments need to be seen not only by those who created them but also by the many stakeholders in education, so that we create a culture that fosters educational change.

9. Atif Saleem, Philip Saagyum Dare, and Guoyuan Sang, "Leadership Styles and the Process of Organizational Change During the Pandemic," *Frontiers in Psychology* 13 (September 12, 2022), https://www.frontiersin.org/articles/10.3389/fpsyg.2022.920495/ full; "Leadership During a Pandemic: Leadership, Complexity, and Inclusion," Midlands Partnership University, NHS Foundation Trust, n.d., https://www.mpft.nhs.uk/about-us /pep-talk-extra/leadership-during-pandemic-leadership-complexity-and-inclusion; Chidinma Ukah, "Reflective Report on Varied Leadership Approaches Taken by Different Leaders in Managing the Changes Arising From Contemporary Issues (Covid-19)," LinkedIn, March 11, 2023, https://www.linkedin.com/pulse/reflective-report-varied-leadership -approaches-taken-different-ukah; Michaela J. Kerrissey and Amy C. Edmondson, "What Good Leadership Looks Like During This Pandemic," *Harvard Business Review*, April 13, 2020, https://hbr.org/2020/04/what-good-leadership-looks-like-during-this-pandemic.

10. Maria Eliophotou Menon, "Transformational School Leadership and the COVID-19 Pandemic: Perceptions of Teachers in Cyprus," *Educational Management Administration and Leadership*, April 6, 2023, https://www.ncbi.nlm.nih.gov/pmc/articles /PMC10080167; Siphokazi Kwatubana and Vivian Molaodi, "Leadership Styles That Would Enable School Leaders to Support the Wellbeing of Teachers During COVID-19," in *New Challenges to Education: Lessons From around the World*, BCES Conference Books, vol. 19, ed. Nikolay Popov et al. (Bulgarian Comparative Education Society, 2021), 106–12, https://files.eric.ed.gov/fulltext/ED614047.pdf; Kelsey Ann Lewis, Carol Campbell, and Joseph Flessa, "School Leaders' Experiences of Navigating Through the Pandemic," EdCan Network, September 19, 2022, https://www.edcan.ca/articles/school-leaders-experiences-of -navigating-through-the-pandemic.

For what educators want to see in their leaders in a crisis, see Seher Yıldız Şal and Ahmet Göçen, "Teachers' Views on Leadership in the New Normal," *Asian Journal of Distance Education* 17, no. 1 (2022), https://files.eric.ed.gov/fulltext/EJ1350104.pdf.

For leading by role modeling, see Karen Gross, "What Does Role Modeling Mean in Today's Pandemic World? It Means Showcasing Good and Eliminating Abuse," Medium, April 3, 2020, https://karengrossedu.medium.com/what-does-role-modeling-mean-in -todays-pandemic-world-d0004c6bd863. For a look at leadership prepandemic, see Karen

Gross, "Our Leaders on Campuses Get Too Scared and Wimp Out," LinkedIn, August 27, 2018, https://www.linkedin.com/pulse/our-leaders-wimpy-scared-karen-gross.

For failed school leadership, see Jeff Bryant, "Bad Leadership Is Plunging Public Schools Into a Crisis," *Progressive Magazine*, October 29, 2020, https://progressive.org /public-schools-advocate/bad-leadership-public-school-crisis-bryant-201029.

11. Jason A. Grissom, Anna J. Egalite, and Constance A. Lindsay, "How Principals Affect Students and Schools: A Systematic Synthesis of Two Decades of Research," Wallace Foundation, 2021, https://www.wallacefoundation.org/knowledge-center/Documents /How-Principals-Affect-Students-and-Schools.pdf; Stephanie Levin and Kathryn Bradley, "Understanding and Addressing Principal Turnover: A Review of the Research," National Association of Secondary School Principals and Learning Policy Institute, 2019, https:// www.nassp.org/wp-content/uploads/2020/06/nassp_edit06-WEB.pdf; forthcoming dissertation from Southern New Hampshire University EdD candidate Allyson Hoffman on the negative impact of changing school leadership on educators, 2024 (draft available from Karen Gross).

12. "How Can You Succeed as an Educational Leader in the 21st Century?" LinkedIn, last updated August 5, 2023, https://www.linkedin.com/advice/1/how-can-you-succeed -educational-leader-21st; "The Difficult Job of Schools Leaders," ASCD, October 1, 2022, https://www.ascd.org/el/articles/the-difficult-job-of-schools-leaders; Jen Barker and Tom Rees, "The Persistent Problems of School Leadership," Ambition Institute, n.d., https:// www.ambition.org.uk/blog/persistent-problems-school-leadership; "The Higher Education Leadership Challenge," Maryville University, September 22, 2016, https://online .maryville.edu/blog/the-higher-education-leadership-challenge; Megan Zahneis, "Why Higher Ed Is Seeing a Spate of High-Profile No-Confidence Votes," *Chronicle of Higher Education*, September 29, 2023, https://www.chronicle.com/article/why-higher-ed-is -seeing-a-spate-of-high-profile-no-confidence-votes; Josh Moody, "Presidents Can't Win," *Inside Higher Ed*, October 18, 2023, https://www.insidehighered.com/news/governance /executive-leadership/2023/10/18/college-leaders-mideast-statements-spark?utm_source =Inside+Higher+Ed.

13. Michael Hansen and Diana Quintero, "School Leadership: An Untapped Opportunity to Draw Young People of Color Into Teaching," Brookings, November 26, 2018, https://www.brookings.edu/articles/school-leadership-an-untapped-opportunity-to-draw -young-people-of-color-into-teaching; Gene Bottoms and Kathy O'Neill, *Preparing a New Breed of School Principals: It's Time for Action* (Southern Regional Education Board, April 2001), https://www.wallacefoundation.org/knowledge-center/Documents/Preparing -a-New-Breed-of-School-Principals.pdf; Center for Comprehensive School Reform and Improvement, "Role of Principal Leadership in Improving Student Achievement," review of Kenneth Leithwood, Karen Seashore Louis, Stephen Anderson, and Kyla Wahlstrom, *How Leadership Influences Student Learning* (Wallace Foundation, 2004), Reading Rockets, https://www.readingrockets.org/topics/school-wide-efforts/articles/role-principal -leadership-improving-student-achievement.

14. James S. Rosebush, "Why Great Leaders Are in Short Supply," *Harvard Business Review*, March 30, 2012, https://hbr.org/2012/03/why-great-leaders-are-in-short.

15. Chris Minnich, "Strong School Leaders Will Be Essential in Next Phase of Pandemic," EdSource, January 28, 2022, https://edsource.org/2022/strong-school-leaders-will -be-essential-in-next-phase-of-pandemic/665547.

16. Sanyin Siang, "Build a Culture of Hope," Duke Corporate Education, December 2020, https://www.dukece.com/insights/build-a-culture-of-hope; Michael Mauro,

"Hope: The Other Essential Leadership Skill," March 7 [no year], Michael Mauro, https://www.michaelmauro.co.uk/thought-leadership/hope-the-other-essential-leadership-skill.

17. Matthew X. Joseph, "How to Lead With Positivity," Edutopia, December 8, 2020, https://www.edutopia.org/article/how-lead-positivity; Magdalena Ponurska, "7 Lessons in Leadership: The Power of Mindset in the Field of Education," LinkedIn, July 15, 2023, https://www.linkedin.com/pulse/7-lessons-leadership-power-mindset-field-education-magdalena-ponurska.

18. Ronald Williamson and Barbara R. Blackburn, "Leadership: Listening to Others in Volatile Times," MiddleWeb, January 16, 2022, updated January 17, 2022, https://www.middleweb.com/46407/leadership-listening-to-others-in-volatile-times; Abner Oakes, "Communication Skills of Leaders," Institute for Student Achievement, April 29, 2015.

19. Williamson and Blackburn, "Leadership"; Oakes, "Communication Skills of Leaders."

20. "Creating a Culture of Creativity: Think Different, Lead Different," *Wharton @ Work* (blog), Wharton School, University of Pennsylvania, February 2012, https://executiveeducation.wharton.upenn.edu/thought-leadership/wharton-at-work/2012/02/culture-of-creativity; Sharon Friesen with Candace Saar et al., "Creating a Culture of Creativity, Risk-Taking, and Innovation," Galileo Educational Network, 2015, https://inquiry.galileo.org/ch6/instructional-leadership/creating-a-culture-of-creativity-risk-taking-and-innovation; "Reframing Creativity: Considering School Culture and the Conditions to Support Creative Leadership," Creative Learning Plan Partners and National Creative Learning Network, n.d., https://education.gov.scot/media/fnjftxhy/reframing-creativity-cll-conference-22-03-21.pdf; Elif Suner, "Why Leaders Should Focus on Strengths, Not Weaknesses," *Forbes*, February 6, 2020, https://www.forbes.com/sites/forbescoachescouncil/2020/02/06/why-leaders-should-focus-on-strengths-not-weaknesses/?sh=4d0ffbd83d1a.

21. "Creativity & COVID: A Lesson From Art Educators on the Importance of Creativity in a Crisis," *National Geographic Education Blog*, May 29, 2020, https://blog.education.nationalgeographic.org/2020/05/29/creativity-covid-a-lesson-from-art-educators-on-the-importance-of-creativity-in-a-crisis; Yvonne Görlichm, "Creativity and Productivity During the COVID-19 Pandemic," *Scientific Reports* 13, article 14615 (2023), https://www.nature.com/articles/s41598-023-40493-y; Robby Berman, "COVID-19: Did Lockdown Help or Hinder Our Creativity?" *Medical News Today*, May 19, 2022, https://www.medicalnewstoday.com/articles/covid-19-did-lockdown-help-or-hinder-our-creativity; Karen Gross, "Art as a Tool for Addressing Trauma," Karen Gross Education, n.d., https://karengrosseducation.com/artwork; Karen Gross, "The Role of Art in Our Violent World," Medium, June 4, 2017, https://karengrossedu.medium.com/the-role-of-art-in-our-violent-world-6543b9a6043d.

22. Bill Lucas, Ellen Spencer, and Louise Stoll, *Creative Leadership to Develop Creativity and Creative Thinking in English Schools: A Review of the Evidence* (Mercers' Company, 2021), https://www.creativityexchange.org.uk/asset/223; Lisa Dabbs, "How Should Successful and Innovative Teaching Be Rewarded?" Edutopia, April 15, 2010, https://www.edutopia.org/rewarding-teachers-edchat-lisa-dabbs; Jordan Pruitt, "Teacher Rewards That Will Supercharge Your School Culture," LiveSchool, April 22, 2022, https://www.whyliveschool.com/blog/teacher-rewards.

23. Dru Tomlin, "Professional Learning Through Cross-Pollination!" AMLE, n.d., https://www.amle.org/professional-learning-through-cross-pollination; Harsh Tuli, "Academic Cross Pollination: A Way Forward," *Journal of Management* 5, no. 3 (2018): 192–196,

https://iaeme.com/MasterAdmin/Journal_uploads/JOM/VOLUME_5_ISSUE_3/JOM_05
_03_025.pdf.

   24. Regional Educational Laboratory West at WestEd (REL West), *A Compilation of Research on Cross-Sector Education and Career Partnerships* (REL West, October 2017), https://ies.ed.gov/ncee/edlabs/regions/west/relwestFiles/pdf/APECS_5-2-1_Literature _Compilation_clean.pdf; "Building Impact: A Closer Look at Local Cross-Sector Collaborations for Education," Wallace, December 2019, https://wallacefoundation.org /sites/default/files/2023-09/Building-Impact.pdf (this piece from the Wallace Foundation ties into the three-legged stool and the centrality of trust in cross-sector efforts). See Nina Kolleck, "Trust in Cross-Sector Alliances: Towards a Theory of Relational Trust in Multi-Professional Education Networks," *Educational Management Administration and Leadership* 51, no. 6 (2023): 1362–1382, https://journals.sagepub.com/doi/10.1177 /17411432211043876.

   25. Kasia Lundy and Haven Ladd, "Why Collaboration Is Key to the Future of Higher Education," EY-Parthenon, December 18, 2020, https://www.ey.com/en_us/strategy /strategies-for-collaborating-in-a-new-era-for-higher-education.

   26. "Research–Practice Partnerships: Collaborative Research for Educational Change," Spencer Foundation, n.d., https://www.spencer.org/grant_types/research-practice-partnerships; "Regional Partnership Grant Program," National Center on Substance Abuse and Child Welfare, n.d., https://ncsacw.acf.hhs.gov/technical/rpg; "STARS Residencies," Mass Cultural Council, https://massculturalcouncil.org/education/stars-residencies.

   27. Edward K. Wang, "A Journey of Public Stewardship on Asian American and Pacific Islander Mental Health: Massachusetts's Approach to Addressing Disparities," *Asian American Policy Review* 29 (Spring 2019): 57–66, https://www.proquest.com/docview /2317571852?pq-origsite=summon&sourcetype=Scholarly%20Journals.

   28. Christine Lehmann, "Psychiatrists Rush to Aid of World Trade Center Victims," *Psychiatric News*, October 5, 2001, https://psychnews.psychiatryonline.org/doi/full/10 .1176/pn.36.19.0001; "Twenty Years Later: A Grim Anniversary as Mount Sinai Remains a Lifeline for 9/11 Responders," *Today* (blog), Mount Sinai, September 8, 2021, https:// health.mountsinai.org/blog/twenty-years-later-a-grim-anniversary-as-mount-sinai-remains -a-lifeline-for-9-11-responders.

   29. Robert D. Putnam, *Bowling Alone: The Collapse and Revival of American Community*, revised and updated (Simon and Schuster, 2021); Hannah Dellinger, Matt Barnum, and Collin Binkley, "Schools Are Cutting Recovery Programs as U.S. Aid Money Dries Up. Students Are Still Struggling," Chalkbeat, September 6, 2023, https://www.chalkbeat .org/2023/9/6/23851143/covid-relief-schools-esser-spending-learning-loss; Matt Barnum, "Schools Face a Funding Cliff. How Bad Will the Fall Be?" Chalkbeat, September 13, 2023, https://www.chalkbeat.org/2023/9/13/23871838/schools-funding-cliff-federal-covid -relief-esser-money-budget-cuts.

   30. Kit Harrington and Infinite Culcleasure, "Journeying Through Histories of Community Schools," Voices for Vermont's Children, August 4, 2022, https://www.voicesforvtkids .org/blog/a-journeying-through-history-with-community-schools?format=amp.

   31. Lisa Rabasca Roepe, "When Leaders Make Mistakes," SHRM, February 27, 2020, https://www.shrm.org/hr-today/news/hr-magazine/spring2020/pages/when-leaders-make -mistakes.aspx; Gustavo Razzetti, "Why Leaders Fail to Realize They're Wrong," *Psychology Today*, November 12, 2021, https://www.psychologytoday.com/us/blog/the-adaptive-mind /202111/why-leaders-fail-to-realize-theyre-wrong; Nicole Lipkin, "Leaders, Can You Admit

When You're Wrong?" Thrive Global, February 22, 2019, https://community.thriveglobal
.com/leaders-can-you-admit-when-youre-wrong.

There are some leaders who do admit their mistakes. See Glenn Llopis, "4 Reasons Great Leaders Admit Their Mistakes," *Forbes*, July 23, 2015, https://www.forbes
.com/sites/glennllopis/2015/07/23/4-reasons-great-leaders-admit-their-mistakes/?sh
=48dc24534628; Karen Gross, "'Doctor of Humane Lettuce,'" *Inside Higher Ed*, June 2,
2008, https://www.insidehighered.com/views/2008/06/03/doctor-humane-lettuce; Karen
Gross, "How Co-Presidents Could Improve Leadership in Higher Education," Aspen Institute, February 1, 2018, https://www.aspeninstitute.org/blog-posts/co-presidents-improve
-leadership-higher-education.

32. Gladwell, *The Tipping Point*; Sam Thomas Davies, "This Study Reveals the Tipping Point in Behaviour Change (and How You Can Use It)," Sam T. Davies, last updated
May 29, 2023, https://www.samuelthomasdavies.com/tipping-point.

33. Bill Murphy Jr., "Google Says It Still Uses the '20-Percent Rule,' and You Should
Totally Copy It," Inc., n.d., https://www.inc.com/bill-murphy-jr/google-says-it-still-uses
-20-percent-rule-you-should-totally-copy-it.html; Shaun Crawford, "The New 80/20
Rule—Why Passion Is a Stronger Motivator Than Innovation," Medium, August 19,
2020, https://medium.com/mammoth-xr/the-new-80-20-rule-why-passion-is-a-stronger
-motivator-than-innovation-2b812319445c.

34. "Why Does Water Pouring From a Glass Sometimes Travel Down the Side of
the Glass?" Physics Stack Exchange, n.d., https://physics.stackexchange.com/questions
/28982/why-does-water-pouring-from-a-glass-sometimes-travel-down-the-side-of-the
-glass.

35. Gladwell, *The Tipping Point*; Davies, "This Study Reveals the Tipping Point in
Behaviour Change; "The Tipping Point: Chapter Three Summary and Analysis," LitCharts,
n.d., https://www.litcharts.com/lit/the-tipping-point/chapter-three-the-stickiness-factor;
Amanda Penn, "The Stickiness Factor: Make Your Ideas Catch On and Spread," Shortform, November 29, 2019, https://www.shortform.com/blog/the-stickiness-factor.

36. Gladwell, *The Tipping Point*; Davies, "This Study Reveals the Tipping Point in
Behaviour Change; "The Tipping Point: Chapter Three Summary and Analysis"; Penn,
"The Stickiness Factor."

37. Heath and Heath, *Made to Stick*.

38. Roger Martin, "The Strategy Lesson From the Bud Light Fiasco," Medium, August 7 [no year], https://rogermartin.medium.com/the-strategy-lesson-from-the-bud-light
-fiasco-874ef8db4f49.

39. Amelia Burke-Garcia, *Public Health Messaging Across Differing Viewpoints*
(NORC at the University of Chicago, January 27, 2022), https://amchp.org/wp-content
/uploads/2022/03/Concurrent-3_Public-Health-Messaging_slides-polls-q-and-a.pdf; Leonard A. Schlesinger and Charlie Kiefer, "Prevent Conflicting Messages From Confusing
Your Team," *Harvard Business Review*, September 26, 2014, https://hbr.org/2014/09
/prevent-conflicting-messages-from-confusing-your-team.

40. Selected Karen Gross testimony: Vermont House of Representatives, Education
Committee, February 2010 (vulnerable-student retention strategies); New York City
Department of Consumer Affairs, June 2006 (debt collection: what needs to be done to
improve the process); United States House of Representatives, Committee on the Judiciary, February 2001 (the impact of H.R. 333 on women and children); United States
Senate, Committee on the Judiciary, Subcommittee on Courts and Administrative Practice,
June 1988 (bankruptcy study results).

For Ed Wang, rather than direct testimony, the involvement came in the form of preparing testimony and reports for the Department of Mental Health.

41. "Harvard Seminar for New Presidents," Harvard Graduate School of Education, n.d., https://www.gse.harvard.edu/professional-education/program/harvard-seminar-new-presidents.

42. Hollie Russon Gilman and Amy Eisenstein, "It's Like Jury Duty, but for Getting Things Done," *Boston Globe*, updated August 18, 2023, https://www.bostonglobe.com/2023/08/18/opinion/citizens-assemblies.

43. James E. Ryan, *Wait, What? and Life's Other Essential Questions* (HarperOne, 2017).

44. Glenn Branch, "Whence Lumpers and Splitters?" National Center for Science Education, December 2, 2014, https://www.bostonglobe.com/2023/08/18/opinion/citizens-assemblies; Brian Hopkins, "Lumping (Versus Splitting)," Lancaster Glossary of Child Development, May 22, 2019, https://www.lancaster.ac.uk/fas/psych/glossary/lumping_-versus_splitting; Jennifer L. Hochschild, "Lumpers and Splitters, Individuals and Structures," in *Racialized Politics: The Debate About Racism in America*, ed. David Sears, Jim Sidanius, and Lawrence Bobo (University of Chicago Press, 2000), 324–43, https://scholar.harvard.edu/jlhochschild/publications/lumpers-and-splitters-individuals-and-structures.

45. "When Can Jury Verdicts Be Challenged or Overturned?" Brill & Rinaldi, n.d., https://www.forpeopleforjustice.com/can-jury-verdicts-challenged-overturned; Emmett E. Robinson, "Reversing a Jury Verdict on Appeal," Robinson Law Firm, February 17, 2020, https://robinsonlegal.org/reversing-a-jury-verdict-on-appeal.

46. "Why Is It So Difficult to Stick to Resolutions? Six Reasons Why You Fail to Follow," *Economic Times*, last updated, December 28, 2022, https://economictimes.indiatimes.com/news/how-to/six-reasons-why-your-new-year-resolutions-dont-work/articleshow/88658576.cms?from=mdr; "Why Most New Year's Resolutions Fail," The Ohio State University, February 2, 2023, https://fisher.osu.edu/blogs/leadreadtoday/why-most-new-years-resolutions-fail.

47. Rhonda Barlow, "'He Plants Trees for the Benefit of Later Generations': John Quincy Adams's Motto," *The Beehive*, Massachusetts Historical Society, updated May 8, 2019, https://www.masshist.org/beehiveblog/2017/06/he-plants-trees-for-the-benefit-of-later-generations-john-quincy-adamss-motto; Afrikindness, "Teaching the Next Generation About the Importance of Planting Trees," LinkedIn, April 29, 2023, https://www.linkedin.com/pulse/teaching-next-generation-importance-planting-trees-afrikindness.

48. For community tree plantings, go to "Plant a Tree," Newtown Tree Conservancy, n.d., https://www.newtontreeconservancy.org/plantings.

49. Richard H. Thaler and Cass R. Sunstein, *Nudge: The Final Edition* (Penguin, 2021); Joshua Blumenstock, Michael Callen, and Tarek Ghani, "How Employers in Poor Countries Are Using Nudges to Help Employees Save Money," *Harvard Business Review*, June 15, 2018, https://hbr.org/2018/06/how-employers-in-poor-countries-are-using-nudges-to-help-employees-save-money; "10 Examples of Nudge Theory," Skip Pritchard, April 20, 2018, https://www.skipprichard.com/10-examples-of-nudge-theory; Sarah D. Sparks, "Small 'Nudges' Can Push Students in the Right Direction," *Education Week*, n.d., https://www.edweek.org/leadership/small-nudges-can-push-students-in-the-right-direction; Utpal Dholakia, "The Ethical Quandary of Default Opt-Ins," *Psychology Today*, April 5, 2021, https://www.psychologytoday.com/us/blog/the-science-behind-behavior/202104/the-ethical-quandary-default-opt-ins.

50. "Fact Sheet: Reforms to Protect American Credit Card Holders," The White House Office of the Press Secretary, May 22, 2009, https://obamawhitehouse.archives.gov /the-press-office/fact-sheet-reforms-protect-american-credit-card-holders; "Obama Signs Credit Card Reform Bill Into Law," Credit Unions Online, May 22, 2009, https://www .creditunionsonline.com/news/2009/Obama-Signs-Credit-Card-Reform-Bill-Into-Law .html; Shlomo Benartzi et al., "Should Governments Invest More in Nudging?" *Psychological Science* 28, no. 8 (2017): 1041–55, https://www.ncbi.nlm.nih.gov/pmc/articles/ PMC5549818; Karen Gross, "Student Loan Forgiveness and Forms: The Devil Is in the Details," Medium, August 25, 2022, https://karengrossedu.medium.com/student-loan -forgiveness-and-forms-the-devil-is-in-;the-details-380b122de403.

51. "Jonas Salk on Humanity's Greatest Responsibility," Big Think, September 24, 2014, https://bigthink.com/words-of-wisdom/jonas-salk-on-humanitys-greatest-respon- sibility; Diego Arguedas Ortiz, "'Are We Being Good Ancestors?' Should Be the Central Question of Our Time," *MIT Technology Review*, October 21, 2020, https://www .technologyreview.com/2020/10/21/1009456/saving-future-generations-roman-krznaric; Roman Krznaric, *The Good Ancestor: A Radical Prescription for Long-Term Thinking* (The Experiment, 2021), https://theexperimentpublishing.com/catalogs/fall-2021/the -good-ancestor.

52. "Small and Incremental Changes for a Lasting Effect," Doctorpedia, January 6, 2023, https://www.doctorpedia.com/channels/small-and-incremental-changes-for-a -lasting-effect; Kelly Teng, "One Small Step: The Power of Incremental Change to Make a Big Difference," TVI, September 19, 2022, https://www.thevectorimpact.com/incremental -change.

53. Karen Gross, *Failure and Forgiveness: Rebalancing the Bankruptcy System* (Yale University Press, 1996). Negative review example: James J. White, "Failure and Forgiveness: A Review," *American Bankruptcy Law Journal* 73, no. 2 (1999): 435–47, https:// repository.law.umich.edu/reviews/107; positive review example: Jean M. Lown, "Failure and Forgiveness: Rebalancing the Bankruptcy System," *Journal of Consumer Affairs* 33, no. 1 (1999): 212–15, https://www.proquest.com/docview/195907228.

For the current debates and the movement toward taking community interests into account in bankruptcy across the globe, see Melissa B. Jacoby, "Corporate Bankruptcy Hybridity," *University of Pennsylvania Law Review* 166 (2018), https://scholarship.law .upenn.edu/cgi/viewcontent.cgi?article=9635&context=penn_law_review; Janis Sarra, *Creditor Rights and the Public Interest: Restructuring Insolvent Corporations* (University of Toronto Press, 2003), https://www.researchgate.net/publication/303414716_Creditor _Rights_and_the_Public_Interest_Restructuring_Insolvent_Corporations.

54. "Head on the Chopping Block and on the Chopping Block," Grammarist, n.d., https://grammarist.com/idiom/head-on-the-chopping-block-and-on-the-chopping-block.

Chapter 12

1. See "Throwaway Culture Is Drowning Us in Waste," Earth.org, n.d., https://earth .org/throwaway-culture; Kayla Vasarhelyi, "Trashing a Throw-Away Society," February 9, 2021. The United States contrasts with other nations in its throwaway culture; however, countries in Asia now are more likely to discard broken objects. "Throwaway Culture: A World Wallowing in Waste," Heinrich-Böll-Stiftung, April 22, 2021, https://hk.boell.org/en /2021/04/22/throwaway-culture-world-wallowing-waste.

2. While both Kintsugi and Ju Ci involve repair of what is broken, they do so in different ways, leading to different cultural interpretations. See "How the Philosophy Behind

the Japanese Art Form of *Kintsugi* Can Help Us Navigate Failure," *The Conversation*, November 8, 2022, https://theconversation.com/how-the-philosophy-behind-the-japanese-art-form-of-kintsugi-can-help-us-navigate-failure-193487; "'Ju Ci': Traditional Art of Mending Comes Back," China Culture.org, January 4, 2017, http://en.chinaculture.org/2017-04/01/content_980119_4.htm; Evan Nicole Brown, "The Art of Repairing Broken Ceramics Creates a New Kind of Beauty," February 15, 2019, Atlas Obscura, https://www.atlasobscura.com/articles/repairing-broken-ceramics; "Porcelain Restoration Craftsmanship Makes Broken Art Complete," *China Daily*, September 8, 2018, https://www.chinadaily.com.cn/a/201808/09/WS5b6baa00a310add14f384d59.html.

A growing literature is extending the approaches of Kintsugi and Ju Ci to mental wellness and healing. See Tomás Navarro, *Kintsugi: Embrace Your Imperfections and Find Happiness—the Japanese Way* (Yellow Kite, 2018); Céline Santini, *Kintsugi: Finding Strength in Imperfection* (Andrews McMeel, 2019).

3. See Gross, *Breakaway Learners*, 45–46; Karen Gross, "Why I Have Hope for the Future of Higher Ed," New England Board of Higher Education, https://nebhe.org/journal/why-i-have-hope-for-the-future-of-higher-ed; Karen Gross, "Karen Gross: Good Things Have Happened in Higher Education During the Pandemic," *New England Diary* (blog), https://newenglanddiary.com/blog/y3qnvvpdm67xub6v03hmd39dxz1e02/12/1/2022.

Index

About the Authors

Karen Gross is an educator, author, and artist, as well as an adviser to nonprofit schools, organizations, and governments. Based in Gloucester, MA, and Washington, DC, she focuses her work on student success across the educational landscape and on the impact of trauma on learning and psychosocial development. She has dealt with institutions planning for and dealing with human-made and natural disasters, including the COVID pandemic, shootings, suicides, hurricanes, and floods. She works with leaders to stabilize their institutions in the midst and aftermath of crises (e.g., student dysregulation, harassment, and discrimination).

She currently is a continuing education instructor at the Rutgers School of Social Work and sits on the advisory council at the Center for Minority Serving Institutions at Rutgers Graduate School of Education. She has been a visiting professor at colleges and universities across the United States and Canada. She is a cofounder of the Virtual Teachers' Lounge, which serves educators across the globe and conducts workshops and seminars for organizations dealing with student and educator struggles, including the impact of trauma on students, educators, families, and communities.

Previously, she served for 8 years as the president of Southern Vermont College and as senior policy adviser to the U.S. Department of Education during the Obama administration. Prior to that, she was a tenured law professor for more than 2 decades in New York City. She has served on a number of local and national boards of nonprofit institutions. She also served on the domestic policy committee of President Joe Biden's campaign, focusing on education.

Her award-winning adult books include *Breakaway Learners: Strategies for Post-Secondary Success With At-Risk Students* and *Trauma Doesn't Stop at the School Door: Strategies and Solutions for Educators, PreK–College*, the first two books in a trilogy of which the current book is the third.

She is the author of a book series for children, Lady Lucy's Quest, several books of which have been translated into Spanish. Her artwork, which is trauma responsive, has been shown in online and brick-and-mortar galleries, appears in online magazines and catalogs, and hangs in educational institutions across the United States. Since she is a frequent blogger and commentator on issues of education, her work has appeared in *The Evolllution, Collegiate Exchange, Newsweek, The New England Journal of Higher Education, Inside Higher Ed, The Chronicle of Higher Education, Age of Awareness* (Medium), and *Authentic Insider* and on Forest of the Rain Productions, among other outlets. During the pandemic, she conducted more than 50 podcasts on trauma's impact on education. She has been cited in numerous articles, including in *Forbes*, *Parents*, *The Atlantic*, *Romper*, and *The New York Times*.

For more information, visit her website at www.karengrosseducation.com.

Edward K. S. Wang loved to listen to stories when he was a child. He is naturally drawn to individual, family, and community narratives professionally to promote growth and healing in tumultuous times. His domestic and international work focuses on improving adolescents' and young adults' social and emotional well-being, strengthening families, and community resiliency.

As the director of policy and planning at the Division of Global Psychiatry at Massachusetts General Hospital and assistant professor of psychology at Harvard Medical School, he coauthored the Project One Billion Global Mental Health Survey and the Liberia National Mental Health Policy. He mentors fellows on violence reduction and trauma recovery initiatives.

He was born in Hong Kong and came to the United States alone at age 16. The lived experience of migration and family members who have mental illness pulls him toward an interest in cross-cultural psychology and communication, trauma, and the practice of cultural humility. After practicing as a clinical psychologist, he became a steward of public mental health and developed an integrated policy, program, and practice model toward equitable care for racially and ethnically diverse populations. He has shared his approaches with mental health authorities and providers of care across the country affiliated with the national Training Institutes of System of Care for decades. Others often use his strategic template published in Beth A. Stroul and Gary M. Blau's *The System of Care Handbook: Transforming Mental Health Services for Children, Youth, and Families*. He retired as director of the Office of Multicultural Affairs Department of Mental Health, where he built the foundation and scaffoldings of care systems to reduce disparities. Reflecting on his Chinese roots, he shared his experience in an article in the Harvard Kennedy School of Government's *Asian American Policy Review*, "A Journey of Public Stewardship on Asian American and Pacific Islander Mental Health: Massachusetts's Approach to Addressing Disparities."

Two knowledge- and skill-based interactive training curricula that he developed, Trauma-Informed Care: Hope, Strengths, Resilience, Growth, and Healing, and Wellness and Resilience in Families and Children, integrate the science of toxic stress and trauma with practice-based evidence. Both curricula are customized and used widely in mental health, child welfare, education, and social services domestically and internationally. He cofounded the Virtual Teachers' Lounge, an online forum to support educators.

He is the first Asian American clinical psychologist appointed to the Substance Abuse and Mental Health Services Administration National Advisory Council. He received many state senate and house citations for his achievements and recognition from community-based organizations for his advocacy and dedication. He is proud to be honored as a community hero by the Commonwealth of Massachusetts Asian American Commission and served as board president of the National Asian American Pacific Islander Mental Health Association.

Dr. Wang promotes the importance of work–life balance and enjoys its benefits. He is the proud grandfather of two beautiful granddaughters, who inspire him to focus work on healthy childhood, family development, and writing children's stories. He enjoys his daily swim and 10,000 steps, gardening, and repurposing items into decorative art.

Contact information: ekwang@mgh.harvard.edu; ed.global.diversity@gmail